Susan J. Paik and Herbert J. Walberg
Editors

Narrowing the Achievement Gap

Strategies for Educating Latino, Black, and Asian Students

Foreword by
EDMUND W. GORDON

 Springer

Susan J. Paik
Claremont Graduate University
USA

Herbert J. Walberg
University of Illinois at Chicago
USA

Library of Congress Control Number: 2006939321

ISBN-10: 0-387-44609-5   e-ISBN-10: 0-387-44611-7
ISBN-13: 978-0-387-44609-7   e-ISBN-13: 978-0-387-44611-0

Printed on acid-free paper.

9 8 7 6 5 4 3 2 1

springer.com

Foreword

The subject of minority children's learning has long been the concern of civic leaders, parents, scholars, and educators. The federal legislation, 'No Child Left Behind' emphasizes the concern even more. It specifically requires assessing the academic achievement of minority students, particularly in economically disadvantaged areas, and holding schools accountable for their progress. Schools that fail to attain "Adequate Yearly Progress" face the real possibility of being forced to close if they continually fail to perform. Unlike the past, these are increasingly "high stakes" consequences for educators, parents, students and the schools that serve them. This book is timely and relevant because it addresses these issues, and recommends solutions for Latino, Black, and Asian students. This book also has implications for the problems the nation faces in helping all students to learn well, particularly those that lag in academic achievement.

In considering the broad problems and in recommending solutions, the book provides breadth, concision, and unique organization. As the introductory chapter makes clear, the book simultaneously considers not only the three most visible minority groups in the U.S., but draws upon the perspectives of anthropology, education, ethnic studies, psychology, and sociology. From these several perspectives, this book is organized within three broad sections: 1) culturally diverse families and schooling; 2) issues of immigration and schooling experiences; and 3) socio-cultural perspectives on teaching, learning, and development. Within each section, the authors marshal research literature regarding each ethnic minority group. The book not only summarizes and evaluates voluminous scholarship but sets forth policy and practice recommendations in each chapter for scholars, legislators, and practitioners.

As a participant in the national conference in Washington, DC, I saw that the contributing scholars were truly interdisciplinary in spirit. Not only did they draw from their deep scholarship in their special fields but they also reached out to sister disciplines both in their writing and in the discussions. During the conference, the scholars, practitioners, and policymakers collaborated in developing recommendations and next steps. The ideas and recommendations in this book will certainly contribute to the national debate concerning how we face the challenge to help all our children learn well.

EDMUND W. GORDON
Senior Scholar in Residence
The College Board
John M. Musser Professor of Psychology, Emeritus
Yale University
Richard March Hoe Professor of Education and Psychology, Emeritus
Teacher's College, Columbia University

Series Preface

Narrowing the Achievement Gap: Strategies for Educating Latino, Black, and Asian Students is a volume in The University of Illinois at Chicago (UIC) Series on Issues in Children's and Families' Lives. The UIC series began in response to the "Great Cities" initiative taken by our former chancellor and president of the University of Illinois system, James Stukel. At its inception, Lascelles Anderson helped establish a working group of UIC faculty to design and offer advice on this series. Currently, the series is sponsored by Sylvia Manning, the current UIC chancellor, as well as other senior administrators, trustees, and civic leaders in Chicago. The purpose of this series is to marshal scholarly resources to facilitate understanding and solutions to problems within American cities by including ideas with far-reaching implications.

Books in this series provide an interdisciplinary and "interprofessional" approach to problems facing children and the adults who care for them. The intended readers for the series includes policymakers, practitioners, scholars, students, and lay citizens who seek a greater understanding of ideas for social and educational reform. Given the wide spectrum of intended audiences, the volumes in the series are unlike many other academic volumes. Rather than emphasizing norms within a particular discipline, the series draws upon knowledge and guidance from nearly all the social, educational, and health sciences. These fields include psychology, sociology, education, economics, social work, criminal justice, law, public policy, and the allied health fields. The common thread within each book concerns programs and policies for use in solving particular social and individual problems.

Reflecting this broad approach, the first volume in the UIC Series set the stage for later more specialized volumes. Titled *Children and Youth: Interdisciplinary Perspectives*, it reviews diverse ways in which families, schools, and the health care system influence and enhance the social, emotional, cognitive, and physical development of young people (Walberg, Reyes, & Weissberg, 1997). The second volume, *Promoting Positive Outcomes*, focuses on solutions to the problems facing children and youth. It features education and child development programs, policies, and practices (Reynolds, Walberg & Weissberg, 1999). *Long Term Trends in the Well-being of Children and Youth* shows scholars and practitioners how successive cohorts of children and youth have been changing over long time periods with respect to a variety of specialized fields such as education and health (Weissberg, Walberg, O'Brien, & Kuster, 2003).

Early Childhood Programs for a New Century highlights trends in preschool education and care, evidence-based programs and practices, and policies that will enhance the quality of wide-scale programming for children (Reynolds, Walberg, & Wang, 2003). *Preventing Youth Problems* discusses policies and practices that prevent smoking, alcohol and drug abuse, sexual risk behaviors, and antisocial behavior (Biglan, Wang, & Walberg, 2003). The title of *Changing Welfare* is intended to reflect both how welfare policy and practice has been changing in recent years and how it should be changed (Gordon & Walberg, 2003). *Nurturing Morality* (Thorkildsen & Walberg, 2004) addresses personal and environmental supports as well as impediments to moral functioning in a wide variety of societal institutions. This current volume, *Narrowing the Achievement Gap: Strategies for Educating Latino, Black, and Asian Students* provides insight on issues regarding culturally diverse families and schooling experiences for the three most visible minority groups in the United States.

We greatly appreciate the many people who helped make both this volume and the UIC Series on Children and Youth a reality. We thank the distinguished members of our UIC Advisory Board and our National Advisory Board. They provided helpful comments and recommendations on the proposed structure and topic for these volumes.

The initial drafts of these chapters were reviewed by participants in a conference sponsored by the Laboratory for Student Success (LSS), through a contract with The Institute of Education Sciences (IES) of the U. S. Department of Education. We are grateful to LSS for their support and help in organizing the conference and disseminating the ideas in this book to interested constituencies. We are also grateful for the thoughtful conversations sustained by everyone who participated in the event.

Finally, we thank Susan J. Paik for her intellectual leadership in organizing this volume and recruiting a highly talented group of scholars to share their ample wisdom, for which we are also grateful. We also are very appreciative of the professionals at Springer in producing this volume effectively and efficiently.

HERBERT J. WALBERG
ROGER P. WEISSBERG
THOMAS P. GULLOTTA
Series Editors

Contents

1
Introduction and Overview

Susan J. Paik and Herbert J. Walberg

We must teach our children to prepare for the future – how to set goals for their lives and for their careers. We must do more to inspire, train, and motivate them. (p. 82) Every home and neighborhood [school and community] in this country needs to be a safe, warm, healthy place – a place fit for human beings as citizens of the United States. It is a big job, but there is no one better to do it than those who live here. (p. 44)

– Rosa Parks (1994)

The chapters of this book originated from a national invitational conference in Washington D.C. sponsored by the Laboratory for Student Success in November of 2005. The conference took place just blocks away from the Capitol Rotunda where, days before, Rosa Parks' body laid in state as the nation mourned her passing. The conference began with the quotes above that reflected her views. The quotes, though simple, were profound as was the life of Rosa Parks. Her life and efforts were significant not only because of her leadership in the civil rights movement but also because of her other passion, "young people and education."

The purpose of the book and conference was founded on the importance of education for minority children and a belief that research should be useful in practice and policy. The conference participants included researchers, practitioners, and policymakers who shared the same passions and were eager to develop recommendations for improving minority education. The book is a means to that end since it discusses both the strengths and challenges of minority children and provides recommendations in each chapter. Based on work group sessions at the conference, the last chapter summarizes consensual recommendations for research, policy, and practice.

In developing this conference and subsequent book, several important questions were asked, such as:

Who are these minority students?
How can we best understand them?
What are their challenges and strengths?
What are the similarities and not just the differences among the groups?

How can we collaborate and develop a collective voice in discussing the three
   groups?
How can we best serve them?
What recommendations can we provide?

We wanted to understand these questions by developing a systematic design
focused on three minority groups: Latino, Black, and Asian students in each of
the three sections in the book.

Why were these groups chosen? Latino, Black, and Asian ethnic minority
groups are the most visible, and are rapidly growing as shown by U.S. Census
data. As suggested by the book title, the groups are listed in terms of their
population size. Latinos, for example, are now the largest minority group in the
U.S. The No Child Left Behind Act (NCLB) has also emphasized these groups as
a concern, especially in economically disadvantaged areas. A growing number of
minority and immigrant families now reside in urban areas (Fix & Passel, 2003);
and these families tend to be poorer, less educated, and have lower proficiency
levels in English (Rong & Preissle, 1998). For purposes of accountability, the
NCLB Act also mandates that educators report separate achievement scores for
each of these minority groups as well as English language learners.

The achievement gap continues to persist between minority and non-minority
groups in the U.S., as well as growing gaps even within minority groups. How
can we diminish the achievement gaps especially with the growing number of
minority students? Educators and allied professionals are interested in improving
the efforts of these growing minority populations.

In trying to understand these groups, we found that there were few books
that offered an array of research expertise on Latino, Black, and Asian children
in a single collective volume. This motivated us to bring together the research
represented in this book. In addition, a better understanding of socio-cultural
issues and experiences regarding the home, school, and community provide
insight into the three groups. Consequently, the following three themes emerged:

Part 1: Culturally Diverse Families and Schooling
Part 2: Histories, Issues of Immigration, and Schooling Experiences
Part 3: Socio-cultural Issues on Teaching, Learning, and Development

Within each section is a chapter on each of the three minority groups. Rather
than sorting themes by three distinctive groups, this organization allows comparisons and contrasts of the cultural groups within each section. Learning about
similarities and differences among the groups provides greater insight into the
myriad of problems and contexts that affect minority and immigrant children.

The invited authors are top scholars and leaders in the fields of psychology,
anthropology, sociology, education, and ethnic studies. The interdisciplinary
selection of scholars was a challenging task, but the editors went to great lengths
to identify the most qualified contributors. Without question, the authors comple-
mented each other in terms of the purpose and scope of this book.

We are aware of the complexities in cultures, subcultures, and topics in this area of research. In inviting the chapter authors, we acknowledged the cultural differences within each minority group. Although there are differences among and within the groups, there are also some similarities in history, culture, language, customs, and traditions both in the originating countries and their experiences in the U.S. Since it was impossible to represent all the groups, we sought to represent not only the largest minority groups, but those subgroups addressed in the NCLB Act.

The chapters in the book are represented by a variety of perspectives, and we acknowledge they are a starting point in understanding the complexities involved in minority groups and subgroups. Each of the authors brought their own expertise and perspectives to address these points and was asked to provide clear recommendations based on their research. The authors also defined and used various terms as appropriate in their respective chapters (e.g., Latino, Hispanic, Black, African American, Asian Pacific American, or Asian American usage, etc.). They also employed language and distinctions in their field of expertise that would make most sense particularly with respect to how minority children can best be served.

While it was impossible to cover everything, this book provides the breadth and organization of synthesized research on the three groups. The chapters synthesize research-based findings on the practices in homes, schools, and communities to help increase our understanding of psychological resilience, academic performance, and pro-social behavior. Classrooms have now changed and it is imperative to understand the background of culturally diverse families and students in order to shape effective schooling experiences. Each author offers recommendations for policymakers, researchers, and practitioners to improve their success in school and life.

The following sections in this chapter provide descriptive statistics about the school and life experiences of the three minority groups in general. This information is presented to the reader to provide a demographic overview in the context of minority education. Followed by summaries of each chapter, the chapter ends with concluding remarks regarding the conference and book.

1.1. Background on Minority Learning

On January 8, 2002, Congress enacted the No Child Left Behind Act (NCLB), which has strongly affected education for all students and minority students in particular. The NCLB Act requires new state academic standards for stronger accountability, better teacher training, and research-based educational practices. Allocating an additional $26.5 billion for the support of public K-12 schools, Republicans and Democrats joined to support this legislation to help all children learn as implied by the Act's title (U.S. Department of Education, 2003). The Act mandates that academic achievement progress be reported separately for students by race, ethnicity, SES, English proficiency, and disability. The information on test performance must be publicly available, and policy makers, educators, parents, and others will be able to see results for each of these student groups (U.S. Department of Education, 2002).

Though bold and providing large increases in federal funding for the education of disadvantaged students, NCLB continues national efforts to increase achievement. Since 1965, more than $242 billion was spent to educate economically disadvantaged students, and indeed, spending has more than doubled since 1996. Achievement gaps, however, persist among low-income, minority, and English language learners. Despite increased spending, performance in reading has not improved in the last 15 years. Currently, less than one-third of the nation's fourth graders read proficiently. Less than 20% of 12th grade students score proficiently in mathematics, and they continue to rank near the bottom on international surveys (U. S. Department of Education, 2003).

Title I of the Elementary and Secondary Education Act of 1965 was amended in the new NCLB Act (Sec. 1001) "to ensure that all children have a fair, equal, and significant opportunity to obtain a high-quality education and reach, at a minimum, proficiency on challenging State academic achievement standards and state academic assessments. This purpose is to be accomplished by:

(1) ensuring that high-quality academic assessments, accountability systems, teacher preparation and training, curriculum, and instructional materials are aligned with challenging State academic standards so that students, teachers, parents, and administrators can measure progress against common expectations for student academic achievement;

(2) meeting the educational needs of low achieving children in our nation's highest poverty schools, limited English proficient children, migratory children, children with disabilities, Indian children, neglected or delinquent children, and young children in need of reading assistance; and

(3) closing the achievement gap between high and low performing children, especially minority and non-minority students, and between disadvantaged children and their more advantaged peers" (U.S. Department of Education, 2002). Students and families from disadvantaged homes, especially those ethnic minority populations who are rapidly growing in the United States are of particular concern.

1.2. Minority Students: A Growing Population

Minority children and youth, particularly immigrant children, are the fastest growing population in U.S. schools. It is estimated that the ratio of immigrant children in grades K-12 is one in five, representing 19% of schoolchildren (Fix & Passel, 2003). Furthermore, an estimated 1,000 immigrant children enter U.S. schools each day (Rong & Brown, 2002, p. 125). The foreign-born population is currently over 31.1 million, which is at an all-time high (Fix & Passel, 2003). Currently, 10.5 million students are children of immigrants; roughly one-fourth are foreign-born and three-fourths are U.S. born (Fix & Passel, 2003).

The largest immigrant groups seeking education in the U.S. are Latinos, Asians, and Caribbean and African Blacks (Rong & Preissle, 1998). Latinos are currently the largest minority population representing over 13% of the population in the U.S. (U.S. Census, 2004). Latinos include Mexican Americans, Cuban Americans, Puerto Ricans, Dominican Republicans, and other Central and South Americans. The U.S. Census reports foreign-born and U.S. born Mexicans constitute roughly 38% of all immigrant children (Fix & Passel, 2003). Educational researchers have long been concerned with achievement, enrollment, and high school dropout rates for Latino students (Tutwiler, 1998; Rong & Preissle, 1998).

Asian Americans are also one of the fastest growing minority populations comprised of both high and low achieving groups as illustrated in the chapters. Census data show that Asian and Pacific Islander Americans total nearly 12 million, which is about 4% of the entire U.S. population. Since 1965, 90% of Asian Americans are recent immigrants (Rong & Preissle, 1998). A particularly diverse group, Asian Americans represent all the countries of East, South, Southeast Asia, and the Pacific Islands. Among the most common are Chinese, Japanese, Korean, and Indians who are typically high-achievers in school, whereas Cambodians, Hmong, and Vietnamese have traditionally achieved less well.

Of post-1900 immigrants, Blacks are the smallest group; they accounted for less than 5% of immigrants in 1994. Census projections, however, suggest that the foreign-born Black population will grow from 1.6 million to roughly 2.7 million in 2010 (Rong & Preissle, 1998). Foreign-born African groups are largely comprised of Non-Hispanics from the Caribbean (mostly Grenadine, Haitian, Jamaican, Trinidadian, and Tobagian) and Africans (mostly Ethiopian, Ghanaian, Nigerian, and South African).

Though the Black immigrant population is smaller than Asians and Latinos, the U.S. born Black population is the second largest minority group and constitutes over 12% of the population based on Census data. Researchers have long been concerned with the educational achievement of African Americans. The U.S. Census reports that substantial numbers of minorities, particularly African Americans, live in urban areas, where inequities continue to persist in achievement, employment, and quality of life.

Scholars have long noted the relationship between educational success and family income. In the United States, many ethnic minority groups, particularly immigrant families, tend to be among the poorer income groups. By 1991, one-third of immigrant children (foreign-born and U.S. born) lived in families with incomes below the poverty line (Fix & Passel, 2003). According to the National Center for Children in Poverty (2006), growing trends show that 63% of Latino children (8.9 million), 61% of Black children (6.6 million), 30% of Asian children (0.9 million), and 27% of White children (11.7 million) lived in low-income families in the U.S. in 2002. Although the largest group is White, minority populations, particularly Latino and African American populations are more likely to live in low-income families.

In general, low-income, minority children face additional challenges to succeeding in school, which widen the achievement gap throughout the school years. Some studies have shown as the number of family risk factors for a child increase (e.g., living in a single-parent household, living below the federal poverty level), that child performs less well in both reading and mathematics (Rathbun & West, 2004, p. v).

In a nation of more than 3 million kindergarteners, the Early Childhood Longitudinal Study of the Kindergarten class of 1998–1999 (ECLS-K) follows a nationally representative sample of 22,782 kindergarteners through fifth grade, revealing important challenges facing minority children. Among the sample, it was found that 45% live in low-income families accounting for all groups (e.g., White, Latino, Black, Asian and other) involved the study. Concerns for disadvantaged minority students continue to grow given the dismal predictions. The study found on average that Black and Latino third-graders had lower proficiency in advanced reading skills and mathematics (Rathbun & West, 2004, pp. vii–viii). Ongoing research from the ECLS-K demonstrates that achievement gaps between disadvantaged and more advantaged children identified at the beginning of school grew wider over the first 4 years of school attendance (West, Denton, Germino Hausken, 2000 as cited in Rathbun & West, p. x).

While the research on Latino and Black populations is well cited regarding the achievement gap, there is also a growing concern over Asian populations, who don't achieve as well. Typically, East Asians have done considerably well, but recent research shows that some students from South or Southeast Asian groups do not perform as highly. Recent research has also cited that some East Asian groups are also struggling academically (Lew, 2006). Given the reputation of the model minority stereotype, research and services for Asian families and students have been generally lacking in the schools. As the diverse Asian communities are growing, there is concern to disaggregate the data and understand the needs given the little existing research on Asian American students (see Lee, Pang, Zhou, chapter publications in this text).

In addition to the complexities, many students also come from non-English speaking countries (e.g., Asia, Africa, and Latin America). There are over 2.6 million limited English proficient students in grades K-12 (Fix & Passel, 2003). Limited English mastery, economic hardships, and cultural barriers are often obstacles to success in school and life. Many believe that without better opportunities, large numbers of foreign-born and U.S. born Latino, Black, and Asian students will continue to be marginalized in the United States. As a result of these trends, school psychologists, educators from various disciplines, and other allied professionals must work hard to improve the academic and life prospects of minority children and youth.

1.3.   Chapter Overviews

The chapter summaries are provided on each of the three themes on culturally diverse families and schooling; brief histories, issues of immigration and schooling experiences; and socio-cultural issues on teaching, learning, and development.

1.3.1.   Part One: Culturally Diverse Families and Schooling

Chapter 2. *Fostering Latino Parent Involvement in the Schools: Practices and Partnerships*. (Concha Delgado-Gaitan). Employment statistics reveal a strong correlation between college attainment and well-paying employment opportunities. For Latino students, however, college entrance is often unattainable. The under-representation of Latinos prompted Delgado-Gaitan's questions of what needs to be done, beginning at the elementary school level, to increase Latino student college admission. A 4-year ethnographic study involving 20 Latino families from Central America and Mexico, in a Northern California community, traced the social-ization of young Latino students and their families preparing for college admission. Delgado-Gaitan discusses the importance of Latino parent involvement, practices in the home and school, and effective partnerships as exemplified in a Mother-Daughter county schools project. Through interviews, observations, and partici-pation in their off-campus and after-school activities, she was able to construct a multi-faceted picture of the cultural knowledge in families and community educational agencies that is necessary in the long journey of changing the dismal statistics of Latinos in higher education. In summary, Delgado-Gaitan discusses issues regarding Latino families and communities in understanding early academic experiences of students. While there is a need to address the schooling process for Latinas, the implications of this study are applicable for both male and female Latino students as educators consider reforms for preparing students in the early grades.

Chapter 3. *Parenting, Social-Emotional Development, and School Achievement of African American Youngsters* (Ronald D. Taylor). Renewed attention has been devoted to the gap in the achievement between African American and European American students. On a variety of indicators (e.g., grades, SAT scores, college attendance and completion), African American youngsters fare poorly compared to European American adolescents. The gap in the achievement appears before kindergarten and continues into adulthood. Among the factors linked to differ-ences in achievement have been social class, teacher expectations and percep-tions, parental expectations and practices. Ron Taylor discusses family relations, parenting practices and their association with adolescents' school achievement and social and emotional adjustment. Taylor also discusses factors that impact the functioning of African American families and their capacity to rear their youngsters. Taylor's chapter discusses how African American families experience high rates of poverty and stressful living conditions. Thus, the influence of families' economic resources, neighborhood conditions and social networks on family functioning are also discussed. Taylor provides recommendations for policy and practice, aimed at improving youngsters' achievement and the social and psychological well-being of students and their families.

Chapter 4. *Asian Pacific American Cultural Capital: Understanding Diverse Parents and Students* (Valerie Ooka Pang). Pang's chapter provides an informed discussion regarding the cultural values that shape the behaviors and achievement of Asian Pacific American (APA) students. Bronfenbrenner's ecological model of human development is used to explain how families, particularly APA families encourage and reinforce educational achievement. A central idea in this chapter is "cultural capital," which Pang refers to as the attitudes, expectations, knowledge, and behaviors parents pass on to their children that assist them in succeeding in school and society. To illustrate this central idea, she also employs several of Sue and Okazaki's ideas about Asian cultural capital in the educational achievement process. Pang also discusses the experiences, backgrounds, and educational needs of diverse APA groups by providing examples of the various groups (e.g., Cambodian, Chinese, Filipino, Japanese, Korean, Lao, and Vietnamese, etc.). She explains that their educational needs may be similar, but their social and academic experiences may differ due to various elements such as history and generational levels in the U.S. The chapter concludes with recommendations for educators to encourage and collaborate with Asian Pacific American students and their families.

1.3.2.   Part Two: Histories, Issues of Immigration, and Schooling Experiences

Chapter 5. *The Mobility/Social Capital Dynamic: Understanding Mexican American Families and Students* (Robert K. Ream and Ricardo D. Stanton-Salazar). Latinos are the largest minority group in the United States, increasing eight times more rapidly than the population as a whole. Their rising numbers come with concern about the status of Latino students in schools. The two-thirds of all U.S. Latinos who are of Mexican descent are challenged with disproportionately high dropout rates and low test scores. In this chapter, Ream and Stanton-Salazar argue that Mexican American underachievement is partly due to the instability in social relationships that accompanies particularly high rates of transience among them. "Like the frequent re-potting of plants" in their analogy, residential and student mobility disrupts social root systems and the context for interaction. It follows that the *mobility/social capital dynamic*, whereby mobility impacts the resources inherent in social networks, merits attention on the basis of its sway over relationship stability and academic achievement. After reviewing the incidence, consequences, and causes of mobility, Ream and Stanton-Salazar address how school systems can reduce unnecessary student mobility and develop strategies for strengthening the social support networks of Mexican American students and their families.

Chapter 6. *Educational Attainment of Immigrant and Non-Immigrant Young Blacks* (Xue Lan Rong and Frank Brown). As African American experiences move into the 21st century, diverse educational attainment patterns and schooling behaviors have emerged among Black students. Recent immigrant Blacks from the Caribbean and Africa with growing numbers differ from Blacks who have lived in the United States for many generations. To compare and contrast the groups, Rong and Brown first discuss the similarities and differences with respect to immigration experiences and history, family and community environments, and schooling experiences. Rong and Brown then focus the discussion on the variations in educational attainment in African and Caribbean immigrants and non-immigrants affected by region or country of origin, generation in the United States, gender, age, and socioeconomic status. Their chapter draws on insights from direct observations and demographic data from the 2000 census. Their chapter also identifies and differentiates causes for variable patterns in educational attainment (e.g., schooling behaviors and self-defined identities). To improve the educational opportunities of Black students, Rong and Brown state that educators and policy makers must recognize the differences in Black communities and among generations. With increased understanding of the distinctive strengths of these communities, educational opportunities may increase for children and youth in several specific ways suggested in this chapter.

Chapter 7. *Divergent Origins and Destinies: Children of Asian Immigrants* (Min Zhou). There has been relatively little concern with whether or not children of Asian immigrants can make it into the American mainstream, partly because of their comparatively high socioeconomic status upon arrival and partly because of their extraordinary educational achievement. The general perception is that a great majority of them, even those from poor socioeconomic backgrounds, will succeed in school and life, and that the "model minority" image represents a reality rather than a myth. Zhou examines the problems and limitations of the homogenized image of Asian Americans based on the analysis of the U.S. Census data and her own ethnographic case studies in Asian immigrant communities. Zhou argues that Asian immigrants and their US-born or raised children are living in a society that is highly stratified not only by class but also by race. This reality, combined with unique cultures, immigration histories, family and community resources, has shaped and, to an important extent, determined the educational outcomes of the children of Asian immigrants. Her chapter starts with a demographic overview of the diverse Asian American population as impacted by immigration. Zhou then examines how diversity creates opportunities and constraints to affect the trajectories of second-generation mobility. Finally, Zhou draws lessons from two case studies, Chinese and Vietnamese, to illustrate how culture interacts with structure to affect unique social environments conducive to education. The chapter ends with a discussion of the lessons and implications for immigrant education, particularly for Asian American communities.

1.3.3. Part Three: Socio-cultural Issues on Teaching, Learning, and Development

Chapter 8. *Educational Issues and Effective Practices for Hispanic Students* (Hersh C. Waxman, Yolanda N. Padrón, and Andres García). The educational status of Hispanic students in the United States is one of the most challenging educational issues. Although the number of Hispanic students in public schools has increased dramatically in recent decades, Hispanic students as a group have the lowest levels of education and the highest dropout rates. Furthermore, conditions of poverty, health, and other social problems have made it difficult for Hispanics to improve their educational status. Waxman, Padron, and Garcia summarize some of the critical educational problems facing Hispanic students and provide some recommendations to alleviate the problems. Their chapter is divided into four major sections. The first section focuses on the educational status of Hispanic students in the United States. The second section discusses factors associated with the underachievement of Hispanic students. This section includes problems associated with the need for qualified teachers, inappropriate teaching practices, and at-risk school environments. The third section examines factors associated with the success of Hispanic students. Waxman, Padron, and Garcia provide a brief summary of programs, schools, and instructional strategies that have been found to significantly improve the academic achievement of Hispanic students. Finally, their chapter provides recommendations and conclusions on effective practices and programs for Hispanic students.

Chapter 9. *Improving the Schooling Experiences of African American Students: What School Leaders and Teachers Can Do* (Gail L. Thompson). For more than half a century, the greatest failure of the U.S. public school system has been that despite numerous education reforms, the achievement gap persists. Although there now exist numerous achievement gaps–including the gap between economically disadvantaged students and their peers from higher socioeconomic backgrounds, the Latino-White gap, the Latino-Asian gap, the Latino-Black gap, the Latino-Latino gap, and the Asian-Asian gap (gaps among various Latino groups, and among various Asians groups),—Thompson informs us that the Black-White achievement gap has historically received more attention than the other gaps, primarily because of the attention given to it via the U.S. Supreme Court ruling in Brown versus Board of Education. In spite of this attention, educators have failed to close the gap, and today, as a result of the current unprecedented pressure to improve students' standardized test scores as a result of NCLB, narrowing the Black-White gap has become a top priority at school districts nationwide. Because educators and researchers continue to seek solutions, Thompson's chapter presents pertinent research from researchers, and African American parents and students regarding how educators can increase their efficacy with African American students. Thompson begins with a brief summary of research on the role of school leaders and then presents "Seven things that African American students need from their teachers". She emphasizes the importance of professional development and concludes with specific recommendations.

Chapter 10. *The Truth and Myth of the Model Minority: The Case of Hmong Americans* (Stacey J. Lee). Asian Americans are generally depicted as model minorities who have achieved academic, social and economic success through hard work and adherence to Asian cultural values. Asian American students are stereotyped as valedictorians, violin prodigies and computer geniuses. While there are Asian American students who are highly successful, the model minority stereotype hides variation in academic achievement across ethnic groups and among individuals. Lee discusses how disaggregated data on Asian Americans reveals significant differences between East Asian and South Asian groups that have high levels of educational attainment, and Southeast Asians who have relatively low levels of educational attainment. Lee's chapter analyzes the similarities and differences in educational achievement and attainment across various Asian American ethnic groups, but focuses on traditionally lower achieving groups. As a primary example, the chapter examines the case of Hmong Americans, a group that has experienced significant barriers to education. Based on data from Lee's ethnographic study of Hmong American high school students in the Midwest, her chapter discusses economic, racial and cultural barriers that Asian students, Hmong students in particular, face in schools. Her study examines the impact of the model minority stereotype on lower achieving Asian American students. Lee concludes with recommendations for educational policy and practice for educators and policymakers.

1.4.   Concluding Remarks and Acknowledgements

The conference participants included the authors, other scholars, and representatives of Washington education groups such as the Council of Chief State School Officers, the Educational Leaders Council, the National Association of Secondary School Principals, and national parent organizations. Board members and officials from state departments of education and local school districts, superintendents, principals, and teachers also participated.

The main work of the conference took place in small groups. With a chair and recorder for each group, their task, based on the conference papers, discussion, and their own experience, was to develop consensus around "next steps" to improve policy and practice. The synthesized recommendations constitute the last chapter (Ch. 11) of this book, which consists of general recommendations for the three groups. Specific recommendations for Latino, Black, or Asian students can also be found in each of the chapters.

The editors thank the Laboratory for Student Success (LSS), the Mid-Atlantic Regional Educational Laboratory, at Temple University Center for Research in Human Development and Education for funding and supporting the conference. The LSS operates under a contract with the U.S. Department of Education's Institute of Education Sciences. Special thanks to C. Kent McGuire, Dean of the College of Education at Temple University, and Marilyn Murphy, Co-director of LSS, Tracey Myska, Robin Neal, Stephen Page, Robert Sullivan, and Julia St. George at LSS for their support.

We thank the authors for their commitment and dedication to their work and to this book. They are top scholars in the fields of education, psychology, sociology, anthropology, and ethnic studies.

We also thank the conference chairs and discussants. They, too, were carefully selected and contributed greatly to our conference discussion. Chairs Edmund Gordon from Teachers College Columbia University, Reynaldo Baca from the University of Southern California, and Gloria Ladson-Billings from the University of Wisconsin-Madison provided key insights on the three sets of chapters. Discussants Larke Nahme Huang from the American Institutes for Research,

Richard P. Duran from the University of California – Santa Barbara, Margaret Gibson from the University of California-Santa Cruz, Grace Kao from the University of Pennsylvania, A. Lin Goodwin from Teachers College Columbia University, and Marc Hill from Temple University provided insightful perspectives to the papers.

We appreciate the efforts of the small group chairs where most of our collaborative work was conducted: Norma Jimenez-Hernandez and William Perez from Claremont Graduate University (CGU), and Marilyn Murphy from LSS. We would like to thank rapporteurs Patricia Felton-Montgomery, Fred McCoy, and Celeste Merriweather of LSS. Special thanks goes to Margarita Jimenez-Silva from Arizona State University for her support and assistance at the conference.

We acknowledge our close colleagues at Claremont Graduate University and the University of Illinois at Chicago for their participation and support of the conference and book. We appreciate the assistance of CGU graduate students, Belinda Butler Vea, Cindy Chia-Hui Wang, and Jocelyn Chong in helping review the final chapters.

Finally, we would like to acknowledge John Griesinger, Judith Griesinger, Ward Weldon, Deborah Williams, Mary Poplin, and Linda Perkins in reviewing the editors' chapters and their support throughout this project.

We are deeply grateful to all those involved in this project for their help in supporting the efforts to improve education for minority children and youth. May we be reminded of Rosa Parks' views in which this chapter began: respectful integration of all ethnic groups and the empowerment of education for all of our children and youth.

References

Basic Facts About Low-Income Children: Birth to Age 18 (2006, January). National Center for Children in Poverty of Columbia University. Retrieved on June 21, 2006 from the National Center for Children in Poverty of Columbia University. http://www.nccp.org.

Fix, M. & Passel, J. (2003, January). *U.S. Immigration – Trends & Implications for Schools*. Paper presented at the meeting of the National Association for Bilingual Education, NCLB Implementation Institute, New Orleans, LA.

Lew, J. (2006). *Asian Americans in Class: Charting the Achievement Gap Among Korean American Youth*. New York: Teachers College Press.

Parks, Rosa, with Gregory Reed. (1994). Quiet Strength: The Faith, the Hope, and the Heart of a Woman who Changed a Nation. *Grand Rapids*, Michigan: Zondervan Publishing House.

Rathbun, A. & West, J. (2004, August). *From Kindergarten Through Third Grade: Children's Beginning School Experiences* (NCES 2004–007). U.S. Department of Education, National Center for Education Statistics. Washington, DC: U.S. Government Printing Office, see: *http://nces.ed.gov/pubsearch/pubsinfo.asp?pubid=2004007*

Rong, X. L. & Brown, F. (2002, February). Immigration and Urban Education in the New Millennium: The Diversity and the Challenges. *Education and Urban Society*, 45 (2), 123–133.

Rong, X.L. & Preissle, J. (1998). *Educating Immigrant Students: What We Need to Know to Meet the Challenges*. California: Corwin Press.

Tutwiler, S.W. (1998). Diversity Among Families. In Fuller, M.L. and Olsen, G. (eds). *Home–School relations*. Needham Heights, MA: Allyn & Bacon, pp. 40–64.

U.S. Census. (2004). *http://quickfacts.census.gov/qfd/states/00000.html*

U.S. Department of Education (2002). *Title 1 – Improving the Academic Achievement of the Disadvantaged* (Public Law 107 – 110-Jan. 8, 2002). Washington DC: Author. Retrieved on May 19, 2003 from the No Child Left Behind website: *http://www.ed.gov/legislation/ESEA02/pg1.html*

U.S. Department of Education (2003). *Overview: No Child Left Behind* (NCLB). Retrieved on May 19, 2003 from the NCLB website: *http://www.nclb.gov/next/ overview/overview.html*

Part 1
Culturally Diverse Families and Schooling

2
Fostering Latino Parent Involvement in the Schools: Practices and Partnerships

Concha Delgado-Gaitan

Remember the days of class "room mother"? Long before there was research on parent involvement, I was convinced that learning was a family and school partnership. Both of my parents spoke limited English and neither had formal schooling in Mexico. But that didn't stop my mother from showing up with armloads of cupcakes for our classroom on Fridays when she was "room mother". Although she didn't speak much English when we immigrated, she was a strong and visible influence both in my school and home life. It mattered to me that my mother held high expectations for my sisters and me to succeed in school because I knew that I had to try my best. She got involved in whatever way she could and she wanted to hear good reports about me from my teachers.

Later when I became a teacher, the notion of involving parents in the school made even more sense. I met my students in their homes with their families, two weeks before school began. I knew that if I enlisted parental support for the educational program and included them in the classroom as much as possible, the children would understand that the teacher and parents worked together for their benefit.

As a school principal, I made the community coordinator a key person in the school's operation. Our effort was to make the school the center of the community. It was a difficult partnership to build, but as the graffiti and vandalism decreased significantly after only one year, we knew the effort was worth it.

Parent involvement is a rich resource, a tool, much like a book that informs us and moves children forward in their schooling (Delgado-Gaitan, 2004: 15). Educators that work collaboratively with Latino parents find that students perform better academically. Regardless of family size, socioeconomic level, or parental level of education, parents are capable of learning how to participate in their children's education. It is important that schools reach out to Latino parents.

2.1.   Latino Presence in the U.S.

For Latinos in the U.S., parent involvement needs to move more to the center of the school curriculum in order to enhance students' educational opportunities. Before we elaborate on effective parent involvement strategies, we need to have a general profile of Latinos in the US. The Latino population represents many nationalities.

The major groups include Mexican, Puerto Rican, and Cuban groups, with those of Mexican heritage comprising 67% (U.S. Census, 2004). The next largest subgroup is Puerto Ricans, followed by Cubans, immigrants from Central America, South America, Dominican Republic, and Spain. In 2004, Latinos comprised 39.9 million, or over 13%, of the total population of the United States (U.S. Census, 2004). Contrary to the public perception that all Latinos are immigrants or undocumented workers, fewer than 10% fit into that category. Furthermore, the total Latino population is projected to increase to nearly 67 million by the year 2050 (U.S. Census, 2004).

Geographically, Latinos reside in every state across the country, from Florida to Alaska to Hawaii. However, about two-thirds are concentrated in the southwestern US, including Arizona, California, Texas, New Mexico, and Colorado, and in Florida. The US Census Bureau (2004) reports that between 1999 and 2000, the California Latino population increased 37%. In Arkansas, the Latino population grew 196%, Georgia 233% and North Carolina, 274%. Latinos in these states work in the chicken processing, furniture manufacturing, and pig farming industries. Schools face tremendous problems as a result of the increasing Latino population. Many states, including Wisconsin, Illinois, Michigan, and New York also report significant Latino population growth.

2.2.   Latinos at Work

Latino workers in the US are well represented in the lower ranks of the labor force, but they also occupy prominent positions in a variety of professions across the US. For example, the number of Hispanic judges, architects, physicians and surgeons, professors, business executives, governors, athletes, university presidents, scientists, attorneys, legislators, and media workers total 120,750 professionals (Pew Hispanic Center, 2003). Latinos are Rhodes Scholars and Nobel laureates, including Adolfo Perez Esquivel (peace prize), Gabriel Garcia Marquez (literature prize), Luis W. Alvarez (physics prize), Octavio Paz (literature prize), Rigoberta Menchu (peace prize), and Mario Molina (chemistry prize).

Although Latinos have their share of Nobel laureates, scholars, professionals, and celebrities, the big picture still looks dismal for the many poor families. In 2003, Latinos, overall, comprised the principal source of new workers to the U.S. economy. The Pew Hispanic Center estimates that more than 500,000 Latino workers are employed below their potential level. This is a result of the economic slowdown, a shortfall equivalent to 3.5% of the Latino workforce.

Although Latinos share a strong work ethic, roughly 20% of the Latino population is living in poverty (U.S. Census, 2004). Latinos who immigrate to the US arrive with high hopes of expanding educational opportunities for their children, which can lead to economic betterment. But often, they remain trapped in entry-level jobs without the possibility for advancing. This is where education is pivotal in breaking the cycle of poverty for the younger generation (Lopez, 2002).

2.3.   Education Status

The link between educational attainment and employment is clear. On average, someone without a high school degree will earn $18,900 a year, compared with $25,900 for those who complete high school (U.S. Census, 2004). People with a bachelor's degree earn $45,400, and with a master's degree, $54,500. Less than 25% of Latinos are enrolled in a 4-year college and Latinos represent only 5% of graduate students (National Council of La Raza, 2004). Generally, by the time Latino students reach 17 years of age, they have the literacy and math skills of 13-year-old white students. While many complete college and graduate school, a large percentage of Latino students have difficulty completing high school and getting into college. In some communities, as many as 40% of Latino students drop out of school, making parent involvement critical to the educational process throughout the students' academic life (National Center for Educational Statistics, 2002).

Latinos have a particular relationship to schooling in the US. Throughout the history of education, Latinos have encountered prejudice and lack of access to educational resources because of their low-income status and linguistic differences. This is especially true for Mexicans in segregated schools where children were punished for speaking Spanish. In the 1960s, those schools were disbanded in response to the Civil Rights movement and the Bilingual Education Act. Today some schools still fail to provide textbooks for students until months after school begins in the fall. Practices like this further set Latino students behind white middle class students. All the while, Latino parents are blamed for the students' underachievement (Delgado-Gaitan, 2004).

For the most part, Latino adults view education as a vehicle to move their children out of the poverty that plagued them. The desire for their children to have a better life accounts for the sacrifices that parents make for their children (Trueba, 1999). Although parents from poor communities value education, they often lack the knowledge on how to access educational resources to support their children's schooling (Lareau, 2003).

Poverty exacerbates stress in the family. Latino children who live in impoverished conditions have fewer resources than those available to families with higher incomes. The lack of financial, social, and political resources also results in health problems caused by poor nutrition and inferior or nonexistent health care. This, in turn, can negatively impact children's school attendance. In extreme cases, inadequate housing and homelessness interfere with children's schooling because of frequent moving from place to place or insufficient space in the house to make schoolwork a priority (Sleeter, 2003).

Recognizing that poverty by itself does not produce underachievement, we must acknowledge that social conditions can interfere with children's motivation and opportunity to learn. Numerous factors hinder educational attainment of Latino students, including: (1) low societal expectations for Latino youth and children, (2) lack of early childhood education opportunities, (3) lack of resources in schools, (4) poorly trained teachers, and (5) limited parental and community engagement and choices (President's Advisory Commission on Educational Excellence for Hispanic Americans, 2003). The President's Advisory Commission on Educational Excellence for Hispanic Americans makes numerous recommendations including: (1) setting higher expectations for Latino students, (2) improving teacher preparation teachers to meet the needs of Latino students, (3) challenging post-secondary institutions to graduate 10% more Latino Americans each year, and (4) Increasing accountability and coordination of federal programs. All of these recommendations necessitate strong parent involvement; the schools must connect and communicate with Latino families in an on-going, sustained process.

Reaching out to Latino communities is a matter of building trust as a platform for creating sustained collaborations with parents. Latino families need to know that educators are interested in meeting their needs and are respectful of their language and cultural differences (Aspiazu, Bauer, & Spillett, 1998; Decker & Decker, 2003; Delgado-Gaitan, 2001). Latino parents who have little contact with educators may feel self-conscious and limited in their ability to discuss schooling in terms unfamiliar to them. Therefore, whether the contact is personal in the home, at school, or by phone, educators need to be conscious of the parents' lack of knowledge about the educational system. However, parents do know something about the most important topic at hand: their child. Regardless of culture, educational attainment, and socioeconomic standing, all families have strengths. Thus, educators need to make the parents feel at ease and win their trust in order to engage them in a continuous collaboration. Partnerships that begins the first day of school and lasts until the student graduates from high school, promise academic success for students.

2.4.   Preparing for College

Many issues reside under the rubric of parent involvement and family-school partnerships. Getting Latinos to college is one aspect of family-school partnership that deserves close attention. Underemployment and low educational attainment in the Latino community remain high because many Latino students fail to attend college. It is a concern that needs to be addressed long before the application is submitted to the college of choice. How Latinos in professional positions attained college is often a story of hardships and inspiration.

As important as those stories are, they are not the focus of this paper. Instead, the remainder of this chapter will focus on the systematic preparation necessary to get young Latino boys and girls into college, especially as it relates to parent involvement. It's the one part of the story of Latinos in education rarely told. For that reason, I emphasize parent involvement from the perspective of families that participated in a program for socializing young Latina students for college.

Although both Latino and Latina students are underrepresented in the university system, Latinas fare even worse than Latino males. 71% of Latina girls in some school districts do not graduate from high school. The long journey to college begins in the elementary school years and steadily gains importance through high school. Schools, as well as family life, play a central role in socializing students to college. Family influence is often absent in undereducated Latino families. Latino girls in traditional families are often not encouraged to pursue education because parents have heard that it's costly. Thus, just getting through high school is sometimes the "best" they think they can do (Andrade, 1982; Asher, 1984; Delgado-Gaitan, 1994; Flemming, 1982; Gonzalez, 1995; Johnston, Markle & Harshbarger, 1986). The problem is that without a high school diploma or college degree, these young people are relegated to low-income employment thereafter.

As dismal as the statistics are for Latino male and female students in gaining admission to college, there is hope. In this chapter, I focus on the socialization process necessary for getting young Latinos into college, with parent involvement as a critical component. I discuss the findings of a 4-year northern California study—a Mother/Daughter Program (M/D). The M/D Program was a proactive and constructive effort addressing the vast challenges and rewards of academic achievement of young Latina girls and their mothers. They learned about attending college and preparing for professional careers.

There is a significant difference between students who just "get by" in school– those who may graduate from high school but not attend college, and students who "get ahead." Students who just "get by" tend to come from families that may be poor and want their children to succeed in school but lack the knowledge to access the educational resources to support their children. Students who "get ahead" tend to come from families who continuously stress high grades, are involved in school activities, and discuss options for colleges and careers (Gonzalez, 1995). The key difference is the "know how", which some parents possess more than others. And it's that cultural knowledge or "know how" that Latino parents gain through participation that develops parent potential and skills.

2.5. The Mother/Daughter Program

The Mother/Daughter Program (M/D) was the context in which I studied 20 girls whose parents were immigrants from Central American countries and Mexico. Before describing the findings of the Mother/Daughter Program, I want to clarify one point, which I will repeat toward the end of the chapter: the Mother/Daughter Program involved only girls because the funding sources made that specification because of the educational need; that is, statistics show that Latina girls trail the boys in college attendance. But boys, just as much as the girls, can benefit from programs such as the M/D if the program is designed to include boys. Here, I describe the M/D program as it involved the girls and their mothers. Later in the chapter, I present the programmatic features that need to be considered by schools in preparing both Latino girls and boys for college.

The program operated on the premise that mothers exert a powerful influence on their children's decision-making (Andrade, 1982; Gonzalez, 1995) and that getting Latina girls to graduate from high school and enter college requires a systematic partnership between the schools, the families, and the university. The M/D program has been a successful model of such a partnership in four states: Arizona, California, New Mexico, and Texas (Tomatzky, Cutler & Lee, 2002). The M/D Program has operated on a national level since 1985. It began in El Paso, Texas and subsequently was adapted by Tempe, Arizona, Albuquerque, New Mexico and San Mateo, California. The programs in the various states differ according to the number of participants, duration of program, and specific activities. All of these programs have major goals and general operational practices in common. My study, however, involved only the program in San Mateo County in northern California.

Using the knowledge of educational development and the understanding of traditional Latino family dynamics as a guide, the national M/D model and the M/D Program in San Mateo were designed around three innovative components: (1) to provide the daughters with academic support towards meeting specific academic goals, (2) to educate mothers and daughters about getting the girls to college, and (3) to socialize the mother/daughter teams to college through field trip experience.

The first-year participants in the Texas program illustrate the M/D Program's success. The girls began the program in the 5th grade and were juniors at the time of the study, which showed the following results:

- 98% of the girls were still enrolled in school;
- 62% of the girls were enrolled in advanced college-preparation classes;
- 27% of the girls were enrolled in honors classes;
- 76% of the first year and 62% of the second year girls were above average in their academic achievement;

The M/D Program extended to various cities across the country. Committed administrators and local universities have initiated the Program in local school districts. Interested school districts assess their needs and seek funding to initiate M/D Programs. An administrative system is organized to manage the program in the schools. At a school level, the administrator designates a teacher to work with students in academic tutoring at school and conducts classes for them on study skills.

The San Mateo program began in the 5th grade and added one grade level in each of the four subsequent years through the 8th grade. Teachers submitted names of girls who were in academic peril, who were from low-income families, and whose parents had low educational attainment.

2.6.   Mother/Daughter Program Activities

Through the M/D Program, parents participated in well-designed activities to acquire the necessary skills and expertise to exercise parental commitment in their children's education. This is the expected outcome in effective parent involvement processes. The Mother/Daughter Program organized activities for the girls and their mothers around four broad themes: (1) building girls' self-esteem; (2) orienting the girls to higher education and professional careers; (3) improving the quality of preparation for higher education; and (4) increasing Latino parental commitment. The knowledge shared collectively among participants in the M/D Program not only empowered the mother and daughter participants, but school personnel also recognized the fruits of their work as Latino parents became informed. As a consequence, Latino students also became better informed and more independent learners and more interested in their schooling in general.

School activities focused on developing the girls' academic readiness by introducing them to computers. And through presentations, the schools helped the girls and their mothers to focus on their personal identities as individuals, members of Latino families, and members of American society. The M/D Program provided ongoing counseling and mentoring through high school and college. Girls were encouraged and supported academically to complete high school and apply for college. Program activities were also designed to acquaint mothers with careers, especially non-traditional careers, for women in math and science.

The Leadership Conference was an important component of the Mother-Daughter Program. The girls developed a wide variety of service projects for their community. For example, one or more students, in order to improve schools attendance, might organize a school attendance campaign involving students, parents, faculty, staff, and community members. The M/D Program's Leadership Conference provided participants the opportunity to develop leadership skills in planning, budgeting, organizing, negotiating, and risk taking. In the process, the girls gained confidence and increased self-esteem.

On Career Day, outstanding Latino professional women from the community went to the university campus and spoke to the Mother-Daughter participants about the importance of education and strategies for educational success. "Career Day" activities involved development of Latino students' knowledge and choices of careers. Students and parents received information about the educational track to follow for their desired career. Mothers became more effective role models for their daughters. They increased their awareness and use of community resources to develop positive self-esteem and confidence. They learned about the possible postsecondary options available to their daughters.

Tutoring in math and reading was an on-going academic activity provided by college student volunteers who came from the local community and state colleges. They were role models and mentors who inspired learning and retention in school, teaching the girls to budget time, obtain resources, and learn to discipline themselves. Computer classes for students and parents increased family interactions.

The significance of programs such as M/S is that they support cultural change in the home and the community. In immigrant families, cultural knowledge about schooling is incomplete due to low schooling of the parents and lack of awareness of available resources for their children's education in the US. Through M/D type programs, change in one family member means change in the family dynamics. The extended effect of the program benefits other family members. Mothers, like Mrs. Segura, describe how her husband and younger children have benefited from participation in the M/D Program.

Before I began participating in the Mother/Daughter program, my husband wouldn't let me leave the house for anything having to do with the schools. I had about 10 years of schooling in Mexico before leaving there, but then I got here and got married. Then I had my two daughters and there never seemed to be enough time to get an education here. So, when our children began school and the teachers sent notices about meetings, my husband wouldn't let me attend. He said that it wasn't important, and it was a waste of my time. I wanted to go just to see what it was all about, but I was afraid to go by myself since I didn't know anyone. Then my girls got older and fortunately, they were good students.

Then when our youngest daughter, Monica, was in the 5th grade, I received a notice that she was being selected to participate in the M/D Program. It sounded so interesting and I lied to my husband the first few times that I went to the Saturday meetings to meet with other moms and the director. Well, finally I got the nerve to tell him where I was really going on Saturdays. He still said it was a waste of time. But I didn't object to my attending because I convinced him that it was very important that I be there to learn as much as possible about ways to help Monica. By then, he was beginning to see that this daughter needed more direction and support than our oldest daughter, who was very disciplined. I think that's why he didn't object as much.

As the program continued and Monica entered middle school, I learned more and more at the M/D Program. I learned how to discipline her at home and how to advise her about schoolwork. I got information on how to seek the help she needed in middle school, both academically and in her social adjustment.

Now that she's in high school, her challenges are many. But if I wasn't involved in the M/D Saturday group with other Latina mothers, learning how to advocate for her, she wouldn't be doing as well as she's doing. My husband does not say anything against me attending meetings or school functions anymore. Although he doesn't attend meetings with me, he has seen the positive results with both of our daughters. And his way of supporting is by remaining quiet. [Translated from Spanish.]

Mrs. Segura, like other mothers, learned that when one family member grows, other members also learn. In Latino families, the ties are strong and the woman's role holds a great deal of authority in reference to children's schooling. Men commonly relegate the responsibility to women. So, in the absence of school programs like the M/D Program, Latina women miss out on social networks with other women and school personnel where they can obtain critical knowledge.

Volunteering in the community helps develop student awareness of their environment and their place in the community they live in. In the personal identity workshops in San Mateo, students met with counselors to discuss and write about their cultural and gender identity. Students worked with sponsoring teachers, district coordinators, and program staff members to identify, plan, and carry out selected community projects. They presented their projects at the scheduled annual Leadership Conference. Its purpose was the development of leadership skills that come from firsthand involvement in leadership activities in their respective school and community. They are skills that help the girls to become productive members of the community with a responsibility to improve the community's quality of life.

Community activities introduced the participants to the many resources around them. The girls and their mothers visited various community sites, including the medical center, city hall, historic missions, the public library, and the museum of art. They attended theater performances, or participated in a health fair for women, taking place in the community. All of these experiences broadened the participants' development as individuals and community members and as future leaders within their community.

2.7. The University's Role

The San Mateo M/D Program forged a partnership with a Santa Clara University, which sponsored four key on-campus activities during the year: (1) Campus Open House and Tour; (2) Career Day; (3) Leadership Conference; and (4) Summer Camp at the university campus. The Campus Open House Tour was the first visit to a university campus for the mother and daughter participants. Experience with the Latina Mentor Program indicates that the visit to the university is the participants' favorite part of the program. The girls also spent 2 days on campus, giving them a well-rounded view and appreciation of campus life.

2.8. Changing the Vision

Cultural literacy about preparation for college involved parental reflection about their own opportunities for learning. Increasing Latino mothers' confidence and knowledge about their daughters' academic career, meant a journey to the mothers' personal and cultural history. The mothers participated in a personal literacy activity that the Director, Dr. Contreras, called "Mother Stories". This became a significant, empowering, cultural literacy activity for the mothers and daughters.

For three of the four years, in the mothers' story sharing activity, mothers met monthly to discuss topics related to mother-daughter relationships. The literacy process was a three-hour session divided into four-parts: (a) reflecting about a specific topic, decided by the parents and the coordinator; (b) writing; (c) reading their written text to the group; and (d) sharing and discussing. Collectively, the women created a safe environment to think and express themselves. The process was intended to break the cycle of isolation for these mothers, who may feel distant from others when it comes to raising their daughters. Isolation typically breeds fear, intimidation, and non-participation. However, engagement allows for connection with the adults to their own history, culture, family, and others in their community, enabling them to feel more empowered. Initially, specific topics were selected for the mothers, but as the M/D Program moved along, the participants were asked to suggest topics that they believed were relevant to their particular experience.

Mothers met in a local community library and cultural center on Saturdays for 2 hours with the M/D Program coordinator to discuss, write, and share their personal stories on topics. They included: (a) important parts of parents' own childhood relative to school; (b) values, which parents most want to impress on their children; (c) developing their own confidence socially and academically; (d) influencing their children's peer groups; (e) finding their children's life-interest; (f) spending time with their children; and (g) discipline, and setting limits for their children.

Each literacy assignment was designed to have the mothers express their own childhood experience on the topic and their efforts to deal with their own role as mothers. In the literacy activities, mothers increased their awareness of issues and values about which they needed to speak with their daughters as they guided them through schooling. Their stories contained critical elements that are known to be of great influence in shaping young girls' attitudes, awareness, and direction in their schooling and career choices. The personal characteristics present in their stories are intelligence, determination, and faith.

Intelligence is too often confused with attainment of formal schooling. But in reality, intelligence is what we do with the knowledge we have. And the stories that these women told their daughters showed their true intelligence in their ability to interpret the complex society in which they live and raise their families. They manage a household and support a family with fewer financial resources than they need to live comfortably. This requires a great deal of intelligence. The decisions they make on a daily basis are those needed to resolve family problems.

Determination is a quality that ran through many of the personal narratives told to the daughters. The mothers have pushed past what they perceived to be limitations and barriers. They forged ahead against the odds in order to provide their daughters, and family as a whole, the best opportunities for a better life than they experienced in their homeland.

In their stories, *Faith* was transmitted in the way that the women have resorted to a spiritual belief in order to bear the struggles with immigration issues, learning a new culture, and underemployment in a new society.

2.9.   Personal Power

How young Latinas perceive their personal power has much to do with their relationship with their mothers. The interviews with the girls indicated that they listen to and depend on their mothers for guidance about school and career decisions. Although the girls know that their mothers did not have formal education in the US, or Mexico in some cases, they first go to their mothers for advice before turning to their friends or teachers. Mothers are the ones to direct the girls to find the appropriate resources. Often, this means that through the personal stories, they share with their daughters they make the girls look within for their inner confidence to resolve problems in a new way.

When the girls were asked who they chose as their confidants, they said, "My mom." Specifically, they appreciate the stories they heard about how their mothers managed during hard times. This makes the girls believe that their mothers know quite a bit, even if the mothers did not have a great deal of formal schooling.

I recall one time when things weren't going well for me in my first year of high school. It was all just too stressful and I felt nervous about my grades. My mother had stopped helping me with my homework years before because she didn't know how to do the homework that I had to do. She hadn't finished school in Mexico and her English wasn't the best. Anyway, she noticed that I was feeling pretty down about things. Then, I told her about the stress I had and how I didn't know if I could handle high school especially because I want to go to college, which will be more difficult. And mom was very understanding. She sat me down at the kitchen table, and she shared about going to school in Mexico. It was during a time when her family was very poor and she wasn't sure that she'd be able to stay in school and work to help her family. Mom told me that she was so excited about learning, but her mom needed her to help work the farm when her father died. Gosh, mom was just 10 years old and all of her brothers and sisters were younger.

Anyway, mom told me about how her mother didn't want her to leave school, but she couldn't do everything by herself. So, together her mother and my mom decided that they would divide the work on the farm so that mom did most of her share before school, after school, and on weekends. And her mother would let her stay in school as long as the work got done. My mom felt so glad that she could stay in school that she studied hard and managed to work and go to school. Mom's story made me feel that I could do what I needed to do to make it in school. As long as I loved learning and could get mom to help me work through things just like her mom helped her. At least I don't have to work hard in the fields.

And actually, that's what mom told me. She said, "you don't ever have to feel that you're doing this alone. None of us are alone. Even if I don't know how to help you to do the work that you're required to do, I will help you find the tutors at school or I'll talk with your counselor to show me what I need to do. So don't ever feel that you can't talk to me." Her comments made me feel so much better. I wasn't as afraid. I felt more confident.

From the mothers' stories, girls learned to trust their own strength and have confidence in themselves and to think about what they must do to go to college and have a better education.

2.10.   Proactive School Engagement

From the M/D Program, we learn that educators need to take proactive measures to prevent academic and social crises. They must continuously inform parents in Spanish about their children's academic progress. Effective schools design parent involvement activities that provide various levels of involvement. Three basic levels of influence in students' academic lives include the family, the school, and the community. Not only are basic cultural values and beliefs learned in the family, but also daily practices often speak louder than words. In the Latino family, if parents are inactive in their child's schooling, educators tend to perceive this as indifference toward the school.

However, what may be driving their behavior is fear or lack of understanding of their role in the school system. In the San Mateo M/D Program, the teacher/mother support component involved the teachers working with parents in establishing and sustaining an academically supportive environment in the girls' home. When the parents entered the program, they and the teachers signed a contract to participate actively for the duration of the program. And they did.

2.11.   Parents' Continued Learning

For the mothers in the M/D Program, one of the highlights was the sense of personal growth that they experienced. Developing mothers' aspirations for their own personal and professional growth is an important part of the teacher/parent component. The mothers involved in the M/D Programs learned to become leaders. They gained confidence to stand in front of a group and address other women, teach them about ways to advocate for their children in school. In many cases, the mothers of the girls in the program reported feeling so inspired by their daughters' enthusiasm for learning that they returned to school themselves to complete high school. They moved on to community college to improve their English before transferring to a state university for a BA degree, as is the case with Alma Garcia.

Alma Garcia's daughter began the M/D Program in the fifth grade.

Participating with the Mother/Daughter program has taught me what it means to be supportive of my daughter, Marina. Although I felt that I had been supportive before, for Marina it was fine with her to do the very least to get by. But this group taught me how to get my daughter motivated and to go the extra mile for her. Just doing "good" work isn't enough to get to college and pursue a career. I've had to learn how to get my daughter inspired to do the best that she can. That's why talking constantly with her teachers has been the best support net that my daughter has had. She knows that we're all in this together with her. That extra push for Marina has been the constant contact with the other girls who can commiserate with her about not liking school. But she still gets support to do the best work possible.

By the time that my daughter was in her first year of high school, she was so turned on with school that she began pushing me to enroll in college. So, I've done that. I am now enrolled at the state college, working toward a psychology major. What's great is that our getting involved in the Mother/Daughter program helped my daughter and then she inspired me to go to college. We both laugh at the thought of graduating from college together. It may just happen. [Translated from Spanish.]

In addition to school-sponsored M/D Programs, other community programs exist that provide the context to assist Latino students' educational needs. One such organization is College Track. In northern California, this organization is improving communication with teachers, helping high school students stay in school, and supporting high school students to graduate and pursue college. College Track's purpose is to provide intense, comprehensive, individual academic assistance and information to high school students to achieve through high school and college. On the school's end, their responsibility is to inform Latino high school students about local organizations that provide academic, emotional, and financial support toward college. From building leadership among parents to building collaborative relationships between parents and school leaders, College Track effects change in the schools through organizing the grassroots community, one parent at a time. The focus of this community-driven school reform programs such as College Track is that they create the social capital necessary to form equal partnerships between the community and the schools. The community-driven school reform has as its goals to create public policy while obtaining resources and eliminating disparity among groups in the school and in the community.

2.12.   Conclusion and Recommendations

Students whose parents are involved in their schooling are twice as likely to excel academically. To Latino parents, "knowing how to navigate the school system" means understanding the school requirements, learning to access resources, and sustaining advocacy for students throughout their schooling. Where parent involvement is concerned, there is no one size fits all. Although no single model exists, effective programs have certain fundamental premises in common: (1) commitment, (2) communication, (3) continuity, and (4) collaboration. Educators and community members build relationships that support Latino families when they build student and parent power. In addition to developing higher academic benefits, students' social adjustment strengthens. Furthermore, when parents are involved, they develop higher self-esteem, which contributes to students' school success.

However, without a systematic partnership program in place, many Latino parents feel rather isolated when they attempt to participate in schools. Yet, every effort on the parents' part matters significantly as was the case in the Delgado-Gaitan household, where our parents encouraged their 5 daughters to study continuously. And in the early years when mom baked armloads of cupcakes for our classroom, her presence bridged the cultural discontinuity between school and home. My mother communicated with the school by using us as translators. Our parents' efforts produced five daughters who are all college graduates in successful careers. In turn, the five daughters' children have also succeeded in school and attended college. Breaking the cycle of poverty and educational neglect begins with the ties closest to us — the family and the school.

Parent involvement partnerships empower Latino families. It promotes high aspirations for students, and builds a solid commitment to life-long learning. Above all, graduating from high school and college and pursuing a professional career, are most likely to be life goals for students whose parents are involved in their education throughout their entire schooling experience. And these practices are most likely to exist where schools and communities commit to making effective partnerships a priority.

2.13. Recommendations for Family-School-Community Partnerships

Although the San Mateo M/D Program efforts to assist Latinas on their journey to college focused on girls and their mothers, the program model lends itself to including boys and fathers. Thus, the entire family benefits from a well-designed program. Executing parent involvement programs to support Latino girls and boys' academic achievement begins at the elementary school level.

Programs such as the M/D Program have taught us that beginning in the fifth grade and continuing through high school, schools need to develop strong academic socialization programs to support Latino students in their preparation toward college. I identified seven major support activities that helped the students to succeed academically in the M/D Program and which are replicable in schools and communities:

1) *Tutoring* students on a regular basis is possible by bringing college students to volunteer in the schools.
2) *Mentoring* students by pairing them with professionals supports not only their academic program but also their socialization and opportunities to learn about multiple career choices.
3) *Study skill classes* in schools or learning centers, teach students how to budget time, obtain resources, and exercise discipline to achieve academic success.
4) *Computer classes* for students and their parents provide the family with technical knowledge to assist students to complete their nightly homework.

5) *Volunteering* in the community helps students to feel a sense of belonging to and being responsible for the community in which they live.

6) *Personal identity* workshops for students and their parents guide students to address personal cultural identity issues with the assistance of counselors. Effective family-school-community efforts include these major components in their paradigm.

7) *Collaboration with community organizations* such as College Track, which assist less represented students to succeed in school and prepare for college.

References

Andrade, S.J. (1982). *Young Hispanics in the United States – Their aspirations for the future: Findings from two national surveys.* Austin, Texas: Center for Applied Systems Analysis.

Asher, C. (1984). Helping Hispanic students to complete high school and enter college. *ERIC Clearinghouse on Urban Education.* New York: Teachers College, Columbia University.

Aspiazu, G.G., Bauer, S.C. & Spillett, M.D. (1998). Improving the academic performance of Hispanic youth: A community education model. *Bilingual Research Journal*, 22(2), 1–20.

Decker, L.E. & Decker, V. (2003). *Home, School, and Community Partnerships.* Lanham, MD: Scarecrow Press.

Delgado-Gaitan, C. (1994). Consejos: The power of cultural narratives. *Anthropology & Education Quarterly*, 25(3), 298–316.

Delgado-Gaitan, C. (2001). *The Power of Community: Mobilizing for Family and Community.* Boulder, CO: Rowman & Littlefield.

Delgado-Gaitan, C. (2004). *Involving Latino Families in the Schools: Raising Student Achievement Through Home-School Partnerships.* Thousand Oaks, CA: Corwin Press.

Flemming, L. (1982). *Parental Influence on the Educational and Career Decision of Hispanic Youth* (National Report). Washington, DC: National Council of La Raza.

Gonzalez, M.C. (Spring, 1995). "Like mother like daughter: intergenerational programs for Hispanic girls" *Educational Considerations*, 22(2), 17–30.

Johnston, J.H., Markle, G.C. & Harshbarger, M. (1986). "What research says about dropouts?" *Middle School Journal* 17 (August), 8–17.

Lareau, A. (2003). *Unequal Childhoods: Social Class, Race, and Family Life.* Berkeley, CA: University of California Press.

Lopez, G.R. (2002). The value of hardwork: Lessons on parent involvement from an (im)migrant household. *Harvard Educational Review* 71(3), 416–437.

National Center for Educational Statistics (2002). Internet site. *The Condition of Education* (Report), Washington, DC: U.S. Department of Education.

National Council of La Raza (2004). Internet site. *The health of Latino communities in the South: Challenges and opportunities.* Report on the Findings of the National Council of La Raza Institute for Hispanic Health's Health in Emerging Latino Communities Project Funded by the Department of Health and Human Services. Office of Minority Health. Atlanta, GA.

Pew Internet Project (October 7, 2003). Internet site. *An Initiative of Pew Research Center.*

President's Advisory Commission on Educational Excellence for Hispanic Americans (March 31, 2003). *Internet site. From Risk to Opportunity: Filling the Educational Needs of Hispanic Americans in the 21st Century.*

Sleeter, C. (2003). Preparing teachers for culturally diverse schools. *Journal of Teacher Education*, 52(2), 94–106.

Tomatzky, L.,Cutler, R. & Lee, J. (2002). "College Knowledge: What Latino Parents Need to Know and Why They Don't Know It" (published 1990). Now that I've made it into mainstream I must not be Hispanic. *El Paso Times.* 28 (August), p. B4. (Both articles rewritten in the Tomas Rivera Policy Institute Report, 2002.)

Trueba, H. (1999). *Latinos Unidos.* Denver: Rowman & Littlefield.

U.S. Census Bureau Press-Release Hispanic Heritage Month (October 15, 2004). *For Facts for Features.*

3
Parenting, Social-Emotional Development, and School Achievement of African American Youngsters

Ronald D. Taylor

In recent years, with the passage of No Child Left Behind Act (2001) (NCLB), renewed attention has been devoted to the achievement gap and the school achievement of ethnic minority children and youth. Ethnic differences in academic performance appear when children are young and continue into adulthood. For example, there are significant differences in the vocabulary scores of African American and European American three and four year-olds (National Longitudinal Survey of Youth, see Jencks and Phillips, 1998). Among the nation's fourth graders, African American children perform below European American children on all subject areas assessed in the National Assessment of Educational Progress (Campbell, Hombo, & Mazzeo , 2000). The scores of African American 17 year-olds also fall significantly below European American 17 year-olds (Campbell, Hombo, & Mazzeo , 2000).

Ethnic differences in achievement are partially related to ethnic families' economic resources. The rates of poverty among African American, Native American and some Latino families are two to three times higher than the rate for non-Latino White children. McLoyd (1998) noted that African American children are also more likely to experience long-term poverty and live in areas of concentrated poverty. Lee and Burkam (2002) have shown that ethnic differences in achievement decline when families' socioeconomic status (SES) is controlled. Specifically, when SES was taken into account, black/white differences in math achievement declined by nearly 50%. Also, gaps in reading declined by nearly 65%. Thus, in understanding the achievement of African American youngsters it is important to examine the influence of family economic resources on children's functioning, and the processes through which the effects take place.

The present chapter is guided in part by the family economic stress model (Conger & Elder, 1994; Conger, Rueter & Conger, 2000) shown in Figure 3.1. The model suggests that families' economic resources are linked to adolescents' adjustment including their school achievement and psychological well-being

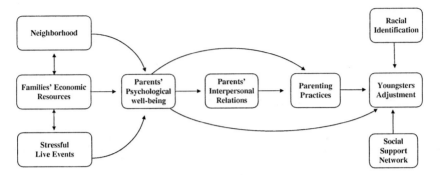

FIGURE 3.1. Conceptual Model Linking Families' Economic Resources And Other Important Social Variables With Youngsters.

through processes occurring in the family. To date, this model is the most comprehensive formulation linking families' economic resources to parents' adjustment, child-rearing practices, and youngsters' outcomes. This chapter also discusses how families' SES is associated with important social variables (e.g., family functioning, neighborhood conditions) that in turn, are linked to adolescents' well-being. Other social contextual variables including families' social networks, schooling, and some personal attributes (e.g., ethnic identity) of youngsters will be examined. The term, youngsters, used throughout the chapter refers to both children and adolescents although the majority of the literature involves studies on adolescents.

3.1.   Economic Resources and Youngsters' Adjustment

Findings have generally shown that families' SES is significantly associated with youngsters' adjustment in the areas of internalizing (e.g., depression) and externalizing problems (e.g., problem behavior, conduct problems; for a review, see McLoyd, 1998).[1] For instance, lower family income is associated with behavioral problems of 3 and 5 year-olds (Liver, Brooks-Gunn, & Kohen, 2002). It appears that social class differences are associated with increasing rates of externalizing problems during the preschool and early school years (Stevenson, Richman & Graham, 1985). For older African American children (10–11 years), low family income, negative financial events, and economic pressures are significantly related to externalizing behavior and internalizing

---

[1] Adolescents' school achievement is one of several indicators of socio-emotional adjustment and well-being that are highly interrelated. In this chapter, school achievement will typically not be distinguished from the larger construct of psychological adjustment. Routinely, correlations found with one indicator of adjustment are likely to have significant implications for other indicators.

symptoms (Conger et al., 2002). Low SES in families is also associated with chronic delinquency and serious offenses (Yoshikawa, 1994), along with poor school performance (Lee & Burkam, 2002).

Advances in theoretical and empirical work on the role of families' economic resources in family functioning have made clear the importance of the duration and timing of economic problems (McLoyd, 1998). The central questions in this work have been whether the length of time children spend in poverty has a predictable effect on their functioning and whether economic problems have more impact in some developmental periods more than others. Signif-icant numbers of African American children typically experience poverty of long duration (Waggoner, 1998). In addition, internalizing and externalizing problems increase the longer children experience poverty and economic problems (Duncan, Brooks-Gunn, Klebanov, 1994; Hanson, McLanahan, & Thompson, 1997). Little available research suggests that links between low income and children's development are stronger for young children than adolescents (Duncan & Brooks-Gunn, 1997).

Two issues are important to note regarding the duration of economic problems and its timing. First, particularly with African American families and adolescents, research is needed on other potentially important outcome measures. For example, economic difficulties may influence adolescents' outlook on the future and may compromise important social and emotional coping skills that affect internalizing and externalizing problems. Second, moder-ating processes that may be linked to attributes of the adolescents have not been adequately assessed in theoretical or empirical work on family income. Thus, for example, personal attributes or capacities (e.g., intellectual functioning, social skills, and self-esteem) that appear to ameliorate the impact of low income need further attention (Masten, 2001). Attributes, such as physical attractiveness or self-confidence have also been found to promote youngsters' capacity to function in the context of economic disadvantage (Elder, 1974).

The families' neighborhood or community is another important social contextual variable linked to families' economic resources and associated with adolescents' well-being. As stated earlier, poor and working-class African American families are more likely to live in economically disadvantaged or distressed neighborhoods. Although research on neighborhood effects remains surprisingly sparse, past work (e.g., Rutter, 1985; Caspi et al., 1993) suggests that variables associated with characteristics of neighborhoods (e.g., rate of poverty or rate of unemployment) are associated with an increase in delinquent behavior, deviant peers, and problems in school. Similar findings have revealed that as the proportion of low-income neighbors increases in a neighborhood, children's externalizing behavior increases (e.g., Duncan, Brooks-Gunn, Klebanov, 1994). Also, research has shown the more that economically disadvantaged African American mothers report their neighborhood has problems the lower the adoles-cents' self-esteem, and the higher their psychological distress and problem behavior (Taylor, 2000). Youngsters in disadvantaged neighborhoods may be more prone to engage in problem behavior than youngsters in more advantaged communities because they have more opportunities to find problem behavior and have fewer social constraints (McLoyd, 1998; Brody et al., 2001; Brody et al., 2003).

3.2. Economic Resources and Parents' Functioning

In the family economic stress model (see Figure 3.1), families' resources impact parents' social and emotional well-being and in turn, affect adolescents' behavior. For example, unemployed men are more depressed, anxious, and dissatisfied with themselves than employed men. Unemployed men also are more likely to engage in risky behavior than employed men (for a review see McLoyd, 1989). When African American fathers' perceive themselves as a failure in providing for the family, their psychological adjustment declines (Bowman, 1988). Financial strain is also positively linked to fathers' pessimism about the future (Galambos & Silberstein, 1987). McLoyd (1989) notes that mental and physical maladies have also been associated with economic problems and may compromise parents' capacity to cope with daily life challenges, including parenting.

Economic resources are also significantly associated with mothers' psychological well-being (Conger et al., 1994; McLoyd et al., 1994; McLoyd, 1998; Taylor et al., 2004). Mothers' depression increases as their economic problems rise (Brody et al., 1994; Conger et al., 2002, McLoyd et al., 1994). In comparison, greater economic resources have been linked to mothers' outlook on the future (Brody et al., 1994; Taylor et al., 2004). For instance, when mothers report financial resources are adequate to meet the families' needs, they are more optimistic about their future (Taylor et al., 2004). Mothers' perceptions of their self-efficacy and self-worth are also negatively associated with economic problems (Brody et al., 1994). Similar to fathers, mothers with economic problems appear to be at risk of physical as well as mental health problems that challenge their coping capacities (e.g., Brody et al., 1994).

Neighborhood conditions and stressful life events are also important factors linked to parents' economic problems and associated with parents' adjustment. The effects of neighborhood conditions on parents' adjustment has revealed that the level of depressive symptoms is higher among residents of economically disadvantaged urban neighborhoods (Ross, 2000). Ross found that in neighborhoods with a high percentage of households below the poverty level and a high number of mother headed households, social disorder was high and in turn, positively associated with depression. Similar findings are apparent when African American families living in rural economically disadvantaged communities are compared to those in economically more secure towns (O'Brien, Hassinger, & Dershem, 1994). It is not surprising that neighborhood disorder (e.g., vacant and deserted buildings, drinking and drug dealing in public) is associated with adults' psychological distress (Cutrona et al., 2000). These stressors add to family distress, particularly for the mother. Other stressors significantly related to self esteem and distress for mothers are family disruption (e.g., divorce, death in family), work related events (e.g., job loss), and health problems (e.g., illness, injury) (Taylor, 1997).

3.3. Parents' Psychological Adjustment, Interpersonal Relations, and Parenting Practices

In the family economic stress model, family income is linked to adolescents' functioning through the influence of parents' well-being and their interpersonal relations (see Figure 3.1). The link between parents' well-being and the experience of conflict and problematic relations have shown that parents' psychological distress is associated with an increase in angry interactions among parents or caregivers (Brody et al., 1994; Conger & Elder, 1994; Conger et al., 2002). For example, parental depression is associated with a decrease in warm, harmonious relations and positively associated with parents' conflict concerning child-rearing (Brody et al., 1994). Lower depression in caregivers is significantly related to higher warmth and lower hostility (Conger et al., 2002). Mental health problems of parents (e.g., depression, anxiety, social dysfunction, somatic symptoms) are negatively associated with maternal and paternal support (e.g., Solantaus, Leinonen, & Punamaki, 2004).

Parents' psychological functioning and marital relations also spill over into parenting practices and relations with youngsters. Marital strife is often linked to the quality of parenting exhibited in the family (Conger et al., 2002). Nurturing, involved parenting decreases as parents display hostile, aggressive behaviors with one another. Marital conflict is associated with greater hostility toward adolescents (Conger & Elder, 1994; Solantaus et al., 2004). In addition, mothers experiencing marital problems are more likely to perceive their youngsters' behavior as more deviant and are more likely to issue commands and to be critical of the youngsters' actions (Webster-Stratton, 1988).

The model also suggests parents' adjustment and well-being have a direct impact on parenting practices (see Figure 3.1). Thus, parents' low self-esteem, depression or anxiety, are expected to have a direct effect on the practices they administer in the home. Depression in parents is associated with increased punitive behavior (Ge et al., 1994; McLoyd et al., 1994). Mothers' depression is also associated with more negative and hostile forms of punishment (scolding, yelling, hitting, threatening to send the child away, McLoyd et al., 1994). In addition, mothers' depression is associated with negative perceptions of maternal responsibilities. Based on mothers' self-report and the report of her spouse, depression may be associated with lower involvement and emotional support of their children (Conger et al., 1992). Finally, other indicators, such as drugs or alcohol are associated with less adequate parenting practices including less control of adolescent behavior (King & Chassin, 2004).

3.4.   Parenting Practices and Youngsters' Adjustment

Economic resources influence parents' functioning, spousal relations and parenting practices, which in turn, influence children's positive or negative adjustment (see Figure 3.1). Research has examined parenting dimensions including control, support, and organization and their links to youngsters' adjustment. Parental warmth and involvement are positively associated with adolescents' school achievement, positive peer relations, and self-confidence (Conger et al., 1992). High quality parenting including emotional support and involvement are associated with lower externalizing behavior (Solantaus et al., 2004). Lower nurturance and involvement are positively linked to youngsters' externalizing symptoms (Conger et al., 2002). Harsher parenting is also associated with youngsters' conduct problems (Simons et al., 2002).

Evidence on parenting practices in controlling and shaping childrens' behavior have shown that more punitive forms of control and discipline (e.g., yelling, hitting, threatening) are associated with adolescents' cognitive distress (difficulty making decisions) and depressive symptoms (McLoyd et al., 1994). Youngsters' externalizing problems are also associated with increased punitive parenting (Solantaus et al., 2004). A number of sources employing different methodologies have revealed the importance of organization and structure in the family for youngsters' functioning (Clark, 1983; Taylor 1996; Taylor & Lopez, 2005). In families that are organized and structured around order and routine, adolescents obtain higher grades, engage in less problem behavior and experience lower psychological distress (Taylor 1996; Taylor & Lopez, 2005).

3.5.   Moderating Processes

Moderating processes, as described earlier, represent experiences or relations that families may have that lessen the impact of economic resources on their capacity to function well. There are a number of social variables that may be linked to protective processes that diminish the impact of economic strain or enhance the quality of African American parenting. For example, when families are more likely to receive support from kin during economic hardship, moderating processes (e.g., emotional support from adult relatives) may be helpful to the adolescent (Dressler, 1985).

Kin support is positively associated with mothers' and youngsters' adjustment (Taylor et al., 1993; Taylor & Roberts, 1995; Taylor, 1996). For example, kin social and emotional support is positively linked to school achievement and engagement (Taylor, 1996). Kin support may also enhance the quality of parenting, and higher quality parenting is associated with higher adolescent functioning (Taylor, 1996; Taylor & Lopez, 2005). Specifically, the negative association of family income with parent-adolescent communication problems is less apparent for families with high compared to low levels of kinship social support (Taylor & Lopez, 2005). McLoyd (1998) noted that adults outside the home may indirectly influence youngsters' socio-emotional functioning by providing mothers support that enhances parental control. Nonparent adults may also model positive behaviors for both youngsters and their parents.

Other research on moderating processes has shown that the qualities of neighborhood in which families live may either buffer adolescents from problems or make negative behaviors more likely to occur. For example, the negative effects of harsh-inconsistent parenting and low nurturance on youngsters' conduct disorders are strongest among families living in the most disadvantaged neighborhoods (Brody et al., 2003). Also, children early in pubertal maturation residing in more disadvantaged neighborhoods are more likely to affiliate with deviant peers than early maturing children living in less disadvantaged neighborhoods (Ge et al., 2002).

3.6. School Context

Youngsters spend most of their waking hours in school and thus, school experiences may have important links to their functioning. Indeed, schools have been regarded as important social institutions in which to address problems of at-risk youngsters (Roeser, Eccles, & Sameroff, 2000). Eccles and colleagues (e.g., Eccles & Midgley, 1989; Eccles, Wigfield, & Schiefele, 1998; Roeser et al., 2000) have argued that to the extent youngsters perceive the school as an environment in which they feel cared for and supported, they are more likely to develop the psychological resources that promote achievement and good conduct.

Much of the research on school experiences and social-emotional development has focused on school climate and its association with youngsters' functioning. School climate has been defined as organizational, instructional and interpersonal areas of the school environment (Loukas & Robinson, 2004). There is a significant link between school climate and youngsters' academic achievement (Roeser et al., 2000; Schmitt et al., 1999; Taylor & Lopez, 2005). For example, the more that youngsters perceive the school environment as emotionally supportive, organized and safe, the higher their school achievement and school engagement (Taylor & Lopez, 2005). A significant association between school climate and adolescents' psychological functioning exists (Roeser et al., 1998, 2000; Taylor & Lopez, 2005). For example, adolescents' perceptions of school climate (e.g., support for competence and autonomy, quality of relationships with teachers) are significantly associated with their psychological well-being (Roeser et al., 2000).

African American males are among several identifiable groups of students who tend to have multiple problems in school (e.g., poor motivation, poor mental health, poor academic behavior). These youngsters tend to report that the school encourages a competitive, hostile environment in which some ethnic groups are mistreated (Roeser et al., 2000). School climate may also moderate or buffer the effects of risk factors on youngsters' emotional and behavioral problems (Baker, 1998; Kuperminc, Leadbeater, & Blatt, 2001; Loukas & Robinson, 2004.).

Students at risk of interpersonal problems are less likely to report poor adjustment when they perceive that the school climate has several positive features (e.g., high cohesion, low friction, Loukas & Robinson, 2004).

3.7. Other Social Correlates of Adjustment and Achievement

In recent years, there has been discussion of youngsters' ethnic identity and its role in their social and emotional development (Alvarez & Helms, 2001; Lee, 2005; Sellers et al., 1997). Some theorists (Fordham & Ogbu, 1986; Ogbu, 1985) have argued that strong identification with their ethnic group may have a negative impact on the academic achievement and adjustment of African American youngsters. African American youngsters as a consequence of experiencing racial discrimination allegedly develop a social identity that is oppositional in nature and rejects school achievement as an appropriate goal (Fordham and Ogbu, 1986). In comparison, others have argued that strong ethnic identification may promote youngsters' functioning by enhancing their self-esteem and psychological well-being and by moderating the negative effects of racism and discrimination (Azibo, 1992; Baldwin, 1980; Seaton, 2005).

Beyond the work of Fordham and Ogbu (1986), little empirical work has shown that ethnic or collective social identity is negatively associated with African American youngsters' achievement and adjustment. An exception has been work suggesting African American youngsters' racial identity in opposing school achievement is so pervasive, high achieving students must avoid contact with other African American students in order to sustain their performance (Steinberg, Dornbusch, & Brown, 1992). Cook and Ludwig (1998) found no evidence of the negative effects of an oppositional social identity in assessing African American youngsters' alienation from school (e.g., educational expectations, drop-out rate, academic effort) or social standing among their peers. Other studies have also found that youngsters' experiences with racial discrimination are positively associated with racial identity development (Taylor et al., 1994). Students' ethnic identity is positively associated with their school achievement and engagement (Taylor et al., 1994). Other work has also revealed the positive association of youngsters' racial identity with their psychological adjustment. For example, racial identity is positively associated with self-esteem (Rowley et al., 1998; Seaton, 2005). Racial identity is also negatively associated with adolescents' depressive symptoms (Seaton, 2005) and problem behavior (Sellers, et al., 1998). The development of theoretical and empirical work on racial identity has made it clear that is it is important to distinguish whether among other issues, African American youngsters regard their race as a salient and a positive aspect of the self. Indeed, youngsters who regard their race as central and positive function more adequately (Seaton 2005; Sellers, Morgan & Brown, 2001).

The role of racial identity development in moderating the impact of racial discrimination on adolescents' social-emotional adjustment has also been examined. Racial discrimination is negatively associated with the mental and physical health of African American adults (Williams, Neighbors & Jackson, 2003). Perceptions of discrimination are also negatively related to African American youngsters' grades (Powell & Arriola, 2003) and positively associated with problem behavior (Guthrie et al., 2002; Prelow et al., 2004). Youngsters' racial identity appears to buffer them from some of the negative effects of perceived discrimination (Seaton, 2005; Sellers & Shelton, 2003). Among African American college students, those in their racial identification, who believe and accept that other groups perceive African Americans in a negative light, experience less distress as a result of their experiences with racial discrimination (Sellers & Shelton, 2003). Also, adolescents labeled as "Buffering/Defensive" view their race as personally salient and positive; and may perceive and accept that others hold negative views of their race (Seaton, 2005). Among this group, experiences with racial discrimination are not negatively associated with their self-esteem. Interestingly, however, "Buffering/Defensive" adolescents who experience racial discrimination also are more likely to report depression. It may be that youngsters' psychological defenses are not invulnerable. The formation of a racial identity as a central and highly evaluated component of the self-concept may offer some African American youngsters some protection from racial discrimination. However, youngsters' resources may not yet be sufficient to fend off all experiences all the time.

3.8.   Conclusions and Recommendations

The chapter suggests that in order to understand the links between parenting practices in African American families and youngsters' emotional adjustment and achievement, it is important to consider the larger social context in which the family resides. Families' economic resources play a significant role in determining where families live and the nature of social resources to which they have access. To the extent that families have sufficient financial resources, parents and youngsters function more adequately. However, when families' resources fall short of their needs both youngsters' and parents' social and emotional well-being are at greater risk. The resources present in the families' neighborhood have also been linked to parents' and adolescents' well-being. Findings also indicate that youngsters' adjustment and achievement is significantly associated with the manner in which parents are affected by their economic circumstances.

For parents, being unable to provide for the family may lead to questions of self-worth, competence and depression. Parents may also have concerns about the future that further darken their outlook. Research indicates that parents are also prone to experience marital problems when they experience economic difficulties. The stress associated with living with insufficient resources may precipitate family conflict. Both family conflict and parents' depression are linked to parents' childrearing practices. Lower family conflict and lower parental psychological distress are positively associated with youngsters' social-emotional adjustment and achievement. Social support typically from extended family and living in a community with more resources buffers youngsters from potential stressors and enhances the quality of parenting they are likely to experience. Also, the climate (organization, safety, emotional support, academic orientation) of the schools in which youngsters attend is associated with their psycho-social functioning. Finally, the development of adolescents' racial or ethnic identity appears to enhance their adjustment and buffers them from the negative effects of racial discrimination.

From the perspective of policy and practice, in order to address the adjustment and school achievement of African American youngsters, several conclusions are apparent. First, the research reviewed here suggests that it is important to improve the social and financial resources available to African American families. The most advantageous strategies are likely to be those that create employment opportunities, build skills and competencies, and enhance the social organization of communities. The findings reviewed suggest that parents function more adequately when they do not face the stress of struggling to make ends meet for the family. Improving the social conditions, including reducing crime and neighborhood physical deterioration and improving access to social resources should be part of any comprehensive plans for addressing the problematic links between families' resources, parenting practices and youngsters' adjustment.

Second, efforts should be devoted to enhancing families' social network. Research suggests that promoting the web of social networks in families' social surroundings (e.g., based in the family, connected to families' religious observance, originating and maintained in the community) will likely enhance family functioning and youngsters' adjustment and moderate the impact of stressors in the environment. Schools because of their prominent role in the community are in an advantageous position to serve as a conduit for social agents who serve families and the community. Schools also play an important role in promoting youngsters' psychological health. Thus, by creating emotionally supportive, safe, structured climates that are developmentally appropriate and reasonably free of racial bias, schools are likely to promote adolescents' adjustment and achievement. The work on school climate, indeed, suggests that it is those with the most challenges to their school performance and engagement who may benefit the most from positive changes in school environments.

Third, additional research is needed on the mental health and caregiver relations in African American families. In the family economic stress model utilized here, parents' mental health, marital relations and parenting practices are the mechanisms that link economic resources to youngsters' adjustment. Thus, with greater resources parents allegedly enjoy better mental health including less depression, and better marital relations, including less conflict, and in turn, display increased emotional support for their children. Unfortunately, there are important gaps in the literature for African American families. There is a scarcity of research on marital or caregiver relations and the impact on youngsters' adjustment. It is also likely that for economic, social and cultural reasons, African American families are underserved in assistance for problems in mental health and marital relations. Thus, one point of advocacy for those working with African American youngsters and families involves the adequate examination and analysis of mental health challenges and an increase in access to appropriate services.

Finally, it is important to note that while the family economic stress model was developed to explain the social and emotional functioning of economically vulnerable families, there is little reason to believe that the basic processes of that model do not apply to all African American families. Working, middle-class and affluent families may be less likely to experience economic pressures that lead to depression, marital conflict, and less adequate parenting practices. However, the same set of processes is likely to exist for parents with higher SES just on a different scale. Psychological distress and caregiver conflict, no matter what their source, may impede the administration of good parenting practices. Also, the effective parenting practices identified here (e.g., warmth, control and monitoring, organization and structure) have been linked to youngsters' adjustment across families' socioeconomic status.

Recommendations based on the research reviewed in this chapter include:

- Devote greater social and financial resources to disadvantaged communities. Tax breaks and capital investment are possible strategies for investment in struggling neighborhoods. Also, targeted deployment of law enforcement personnel to troubled neighborhoods has proven useful in some urban areas.
- Locate important social services (e.g., well-baby clinic, GED and adult literacy instruction) in schools so that schools in urban communities can connect social networks serving families and the community in a more comprehensive manner.
- Work with city, state and community leaders to increase psychological services devoted to poor communities. Services aimed at addressing psychological distress and marital relations are likely to benefit children and parents.
- Educate parents regarding the role of parenting practices and marital relations in the well-being of youngsters.
- Educate parents concerning the value and importance of good mental health and the availability of services for adults and youngsters.
- Inform educational personnel regarding the relations between non-instructional factors (e.g., poverty, family functioning, school climate) and youngsters' school achievement.
- Educate schools personnel regarding the complexities and challenges of serving an increasingly more racially diverse student population.

References

Alvarez, A.N. & Helms, J.E. (2001). Racial identity and reflected appraisals as influence on Asian American's racial adjustment. *Cultural Diversity and Ethnic Minority Psychology*, 7, 217–231.

Azibo, D. (1992). *Liberation Psychology*. Trenton, NJ: African World Press.

Baker, J.A. (1998) Are we missing the forest for the trees? Considering the social context of school violence. *Journal of School Psychology*, 36, 29–44.

Baldwin, J.A. (1980). The psychology of oppression. In Asante, M.K. and Vandi, A. (eds) *Contemporary Black Thought*. Beverly Hills, CA: Sage.

Bowman, P. (1988). Post-industrial displacement and family role strains: Challenges to the Black family. In Voydanoff, P. & Majka, L. (eds), *Families & Economic Distress*. Newbury Park, CA, pp. 75–101.

Brody, G.H., Ge, X., Conger, R., Gibbons, F.X., Murry, V.M., Gerrard, M., & Simons, R.L. (2001). The influence of neighborhood disadvantage, collective socialization and parenting on African American children's affiliation with peers. *Child Development*, 72, 1231–1246.

Brody, G.H., Ge, X., Kin, S., Murry, V.M., Simons, R.L., & Gibbons, F.X. (2003). Neighborhood disadvantage moderates associations of parenting and older sibling problem attitudes and behavior with conduct disorders in African American children. *Journal of Consulting and Clinical Psychology*, 71, 211–222.

Brody, G.H., Stoneman, Z., Flor, D. McCrary, C., Hastings, L., & Conyers, O. (1994). Financial resources, parent psychological functioning, parent co-caregivering, and early adolescent competence in rural two-parent African American families. *Child Development*, 65, 590–605.

Campbell, J.R., Hombo, C.M., & Mazzeo, J. (2000). U.S. Department of Education. National Center for Education Statistics. *NAEP 1999 Trends in Academic Progress: Three Decades of Student Performance*, NCES 2000–2469.

Caspi, A., Lyman, D., Moffitt, T.E., & Silva, P.A. (1993). Unraveling girls' delinquency: Biological, dispositional, and contextual contributions to adolescent misbehavior. *Developmental Psychology*, 29, 19–30.

Clark, R. (1983). *Family Life and School Achievement: Why Poor Black Children Succeed or Fail*. Chicago: University of Chicago Press.

Conger, R.D., Conger, K.J., Elder, G.H., Lorenz, F.O., Simons, F.L., & Whitebeck, L. B. (1992). A family process model of economic hardship and adjustment of early adolescent boys. *Child Development*, 63, 526–541.

Conger, R.D., Ge, X. Elder, G.H., Lorenz, F.O., & Simons, R.L. (1994). Economic stress, coercive family process, and developmental problems of adolescents. *Child Development*, 65, 541–561.

Conger, K.J., Rueter, M.A., & Conger, R.D. (2000). The role of economic pressure in the lives of parents and their adolescents. The family stress model. In Crockett, L. J. and Silbereisen, R.J. (eds), *Negotiating Adolescence in Times of Social Change*. Cambridge, England: Cambridge University Press, pp. 201–223.

Conger, R.D. & Elder, G.H. (1994). *Families in troubled times*. New York: Aldine de Gruyter.

Conger, R.D., Wallace, L.E., Sun, Y., McLoyd, V.C., & Brody, G.H. (2002). Economic pressure in African American families: A replication and extension of the family stress model. *Developmental Psychology*, 38, 179–193.

Cook, P.J. & Ludwig, J. (1998). The burden of 'acting white:' Do African American adolescents disparage academic achievement? In Jencks, C. & Phillips, M. (eds), *The Black-White Test Score Gap*. Washington, DC: The Brookings Institute Press, pp. 375–400.

Cutrona, C.E., Russell, D.W., Hessling, R.M., Brown, P.A., & Murry, V. (2000). Direct and moderating effects of community context on the psychological well-being of African American women. *Journal of Personality and Social Psychology*, 79, 1088–1101.

Dressler, W. (1985). Extended family relationships, social support, and mental health in a southern black community. *Journal of Health and Social Behavior*, 26, 39–48.

Duncan, G. & Brooks-Gunn, J. (eds) (1997). *Consequences of Growing Up Poor*. New York: Russell Sage Foundation, pp. 190–238.

Duncan, G., Brooks-Gunn, J., & Klebanov, P. (1994). Economic deprivation and early childhood development. *Child Development*, 65, 296–318.

Eccles, J.S. & Midgley, C. (1989). Stage/environment fit: Developmentally appropriate classrooms for young adolescents. In Ames, R.E. & Ames, C. (eds) *Research on Motivation in Education Vol. 3. Goals and Cognitions*. New York: Academic Press, pp. 139–186.

Eccles, J.S., Wigfield, A., & Schiefele, U. (1998). Motivation to Succeed. *Handbook of Child Psychology: Social, Emotional and Personality Development* (5th edn). New York, NY: John Wiley & Sons, Inc.

Elder, G. (1974). *Children of the Great Depression*. Chicago: University of Chicago Press.

Fordham, S. & Ogbu, J.U. (1986). Black students' school success: Coping with the "burden of acting White." *The Urban Review*, 18(3), 176–206.

Galambos, N. & Silberstein, R. (1987). Income change, parental life outlook and adolescent expectations for job success. *Journal of Marriage and the Family*, 49, 141–149.

Ge, X., Lorenz, F.O., Conger, R.D., Elder, G.H., & Simmons, R.L. (1994). Trajectories of stressful life events and depressive symptoms during adolescence. *Developmental Psychology*, 30, 467–483.

Ge, X., Brody, G.H., Conger, R.D., Simons, R.L., & Murry, V.M. (2002). Contextual amplification of the effects of pubertal transition on African-American children's deviant peer affiliation and externalized behavioral problems. *Developmental Psychology*, 38, 42–54.

Guthrie, B.J., Young, A.M., Williams, D.R., Boyd, C.J., & Kintner, E.K. (2002). African American girls' smoking habits and day-to-day experiences with racial discrimination. *Nursing Research*, 51, 183–190.

Hanson, T., McLanahan, S., & Thompson, E. (1997). Economic resources, parental practices, and children's' well-being. In G. Guncan & J. Brooks-Gunn (eds), *Consequences of Growing Up Poor*, New York: Russell Sage Foundation, pp. 190–238.

Jencks, C. & Phillips, M. (1998). *The Black-White Test Score Gap*. Washington, DC: The Brookings Institution.

King, M. & Chassin, L. (2004). Mediating and moderated effects of adolescent behavioral undercontrol and parenting in the prediction of drug use disorders in emerging adulthood. *Psychology of Addictive Behaviors*, 18, 239–249.

Kuperminc, G.P., Leadbeater, B.J., & Blatt, S.J. (2001). School social climate and individuals' differences in vulnerability to psychopathology among middle school students. *Journal of School Psychology*, 39, 141–159.

Lee, R.M. (2005). Resilience against discrimination: Ethnic identity and other-group orientation as protective factors for Korean Americans. *Journal of Counseling Psychology*, 52, 36–44.

Lee, V.E. & Burkam, D.T. (2002). *Inequality at the Starting Gate: Social Background Differences in Achievement as Children Begin School*. Washington, DC: Economic Policy Institute.

Liver, M.R., Brooks-Gunn, J., & Kohen, D.E. (2002). Family processes as pathways from income to young children's development. *Developmental Psychology*, 38, 719–734.

Loukas, A. & Robinson, S. (2004). Examining the moderating role of perceived school climate in early adolescent adjustment. *Journal of Research on Adolescence*, 14, 209–233.

Masten, A.S. (2001). Ordinary Magic: Resilience Processes in Development. *American Psychologist*, 56, 227–238.

Masten, A.S. & Coatsworth, D.J. (1998). The development of competence in favorable and unfavorable environments: Lessons learned from research on successful children. *American Psychologist*, 53, 205–220.

McLoyd, V.C. (1989). Socialization and development in a changing economy: The effects of parental job and income loss on children. *American Psychologist*, 44, 293–302.

McLoyd, V.C. (1998). Socioeconomic disadvantage and child development. *American Psychologist*, 53, 185–204.

McLoyd, V.C., Jayaratne, T., Ceballo, R., & Borquez, J. (1994). Unemployment and work interruption among African American single mothers: Effects on parenting and adolescent socioemotional functioning. *Child Development*, 65, 562–589.

NCLB (2001). No Chlid Left Behind Act of 2001. (Public Law 107–110).

O'Brien, D.J., Hassinger, E.W., & Dershem, L.D. (1994). Community attachment depression in two rural Midwestern communities, *Rural Sociology*, 59, 255–265.

Ogbu, J.U. (1985). A cultural ecology of competence among inner-city Blacks. In Spencer, M.B., Brookins, G.K. & Allen W.R. (eds), Beginnings: *The Social and Affective Development of Black Children*, Hillsdale, NJ: Lawrence Erlbaum Associates, pp. 45–66.

Prelow, H.M., Danoff-Burg, S., Swenson, R.R., & Pulgiano, D. (2004). The impact of ecological risk and perceived discrimination on the psychological adjustment of African American and European American Youth. *Journal of Community Psychology*, 32, 375–389.

Powell, C.L., & Arriola, K.R. (2003). Relationship between psychosocial factors and academic achievement among African American students. *The Journal of Educational Research*, 96, 175–181.

Roeser, R.W., Eccles, J.S., & Sameroff, A.J. (1998). Academic and emotional functioning in early adolescence: Longitudinal relations, patterns, and prediction by experience in middle school. *Development and Psychopathology*, 10, 321–352.

Roeser, R.W., Eccles, J.S., & Sameroff, A.J. (2000). School as a context of early adolescents' academic and social-emotional development: A summary of research findings. *The Elementary School Journal*, 100, 443–471.

Ross, C.E. (2000). Neighborhood disadvantage and adult depression. *Journal of Health and Social Behavior*, 41, 177–187.

Rowley, S.A.J., Sellers, R.M., Chavous, T.M., & Smith, M. (1998). The relationship between racial identity and self-esteem in African American college and high school students. *Journal of Personality and Social Psychology*, 74(3), 715–724.

Rutter, M. (1985). Family and school influences on cognitive development. *Journal of Child Psychology and Psychiatry*, 26, 683–704.

Schmitt, N., Sacco, J.M., Ramey, S., Ramey, C., & Chan, D. (1999). Parental employment, school climate, and children's academic and social development. *Journal of Applied Psychology*, 84, 737–753.

Seaton, E.K. (2005). *Perceived discrimination and racial identity profiles among African American adolescents*. Unpublished manuscript, Institute for Social Research, University of Michigan.

Sellers, R.M., Smith, M., Shelton, J.N., Rowley, S.J., & Chavous, T.M.(1998). Multidimensional model of racial identity: A reconceptualization of African American racial identity. *Personality and Social Psychology Review*, 2, 18–39.

Sellers, R.M. & Shelton, J.N. (2003). The role of racial identity in perceived racial discrimination. *Journal of Personality and Social Psychology*, 84, 1079–1092.

Sellers, R.M., Morgan, L., & Brown, T.N. (2001). A multidimensional approach to racial identity: Implications for African American children. In Neal-Barnett, A. (ed.), *Forging Links: Clinical-Developmental Perspectives on African American Children*. West Port, CT: Praeger, pp. 23–56.

Sellers, R.M., Rowley, S.A.J., Chavous, T.M., Shelton, J.N., & Smith, M. (1997). Multidimensional inventory of black identity: Preliminary investigation of reliability and construct validity. *Journal of Personality and Social Psychology*, 73, 805–815.

Simons., R.L., Lin, K., Gordon, L., Brody, G., Murry, V. and Conger, R. (2002). Community contextual differences in the effect of parental behavior on child conduct problems: A multilevel analysis with an African American sample. *Journal of Marriage and Family*, 64, 331–345.

Solantaus, T., Leinonen, J., Punamaki, R. (2004). Children's mental health in times of economic recession: Replication and extension of the family economic stress model in Finland. *Developmental Psychology*, 40, 412–429.

Steinberg, L., Dornbusch, S.M., & Brown, B.B. (1992). Ethnic differences in adolescent achievement: An ecological perspective. *American Psychologist*, 47, 723–729.

Stevenson, J., Richman, N., & Graham, P. (1985). Behaviour problems and language abilities at three years and behavioural deviance at eight years. *Journal of Child Psychology and Psychiatry*, 26, 215–230.

Taylor, R.D., Casten, R., & Flickinger, S. (1993). The influence kinship social support on the parenting experiences and psychosocial adjustment of African-American adolescents. *Developmental Psychology*, 29, 382–388.

Taylor, R.D., Casten, R., Flickinger, S., Roberts, D., & Fulmore, C. (1994). Explaining the school performance of African-American adolescents. *Journal of Research on Adolescents*, 4, 21–44.

Taylor, R.D. (1996). Kinship support, family management, and adolescent adjustment and competence in African American families. *Developmental Psychology*, 32, 687–695.

Taylor, R.D. (1997). The effects of economic and social stressors on parenting and adolescent adjustment in African American families. In Taylor, R. & Wang, M. (eds). *Social and Emotional Adjustment and Family Relations in Ethnic Minority Families*. Hillsdale, NJ: Lawrence Erlbaum Associates, pp. 35–52.

Taylor, R.D. (2000). An examination of the association of African American mothers' perceptions of their neighborhood with their parenting and adolescent adjustment. *Journal of Black Psychology*, 26, 267–287.

Taylor, R.D. & Lopez, E.I. (2005). Family management practice, school achievement and problem behavior in African American adolescents: Mediating processes. *Journal of Applied Developmental Psychology*, 26, 39–49.

Taylor, R.D. & Roberts, D. (1995). Kinship support and parental and adolescent well-being in economically disadvantaged African-American families. *Child Development*, 66, 1585–1597.

Taylor, R.D., Seaton, E., Dominguez, A., & Rodriguez, A.U. (2004). The association of financial resources with parenting and adolescent adjustment in African American families. *Journal of Adolescent Research*, 19, 267–283.

Waggoner, D. (1998, September). New study finds that poverty is transient for many. *Numbers and Needs: Ethnic and linguistic minorities in the U.S.*, 8(5). Retrieved from http/www.asu.edu/educ.cber/

Webster-Stratton, C. (1988). Mothers' and fathers' perceptions of child deviance: Roles of parent and child behaviors and parent adjustment. *Journal of Consulting and Clinical Psychology*, 56, 909–915.

Williams, D.R., Neighbors, H.W., & Jackson, J.S. (2003). Racial/ethnic discrimination and health: Findings from community studies. *American Journal of Public Health*, 93, 200–208.

Yoshikawa, H. (1994). Prevention as cumulative protection: Effects of early family support and education on chronic delinquency and its risks. *Psychological Bulletin*, 115, 28–54.

4
Asian Pacific American Cultural Capital: Understanding Diverse Parents and Students

Valerie Ooka Pang

The purpose of this chapter is to provide an informed discussion regarding the cultural values that shape the behaviors and achievement of Asian Pacific American (APA) students. Bronfenbrenner's (1979, 1986) ecological model of human development is used to explain how many APA families encourage and reinforce educational achievement. A central idea in this chapter is "cultural capital," which refers to the attitudes, expectations, knowledge, and behaviors parents pass on to their children that assist them in succeeding in school and society. To illustrate this central premise, the chapter also employs Sue and Okazaki's (1990) concept of relative functionalism as a key element in Asian cultural capital as it relates to both educational achievement and upward mobility. In addition, the chapter discusses the experiences and educational needs of diverse APA groups (e.g., Chinese, Filipino, Hmong, Japanese, Korean, Lao, Vietnamese, etc.). Though their educational needs may be similar, their social and academic experiences may differ due to various elements such as history and generational levels in the US. The chapter concludes with recommendations for educators to encourage and collaborate with Asian American students and their families.

4.1. Asian Pacific American Diversity

Asians generally share similar cultural values. For example, researchers find that many APA parents and their children have high regard for education. Nonetheless, their views and behavior may differ depending on ethnic group membership, socio-economic class, generation in the United States, assimilation levels, and other factors (Agbayani-Siewert, 1994; Benham & Heck, 1998; Chang, 2003; Cordova, 1983; Goyette & Xie, 1999; Heras & Patacsil, 2001; Hirschman & Wong, 1986; Kao & Tienda, 1998; Kiang & Lee 1993; Kim, 1980; Kim, 2002; Kitano & DiJiosia, 2002; Lee, 1996; Nordoff, 1985; Pang, 1990;

Rumbaut, 1997; Slaughter-Defoe et al., 1990; Sue & Sue, 1973; Tanabe & Rochon, in press; Uba, 1994). The discussion in this chapter indicates that APA parents employ differing methods to encourage educational success in their children. For this reason, some APA families and groups may be more successful in schools than others as illustrated in this chapter.

Researchers also find that APA youth are in need of educational services that are not being provided in schools (Benham & Heck, 1998; Flores, 1998; Rumbaut, 1997). Unfortunately, educators operate as if the "model minority" myth, a belief that all APA students are high achievers, is true (Hune & Chan, 1997). Zhou (Ch. 7, this volume) and Lee (Ch. 10, this volume) discuss this myth in proceeding chapters of this book. An overgeneralized view of Asian Pacific Americans is a powerful force in society. This viewpoint arises from the belief that "Asians" are a homogeneous group of model minority students. When data are gathered in school districts and aggregated into broad categories such as APA, research on academic achievement seems to indicate high levels of scholarship and thus the label, "whiz kids" has been used to describe many APAs.

Unfortunately, this portrayal does not accurately reflect the performance of individuals and particular ethnic groups. Some research suggests that Samoan Americans, Cambodian Americans, Native Hawaiians, and Lao Americans have not, as separate groups, been highly successful in schools (Lee, 1996; Long, 1996; Pang, 1990; Kiang, 2002; Reeves & Bennett, 2003). The academic achievement profiles of various APA groups differ and disaggregated statistical information can assist researchers in better understanding the specific needs of APA ethnic groups (Hune & Chan, 1997; Nordoff, 1985; Pang, Kiang, Pak, & 2004).

4.2.   Asian Pacific Americans

Presently, there are approximately 12 million Asian Pacific Americans, and they have increased by 72.2 percent since 1990 (Youngberg, 2001). The U.S. Census Bureau predicts that the APA population will increase to 33.5 million by 2050 (Committee of 100, 2005). APAs encompass a number of highly diverse ethnic groups, including those of Cambodian, Chinese, East Indian, Filipino, Guamanian, Hawaiian, Hmong, Indonesian, Japanese, Korean, Laotian, Samoan, Thai, Tibetan, and Vietnamese cultural heritages. The U.S. Bureau of the Census also included the following groups within the category of all other Asians in the 1980 Census (U.S. Bureau of the Census, 1983): Bangladeshi, Bhutanese, Bornean, Burmese, Celbesian, Cernan, Indochinese, Iwo-Jiman, Javanese, Malayan, Maldivian, Nepali, Okinawan, Sikkimese, Singaporean, and Sri Lankan (Gardner & Smith, 1985). In total, APAs are one of the fastest-growing minority groups in the United States. From 1970 to 1980 the APA population increased by approximately 143% (Suzuki, 1988). And from 1980 to 1990 the APA population continued to grow, numbering 7.3 million people and representing almost 3% of the U.S. population in 1990 (Ong & Hee, 1993).

The APA student population has also seen dramatic growth. During the 1980s, the number of Asian and Pacific Islander American children increased from a little over 900,000 to 1.7 million (Kiang & Lee, 1993). In states like California, New York, New Jersey, and Pennsylvania, the number of APA school-age students grew during this decade at a rate of over 100%. Various factors account for the explosive population increase. For example, the numbers of Korean immigrant children have grown because of the expansion in adoption of youth by U.S. families (Chan, 1991). In addition, the number of immigrants from Southeast Asia increased as a result of the Vietnam War. Kiang and Lee (1993) reported that one district in Massachusetts saw the addition of 35 to 50 new Cambodian and Laotian students registering for school each week in 1987. Taking into consideration birthrate and continued immigration, it is projected that the APA student population will continue to increase.

Since the APA community is complex and includes many ethnic groups, it is important to identify the terms utilized in this chapter. The terminology and definitions adopted for this piece were taken from a document written by the Committee of 100, a non-partisan Chinese American leadership organization (Committee of 100, 2005, p. 16):

- *Asians* are persons who have origins in peoples of the Far East (Chinese, Filipino, Japanese, Korean), Southeast Asia or the Indian subcontinent.
- *Native Hawaiians and Pacific Islanders* are persons who have origins in peoples of Hawaii, Guam, Samoa, Palau, Micronesia, Mariana Islands, or other Pacific Islands.
- *Southeast Asian* generally refers to Burmese, Cambodian, Hmong, Laotian, Thai, and Vietnamese.
- *South Asian* generally refers to Asian Indian, Bangladeshi, Bhutanese, Nepalese, Pakistani, Tibetan, and Sri Lankan.

These terms and their definitions demonstrate the diversity found within the APA community. Though many individuals think of Asian Pacific Americans as a homogenous group, the listing above shows the extensive within group diversity.

4.3.   Ecology of Human Development

The interactions of APA parents and their children within their ethnic communities and in general society can be explained by using Bronfenbrenner's (1979, 1986) ecology of human development. Bronfenbrenner identified five environmental systems to explain a range of contexts and factors that contribute to maturation. Since the first four are most pertinent to the experiences of APA children in this chapter, they will be the focus of the discussion. These four ecological systems can be used to explain the complexities involved in how APA parents impart educational values and guide the academic development of their children. In each environmental system, the child is placed at its center and linkages are shown to influence the life of the person. Though more detailed illustrations are given in a subsequent section, here is a summary of these four systems:

1) *Microsystem* – daily interactions with family members, peers, and teachers;
2) *Mesosystem* – influence of the connections of various microsystems. For example, parents who have positive relationships with teachers may be helpful in the child's learning process;
3) *Exosystem* – the influence of other settings that are further removed from a child. For example, state curriculum standards may indirectly shape his/her schooling experiences; and
4) *Macrosystem* – the socio-cultural values of society that influence the development of a child. For example, the lack of APA role models found in mainstream culture may negatively impact the ethnic identity formation of a young person.

Though Bronfenbrenner has identified family relationships as a fundamental ecology in the development of children, he also believed in the importance of other ecological systems that interact with the family system. In his theoretical framework, people are seen as individuals who interact within a range of social contexts. Individuals also have diverse characteristics that include ethnicity, age, immigration history, generation in the United States, gender, religious affiliations, interests, and talents that shape their experiences. For example, APA parents may be first generation immigrants who hold strong traditional cultural values, such as respect for elders and high regard for education. Since many children go to school with these values, students not only assimilate into the school culture, their ethnic beliefs about education become more connected to expected achievement behaviors and norms of society. In addition, their ethnic identity may be generally positive due to ethnic group experiences, such as participation in after-school Chinese school and ethnic churches, which oftentimes reinforce these values. Parents may also engage children in discussions regarding the importance of college and these discussions over time provide a strong educational orientation. Therefore, as children mature, they develop their own systems of beliefs. The examples above indicate how the cultural capital that many Asian Pacific American students may bring to schools work well with mainstream educational expectations.

Bronfenbrenner's ecological system of human development is a multi-layered theory and supports data from different disciplines such as anthropology, sociology, and psychology. The theory explains how an individual interacts in various contexts and through these interactions children develop and mature. In addition, since environments are dynamic and always changing, shifting social influences shape individual development over time. It is important to note that the following section includes studies as examples in understanding the complexities of APA cultures and development. Many of the selected studies were large-scale research projects that encompassed several groups. Other studies are representative of certain APA groups. Due to the limits of this chapter, it was impossible to represent all APA groups equally and should be interpreted carefully. However, since many APAs do share some similar experiences and hold the family as a central unit, this chapter highlights the importance of cultural capital through Bronfenbrenner's model.

4.4.   The Four Ecological Environments and Their Impact on Human Development

The first context that a child finds him/herself in is the *microsystem*. Within this context, the child interacts with and responds to parents, siblings, extended family members, neighbors, and peers. In this ecological paradigm, the child interacts with others and constructs meaning that arises out of life experiences. The interactions are reciprocal rather than passive. At this level, much time is spent with parents and other family members. Since the family is the most important structure in the transmission of cultural values (Sata, 1983), particularly for an APA family, it is essential to provide examples of parent-children interactions. The examples discussed below indicate that though parents may value education and are communicating with their children, parent-child interaction patterns may slightly differ in the APA community depending on factors such as generation in the United States, immigrant status, and ethnic membership.

Research indicates that APA parents are often involved in the education of their children through childrearing practices. One important study conducted by Cabezas (1981) examined the early childhood development of 233 Asian American families (Chinese, Japanese, Korean, and Vietnamese) from the San Francisco-Oakland metropolitan area. He researched parental values and communication styles. The author found in his sample that Asian American mothers, both native born and immigrant, tended to use question-asking behaviors rather than modeling, cueing or direct commands. Native-born Asian American mothers used more question behaviors than others. The Chinese and Filipino mothers who were born overseas used more direct commands and held more authoritarian beliefs than other mothers. In the families where mothers asked more questions, the children (preschool and primary grades) also responded with more questions and sought more verbal approval from their mothers. Other studies, such as the research conducted by Chao (2001) found that Chinese American parents were more authoritarian based on cultural values. In general, researchers have found that authoritarian parenting appears to be effective with Asian students and encourages them to do well in school, however, as noted earlier, generation, ethnic group, and assimilation levels should be considered.

Another study looked at the parent-children relationships of Southeast Asian American refugees. Rumbaut and Ima, (1988) in San Diego collected extensive data on 579 youth, while general comparative information was collected on 1485 junior and senior high students. Vietnamese, Chinese Vietnamese, and Hmong parents stressed and pressured students to achieve more than Lao and Khmer parents. Rumbaut and Ima hypothesized that Vietnamese, Chinese Vietnamese, and Hmong parents exercised stronger parental control over their children. Vietnamese American students were more likely to feel familial obligation and to be competitive in school since parents stressed the critical nature of collective survival. It was important that all members of the family including children contribute to the status and future of the family (Rumbaut & Ima, 1988). In contrast, the Lao and Khmer samples were from more rural areas and were less educated. These parents valued a more individualist orientation and encouraged their children to move out of the house sooner, therefore these children did not hold the same achievement responsibilities to the family. Though the levels of parental styles and expectations varied, along with socio-economic status, parents generally encouraged academic success.

As children mature, Bronfenbrenner's ecology of human development expands to include linkages between several microsystems to form a *mesosystem*. In this level, microsystems, may conflict or reinforce each other. In some cases on a micro level as seen through the earlier examples, Asian Pacific American parents have taught their children to value education, which is reinforced by the ethnic culture. These two microsystems work together to form a belief system that supports academic achievement. The child internalizes the importance of education and is motivated to bring honor to the family and community; this creates a "culturally compatible" orientation (Slaughter-Defoe et al., 1990). The two microsystems demonstrate cultural continuity in the immigrant subculture of the APA families to values found in mainstream schools (Kao, 2004; Kim 1980). The two systems are working collaboratively to reinforce the importance of academic achievement.

This cultural orientation can also be seen in the research of Kao (2004). Kao studied parent-child relationships using the National Education Longitudinal Study of 1988. Asian American and Hispanic eighth graders and their parents were first sampled in 1988 and then additional data was gathered every two years through 1994. Kao's (2004) study reported data from students in the tenth and twelfth grades. Results showed that Asian American immigrant parents exercised more decision-making over their first generation Asian children than the parents of third generation Asian peers. Therefore, the parent-child relationships of immigrant parents were much more authoritarian, a relationship that is more strict and did not allow children as much independence (Kao, 2004).

Like the study by Rumbaut and Ima, Kao found students who held strong traditional cultural values towards education and had solid relationships with parents, were more likely to be successful in school. In addition, Kao found that first and second generation Asian parents talked with their children about college and the importance of studying for standardized tests such as the Scholastic Aptitude Test (SAT). Kao hypothesized that Asian American students of immigrant parents were more likely to feel obligation towards their family and internalize their parents' high academic expectations. This example illustrates how two systems worked closely together to encourage academic achievement: one was the parenting style of immigrant parents and the second was the cultural value belief system of parents.

Research has also been conducted on other APA youth populations. Lee (1996) studied Hmong high school students and found that "1.5 generation" (those who were born in the home country but who came to the US as children), "second generation" (those born in the US to immigrant parents), and "third generation" (those who were born to second generation parents) have taken on various identities. Some youth are more traditional in their identity and others who are successful in school believe educational success will lead to career success, while others do not believe that schooling experiences will lead to increased mobility in society. Other researchers have also found that some second generation Hmong youth had serious conflicts with parents, schooling, and did not feel accepted in mainstream society. A number of these young people became involved in Asian gangs or dropped out of school (Rumbaut & Ima, 1988).

In a follow-up study of Hmong high school students, Lee (2001) found that though many Hmong youth faced influential forces of assimilation, they were still connected to issues of cultural identity, generation, age, and marital status. In fact, some were unusually protective of their cultural background (Lee, 2001). Her research demonstrated how different microsystems come into contact with each other and influence the development of APA youth. Though schools are strong institutions of cultural assimilation, parents and students are working toward finding ways to develop a bicultural orientation. Unfortunately, some teachers operate on the overgeneralized stereotype of the model minority and do not understand that culture is important to many of their Hmong students no matter what generation they represent. Lee (2001) found many Hmong students to have created a dynamic balance between traditional and mainstream US cultures. They value their home cultures, but clearly do not feel accepted by the majority of other students or school faculty.

Exosystem is an ecological environment in which individuals have no power to change or influence the embedded system. Numerous examples show how APA members are affected by school personnel and others. The following discussion on Filipino American parents and children is one example of being part of an environmental context that they did not choose.

The cultural background of Filipino Americans includes the values, history, and cultural behaviors of colonial countries that dominated the Philippines for numerous years. The Philippines was a Spanish colony for more than 350 years from 1521 until 1898. Later the country was controlled by the United States after the US defeated Spain in the Spanish American War (Flores, 1998). As a case study of colonialism, Santos (1983) and Cordova (1983) believed that the domination of these countries created a colonial mindset in many Filipinos and Filipino Americans. A colonial mindset may be an obstacle to feeling full inclusion in society and can impact the success of parents and their children in society (Santos, 1983). Filipinos, however, came to the United States with many cultural assets. Most Filipinos know English and they have been raised in cultural traditions that are similar to those in the United States. For example, many

Filipino immigrants are Christian or Catholic and have attended school systems that were modeled after those in the U.S. Education is an important value in the family and parents work hard to ensure that their children have educational opportunities (Cordova, 1983; Agbayani-Siewert, 1994; Santos, 1983). Children are expected to do well in school. Filipino American parents and children may hold many values and language skills that are culturally compatible with mainstream society (Agbayani-Siewert, 2004), however, it is important to understand the history and background of their experiences.

Macrosystem is an extensive ecological context that includes the general society. Though the child is at the center of the circle, his/her experiences are now influenced by other powerful systems such as mainstream society and global issues. Therefore, the individual encounters more value orientations, perspectives, and ways of being that may support or conflict with his/her socio-cultural expectations. In the macrosystem, APA youth may encounter a variety of these experiences. One powerful force is cultural assimilation and even racism in their maturation process (Pang, 2006). Cultural assimilation is the process in which an individual takes on the culture of the host community and removes aspects of the home and ethnic cultures such as language, behaviors, and attitudes.

As part of the developmental process, APA youth develop an identity, who they are, what they think is important, and where they belong. This can be a difficult process when they encounter consistent messages that they do not belong in US society. APA parents and youth often encounter comments and other forms of prejudice that convey the message that they are foreigners and not Americans (Agbayani-Siewert, 1994; Benham & Heck, 1998; Chang, 2003; Cordova, 1983; Flores, 1998; Hune & Chan, 1997; Kiang, 2002; Louie, 2004; Pang, 2006). In addition, young people face powerful forces of cultural assimilation where they receive continual messages that to be an "American" means the giving up of home languages, cultural behaviors, and cultural values that may differ from the mainstream. As a member of at least two cultural communities, Asian or Pacific Islander and mainstream, the process of identity development can be extremely confusing.

Sue and Okazaki (1990) posed a pragmatic construct of relative functionalism in understanding cultural capital. Since they believe that Asian Pacific Americans have experienced extensive societal oppression, the researchers theorized that many APAs perceive education as one of the few avenues that they can utilize to become successful. Therefore, Sue and Okazaki believe parents teach their children in covert and overt ways to work harder in order to succeed in schools and in society to fight racism. This pragmatic approach was also proposed by Suzuki (1977), who argued that APAs, such as Chinese Americans, Japanese Americans, and Korean Americans pursued education, because of the discrimination they faced in employment. Suzuki believed that some Asian Americans felt that schooling and earning advanced degrees would provide their children with upward mobility. In addition, many Asian Americans believed in a type of meritocracy. Though they may not be able to rise to the same socio-economic level of mainstream Americans with the same degree of accomplishments, they believed education was their most promising pathway for career advancement.

Historically, there are many examples where legalized and covert oppression has shaped the lives of Asian Pacific Americans. For example, in Hawaii, there are many instances that can be identified. To begin with, Hawaiians have had their lands taken from them and were politically marginalized with little voice in the Hawaiian government until recent times. In addition, many Hawaiians have suffered from unemployment, lack of housing, and poor health. Examples can also be found in schools. In 1994, native Hawaiian youth made up 23 percent of the student population in Hawaii, but comprised 33 percent of special education students (Benham & Heck 1998). However, Hawaiian Americans have become politically active and are working towards preserving their cultural heritage. Through this self-empowerment movement, Hawaiians are encouraging their children to go to college and attend high achieving schools. Parents and the community want their young people to be academically successful. One of the most powerful organizations in Hawaii is the Bishop Estate. This institution supports Kamehameha Schools originally founded by Princess Bernice Pau'ahi Bishop to ensure the education of Hawaiian children. In order to attend these schools, children must be part Hawaiian.

Cultural and economic oppression are extremely powerful forces. Initially, Hawaii was one of the most literate communities in the world, however, this changed when non-Hawaiians took control of the islands and forced Hawaiians to eliminate their language and cultural ways of living. However, after statehood was achieved, the revival of community and culture began to take hold. Unfortunately, due to historical racism, one of the major issues for Native Hawaiians is literacy. In 1991, a report issued by the Bishop Estate noted that about one third of Native Hawaiians were functionally illiterate (Benham & Heck, 1998). Scholars believe that severe cultural and political issues act as obstacles to the education of Native Hawaiians. For example, many Native Hawaiian children come to school speaking Hawaiian Creole English. This dialect is an integral aspect of Hawaiian identity and culture (Au & Jordan, 1977; Benham & Heck, 1998).

Students, however, are often criticized and penalized for use of the home dialect and told to speak Standard English. This cultural conflict can result in students retreating from their studies or ignoring their teachers. Culturally relevant teaching has been found to be an excellent approach for teachers to use with Hawaiian students (Au & Jordan, 1977). In this way both the content and context of the students' cultures are integrated into the curriculum and instruction of the classroom (Pang, 2005). Today, in some schools, such as the Kamehameha Schools, Hawaiian history, culture, and language are integrated into the instructional curriculum along with communication styles that are familiar to children (Benham & Heck, 1998; Au & Jordan, 1977). These strategies have been implemented and used to form the foundation of educational reform at the Kamehameha Schools. Parents and community leaders believe that the Hawaiian culture must be protected, integrated, and honored in schools so that children develop a strong sense of who they are. Though macrosystems that include racism and social oppression have discouraged the development of educational opportunities for Hawaiians, parents, students, community leaders, and educators have worked together to provide educational opportunities for students.

In this level of macrosystems, the socialization of Korean American children was effected by racism. Kim (1980) studied a total of 408 Korean American parents and elementary age children who lived in Chicago and Los Angeles. The researcher collected data through interviews and questionnaires. Parents believed strongly in education and had high expectations for their children; they wanted them to be successful in schools and later in their careers. Kim found that approximately three-quarters of mothers worked outside of the home. Within this sample, approximately 30 percent of parents and children in Chicago identified instances of discrimination at school. They reported that children experienced name-calling, being picked on, or were bullied. Parents also described their own personal problems with discrimination. The adults were frustrated with their ability to advance in society because of their Korean ancestry and language limitations. Approximately two-thirds of the Chicago sample, both mothers and fathers, were working in skilled, semi-skilled, unskilled, or had no position outside of the home. Few were professionals, managers, or business owners. Many parents felt that prejudice was an element in their inability to advance. Therefore, parents taught their children to be high achievers in school, and emphasized that they were to learn English well so they could assimilate quickly into school culture.

Parents in the Los Angeles sample reported that about 42 percent of the men and 32 percent of the women were professionals, managers, clerks or business owners. Many had discussed a downward trend in their careers when they migrated to the United States. Many subjects indicated a need for English fluency and this might also add to their inability to secure a position that was equal to their educational accomplishments. Parental attitudes conveyed to children were also studied regarding career aspirations. Korean American children in the Los Angeles sample reported that their parents had high levels of career aspirations for them. For example, 35.5 percent of the children who lived in Los Angeles reported that their parents wanted them to be doctors or lawyers and 7.6 percent felt their parents wanted them to be scientists. These numbers are quite different from a reported 3 percent of the sample indicating that the child thought their parents wanted him/her to be a politician.

Kim, however, also found parents held conflicting beliefs. They wanted their children to do well in mainstream schools and to learn mainstream ways, but they also did not want their children to lose the ability to speak Korean or give up their cultural values. Like Sue and Okazaki, this study indicates that parents are well aware of societal prejudice and believe that children must work hard in order to combat obstacles of racism that they will encounter by achieving in school.

As with other Asian Pacific American communities, Japanese Americans value family and education (De Vos, 1973; Kitano, 1976). However, the macrosystem has been extremely powerful in the rapid cultural assimilation process of Japanese Americans. This is largely due to their historical experiences with institutional and societal racism in the United States during the first half of the Twentieth Century. Historically, their experience has been somewhat different than more recent Asian immigrant groups. Chinese immigrants were the first ethnic group to be denied entry into the United States by name with the passage of the Chinese Exclusion Act of 1882. Racism against Asian Americans continued. During World War II, 120,000 Japanese Americans, two-thirds of whom were US born citizens, were incarcerated by their own government after the bombing of Pearl Harbor. These citizens were perceived as foreigners and traitors.

Because of racism, evidenced by their removal, many lost their homes, farms, businesses, possessions, and sense of self. In addition after the war when they returned to birthplaces such as Seattle, San Francisco, and Portland, they were labeled, humiliated, excluded, and discriminated against in housing, employment, and in schools. Japanese Americans felt their honor and pride had been damaged and wanted to demonstrate their loyalty to mainstream society. Since most of the Japanese at that time held a belief system that was founded on the traditional values of Meiji Japan, they valued community, honor, and education. This also included sensitivity to others and a need to belong to a collective, therefore they were more vulnerable to criticism of others (Kitano, 1976; Sata, 1983; Yamamoto & Iga, 1983).

Due to the extreme racism that Japanese American parents and their children experienced during World War II, outward cultural customs and artifacts were not encouraged. So many third generation and beyond youth were never taught to speak Japanese at home. Parents did not want their children to experience the humiliation and prejudice that they felt, so many parents wanted their children to grow up being "two hundred percent" American (Kitano, 1976). The process of cultural assimilation of Japanese Americans has been one of the most comprehensive in APA ethnic groups. In addition, since the immigration of Japanese Americans was halted in 1924 with the Asian Exclusion Act, the Japanese American community became isolated and tight knit.

These forces contributed to what Sue and Okazaki identified as relative functionalism. Japanese American parents believed that their children had to work hard and to excel in school. Education was one of the few ways that their children could access economic mobility especially in a country that touted the principle of equal educational opportunity. Many Japanese Americans are upwardly mobile because of their belief in effort, importance of family honor and community status, strong sense of pragmatism, higher levels of assimilation, and accessing educational avenues.

In a society where cultural assimilation is expected, a bicultural balance may be difficult to maintain as Tanabe and Rochon (in press) found in working with the Hmong community in Wisconsin. Tanabe and Rochon discovered that Hmong parents and their children were committed to the educational and career success of their young people, however this was a struggle because of less financial resources, lack of language abilities, and lack of educational networks.

Tanabe and Rochon, however, created and implemented the Hmong Leadership Project. The purpose of this program was to develop a pipeline for members of the Hmong community in Wisconsin to become teachers and principals. At the time they started the program, there were no Hmong teachers in the local school districts. Through a comprehensive collaboration between local Hmong elders, university faculty, and local educator organizations, they established a pipeline program. Their program has been successful and over 40 Hmong have become certified teachers and one woman is now a principal in the local district in Wisconsin.

The cultural assimilation process was proceeding at a rapid pace. Many of the new Hmong teachers, who were second generation, could no longer speak Hmong. Though the first language of these young certified teachers was Hmong and they are in their mid twenties, they lacked the vocabulary to effectively communicate with Hmong parents. The process of cultural assimilation had enveloped them so they asked for Hmong interpreters to assist them in parent-teacher conferences. The Hmong teachers found themselves without an extensive vocabulary that allowed them to successfully communicate with Hmong parents. This led to the addition in the Hmong Leadership Project of a cultural preservation component. It became apparent that the Hmong community desired to preserve their culture, but did not know how to do so. They approached Rochon and Tanabe and consequently, cultural and linguistic components were integrated into the program. The collaborative leadership of the project understood that ethnic identity and ethnic community were still critical components of how Hmong teachers identified themselves.

4.5. Conclusion and Recommendations

This chapter demonstrates how Bronfenbrenner's model can be used to explain how multiple forces influence the actions of parents in the development of their children. This model can be taught to teachers so they better understand the complex sociocultural systems that influence the achievement of Asian Pacific American students. Teachers can also understand how to utilize the model in developing programs that will more fully serve APA youth. Though parents and immediate family members are most significant, other influences affect children.

The psychological, sociological, anthropological, and historical research cited in this chapter indicates that parents utilize multiple pathways in various micro-, meso-, and macrosystems to ensure that their children develop the cultural capital they will need to succeed in schools and in their vocations. In addition, many parents are aware that Asian Pacific Americans are marginalized in society. Additionally, parents are often unaware that the process of cultural assimilation also may create issues of identity confusion and the loss of traditional culture in their children. The educational advancement of APA children is a complex one and parents continue to be one of the core factors in their achievement.

Researchers have found Asian Pacific American parents to be actively involved in the achievement process. The cultural capital they have transferred to their children has assisted them in the learning process. It is also important for school personnel to develop programs and activities that are specifically designed to assist Asian Pacific American parents and their children to better understand the ongoing process of cultural assimilation and the practices of schooling (Goodwin, 1997). Though parents may hold high expectations for their children, they may not understand the workings and practices of schools. In addition since 65 percent of APAs are immigrants, school personnel must institute various avenues to engage parents. The following is a short list of recommendations for educators to consider in their quest to improve the delivery of education to APA students:

1) Open and increased communication between parents and school is always important in the education of children. Encourage and invite parents to partic-ipate in school activities and committees. Often parents whose native language is not English may not feel able to express themselves at Parent Teacher Association (PTA) meetings. APA parents are more likely to attend if they are personally invited by other parents and teachers. Interpreters can be on hand so parents whose home language is other than English can understand what is being said and respond.

2) Teachers can bring parents into the classroom as guest experts whether on cooking, history, photography, sports, or other hobbies. When parents are included in classroom learning, teachers and students learn, while this reinforces the importance of parent-school relationships. Parents and students will also feel valued for their knowledge and abilities.

3) Since so many parents are immigrants, school personnel might consider offering English classes in the evening for parents. This again allows schools to become community centers for parents and children. While parents are attending English classes, students could be attending homework or tutoring sessions whether in elementary or high school. This strengthens relationships between parents and schools.

4) Have a school newsletter translated into major languages in the community. Some APA parents may not be able to read proficiently in English, however they are literate in their native language. Get district personnel to translate newsletters into a variety of languages such as Cambodian, Spanish, and Vietnamese if parents speak these languages.

5) Racism is one of the continuing issues that APA parents and children identify. Ask parents and young people what the school can do to address the racism that is being encountered whether through staff development, inclusion of monthly civil rights rallies, and the presentation of plays, books, or displays about famous Asian Pacific Americans such as Fred Korematsu, Dith Pran, Bill Lann Lee, or Patsy Mink.

APA parents and students value education and want to be involved in school activities. Teachers, moreover, can enhance the learning experience. The Bronfenbrenner theory can assist teachers in better understanding that child development is influenced by numerous levels of interactions. As the work of Tanabe and Rochon (2006) has demonstrated, educational programs that tie into all four ecological levels are more effective because they address the comprehensive needs of students. Education is a process that must include important stakeholders; parents are most central to this endeavor.

References

Agbayani-Siewert, P. (1994). Families in society: Filipino-American culture and family. *Journal of Contemporary Human Services*, 75, 429–438.

Agbayani-Siewert, P. (2004). Assumptions of Asian American Similarity: The Case of Filipino and Chinese American Students. *Social Work*, 49, 39–51.

Au, K & Jordan, C. (1977). Teaching reading to Hawaiian children: Finding a culturally appropriate solution. In Trueba, H. & Au, K. (eds), *Culture and the Bilingual Classroom: Studies in Classroom Ethnography*. Rowley, MA: Newbury House, pp. 139–152.

Benham, M. & Heck, R.H. (1998). *Culture and Educational Policy in Hawai' Mahwah*, New Jersey: Lawrence Erlbaum Associates, Inc.

Bronfenbrenner, U. (1979). *The Ecology of the Family as a Context for Human Development: Experiments By Nature and Design*. Cambridge, MA: Harvard University Press.

Bronfenbrenner, U. (1986). Ecology of the family as a context for human development: Research perspectives. *Developmental Psychology*, 22, 723–742.

Cabezas, A. (1981). *Early Childhood Development in Asian and Pacific American Families: Families in Transition*. San Francisco: Asian Inc.

Chan, S. (1991). *Asian Americans: An Interpretive History*. Boston: Twayne.

Chao, R.K. (2001). Extending research on the consequences of parenting style for Chinese Americans and European Americans. *Child Development*, 72(6), 1832–1843.

Chang, I. (2003). *The Chinese in America*. New York: Penguin Books.

Committee of 100. (2005). The Committee of 100's Asian Pacific Americans (APAs) in higher education report card, *http://www.committee100.org/publications/edu/C100_Higher_Ed_Report_Card.pdf* (retrieved November 29, 2005).

Cordova, F. (1983). *Filipinos: The Forgotten Asian Americans*. Seattle: Demonstration Project for Asian Americans.

De Vos, G. (1973). *Socialization for Achievement*. Berkeley and Los Angeles, CA: University of California Press.

Flores, P. (1998). Filipino American students: Actively caring a sense of identity. In Pang, V.O. & Cheng, L. (eds), *Struggling To Be Heard: The Unmet Needs of Asian Pacific American Children*. Albany, NY: SUNY Press, pp. 27–43.

Gardner, R.W., Robey, B., & Smith, P. (1985) *Asian Americans: Growth, Change, and Diversity*. Washington, DC: Population Reference Bureau.

Goodwin, A.L. (1997). *Assessment for Equity and Inclusion: Embracing All Our children*. NY: Routledge.

Goyette, K. & Xie, Y. (1999). Educational expectations of Asian American youths: Determinants and ethnic differences. *Sociology of Education*, 72, 22–37.

Heras, P & Patacsil, J. (2001). Silent sacrifices: Voices of the Filipino American family: A documentary. *The Companion Guide*, San Diego, California: Patricia Heras Publisher.

Hirschman, C. & Wong, M.G. (1986). The extraordinary educational achievement of Asian Americans: A search for historical evidence and explanations. *Social Forces*, 65(1), 1–27.

Hune, S. & Chan, K.S. (1997). Asian Pacific American demographic and educational trends. In Carter, D.J. & Wilson, R. *Minorities in Higher Education: 1996–1997* Fifteen Annual Status Report. Washington, DC: American Council on Education, pp. 39–67.

Kao, G. (2004). Parental influences on the educational outcomes of immigrant youth. *The International Migration Review*, 38, 427–450.

Kao, G. & Tienda, M. (1998). Educational aspirations of minority youth. *American Journal of Education*, 106, 349–384.

Kiang, P.N. (2002). K-12 education and Asian Pacific American youth development. *Asian American Policy Review*, 10, 31–47.

Kiang, P.N. & Lee, V.W. (1993). Exclusion or contribution? Education K-12 policy. In Aguilar-San Juan, K. (ed.), *The State of Asian Pacific America: A Public Policy Report: Policy Issues to the Year 2020*. Los Angeles: LEAP Asian Pacific American Public Policy Institute and UCLA Asian American Studies Center, pp. 25–48.

Kim, B.L.C. (1980). *The Korean-American Child at School and At Home* (Grant No. 90-C-1335 [01]) Washington, DC: US Department of Health, Education, and Welfare.

Kim, E. (2002). The relationship between parental involvement and children's educational achievement in the Korean immigrant family. *Journal of Comparative Family Studies*, 33(4), 529–541.

Kitano, H. (1976). *Japanese Americans: The Evolution of a Subculture* (2nd edn). Englewood Cliffs, NJ: Prentice-Hall.

Kitano, M. & DiJiosia, M. (2002). Are Asian and Pacific Americans Overrepresented in programs for the gifted? *Roeper Review*, 24, 76–81.

Lee, S. (1996). *Unraveling the "Model Minority" Stereotype: Listening to Asian American Youth*. New York: Teachers College Press.

Lee, S. (2001). More than "model minorities" or "delinquents": A look at Hmong American high school students. *Harvard Educational Review*, 71(3), 505–529.

Long, Patrick Du Phuoc. (1996). *The Dream Shattered: Vietnamese Gangs in America*. Boston, MA: Northeastern University Press.

Louie, V. (2004). *Compelled to Excel: Immigration, Education and Opportunity among Chinese Americans*. Palo Alto, CA: Stanford University Press.

Nordoff, Jean F. (1985). Mental health and refugee youths: A model for diagnostic training. In Owan, T. (ed.), *Southeast Asian Mental Health: Treatment, Prevention, Services, Training, and Research*. Washington, DC: U.S. Department of Health and Human Services.

Ong, P. & Hee, S. (1993). The growth of the Asian Pacific American population: Twenty million in 2020. *The state of Asian Pacific America: A public policy report: Policy issues to the Year 2020*. Los Angeles: LEAP Asian Pacific American Public Policy Institute and UCLA Asian American Studies Center.

Pang, V.O. (1990). Asian American Students: A Diverse Population. *Educational Forum*, 55(1), 1–18.

Pang, V.O. (2005). Multicultural Education: A Caring-Centered, *Reflective Approach* (2nd edn). Boston, MA: McGrawHill.

Pang, V.O. (2006). Fighting the marginalization of Asian American students with caring schools: focusing on curricular change. *Race, Ethnicity, and Education*, 9, 69–85.

Pang, V., Kiang, P., & Pak, Y. (2004). Asian Pacific American students: Changing a biased educational system. In Banks, J. and Banks, C. (eds) *Handbook of Research on Multicultural Education* (2nd edn). San Francisco: Jossey-Bass.

Reeves, T. & Bennett, C. (2003). The Asian and Pacific Islander Population in the United States: March 2002 *Population Characteristics*. http://www.census.gov/prod/2003pubs/p20–540.pdf Washington DC: U.S. Census Bureau, retrieved on June 13, 2005.

Rumbaut, R. (1997). Assimilation and its discontents: Between rhetoric and reality. *The International Migration Review*, 31, 923–961.

Rumbaut, R. & Ima, K. (1988). *The Adaptation of Southeast Asian Refugee Youth: A Comparative Study*. Washington, DC: U.S. Department of Health and Human Services, Family Support Administration, Office of Refugee Resettlement.

Santos, R. (1983). The social and emotional development of Filipino American children. In Powell, G.J. (ed.), *The Psychosocial Development of Minority Group Children*. New York: Brunner/Mazel, pp. 131–48.

Sata, L. (1983). Mental health issues of Japanese-American children. In Powell, G.J. (ed.), *The Psychosocial Development of Minority Group Children*. New York: Brunner/Mazel, pp. 362–372.

Slaughter-Defoe, D., Nakagawa, K., Takanishi, R., & Johnson, D.J. (1990). Toward cultural/ecological perspectives on schooling and achievement in African- and Asian-American children. *Child Development*, 61, 363–383.

Sue, S. & Okazaki, S. (1990). Asian-American educational achievements: A phenomenon in search of an explanation. *American Psychologist*, 45, 913–920.

Sue, S. & Sue, D.W. (1973). Chinese American personality and mental health. In Sue, S. & Wagner, N. (eds), *Asian-American Psychological Perspectives*. Palo Alto: Science and Behavior Books.

Suzuki, B.H. (1977). Education and socialization of Asian Americans: A revisionist analysis of the "model minority" thesis. *Amerasia Journal*, 4(2), 23–51.

Suzuki, B. (1988, April). *Asian Americans in Higher Education: Impact of Changing Demographics and Other Social Forces*. Paper presented at the National Symposium on the Changing Demographics of Higher Education, Ford Foundation, New York.

Tanabe, C. & Rochon, R. (in press). Seeking educational justice for Hmong children: The journey of two professors who were given the opportunity to work in the Hmong community. In Pang, V.O (ed.), *Multicultural Education: Principles and Practices*. Westport, CT: Praeger.

Uba, L. (1994). *Asian Americans: Personality Patterns, Identity, and Mental Health*. New York: Guilford Press.

U.S. Census Bureau. (1983). 1980 *Census Population: Characteristics of the Population*. Washington, DC: Government Printing Office.

Yamamoto, J. & Iga, M. (1983). Emotional growth of Japanese-American children. In Powell, G.J. (ed.), *The Psychosocial Development of Minority Group Children*. New York: Brunner/Mazel, pp. 167–178.

Youngberg, F.L. (2001). Census 2000: *Asian Pacific American Americans Changing the Face of America at a Rapid Pace*. In 2001–2002 National Asian Pacific American political almanac. Los Angeles, California: UCLA Asian American Studies Center, pp. 42–64.

Part 2
Histories, Issues of Immigration, and Schooling Experiences

5

The *Mobility/Social Capital Dynamic*: Understanding Mexican American Families and Students

Robert K. Ream and Ricardo D. Stanton-Salazar

From big city mayors and star baseball players to service sector employees and migrant workers, today's 41 million U.S. Latinos will greatly affect our nation in the decades before us. The number of U.S. Latinos is increasing eight times more rapidly than the population as a whole; by 2025 a quarter of all U.S. K-12 students will be of Spanish-speaking origin (U.S. Department of Commerce, Bureau of the Census, 2000a). In fact, Latinos are the largest and fastest growing minority population in the United States (Tienda, 2001). The rising numbers of Latinos brings with it a growing concern regarding their status as students in schools: Latino student underachievement and dropout rates are disproportionately high (Latinos in Education, 1998). In 2001, 1.4 million Latinos between the ages of 16 and 24 were dropouts (U.S. Department of Education, NCES, 2002). The Latino high school dropout rate is twice that of Blacks and more than three times that of non-Latino Whites (see Figure 5.1).[1] These numbers prefigure similar trends in educational attainment at the college level, where Latinos are about half as likely as their non-Latino White peers to complete 4 years of college (Vernez & Mizell, 2002).

Additionally, considerable differences exist in the educational experiences and outcomes *among* U.S. Latinos (Aguirre & Martinez, 2000). In particular, youth of Mexican descent, who are among the most challenged of all U.S. Latino subgroups (Gibson, Gándara, & Koyama, 2004), score significantly lower on

---

[1] It should be noted, however, that Latinos are also making real educational gains over generations—improvements that are obscured by the continuing influx of new immigrants. A recent longitudinal study employing U.S. Census and Current Population Survey data demonstrates impressive Latino advances in educational *attainment* across generations. Illustratively, Mexican immigrants born during 1905–1909 averaged but 4.3 years of schooling. Their American-born sons, averaging 9.3 years, doubled the years of schooling. And their grandsons were high school graduates, averaging 12.2 years of schooling (Smith, 2003).

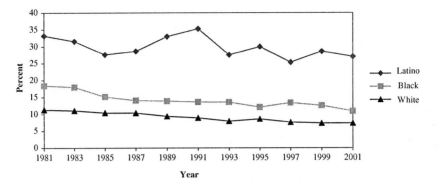

FIGURE 5.1. Status Dropout Rates of 16- to 24-Year-Olds by Race/Ethnicity, 1981–2001. *Source*: U.S. Department of Commerce, Bureau of the Census, Current Population Survey, 1972–2001.

Stanford achievement tests and are dropping out of school at higher rates than their same-age peers (U.S. Census Bureau, 2000b; Portes & Rumbaut, 2001). What's more, the two-thirds of all U.S. Latinos who are of Mexican origin have the lowest college completion rate among Latino sub-groups (Vernez & Mizell, 2002). Hence, the U.S. is presented with a growing problem: Mexican American educational achievement and attainment is significantly below the rest of the nation (College Board, 1999). This is cause for serious concern and it is important for policymakers to think about what should and can be done about these perplexing trends.

5.1.   Understanding Mexican American Student Performance

Contemporary research offers various reasons for Mexican American under-achievement, and yawning economic inequality bears the mark of exceptional culpability in this regard. Still, some of the explanatory pieces continue to be missing from the puzzle. To illustrate, dozens if not hundreds of studies point to poverty as an insidious and fundamental reason why economically disadvantaged children do not perform to their true potential (Brooks-Gunn & Duncan, 1997; Rothstein, 2004). Yet such studies, based on material and human capital (i.e., economic wealth and skills developed through schooling), have yet to explain why some middle-class minority students consistently perform below non-Latino Whites with similar economic and family backgrounds (Jencks & Phillips, 1998; Miller, 1995). And while primary cultural differences (i.e., language and parenting styles) are most frequently cited in association with Mexican American underachievement (Gándara, 1994), relevant research remains the subject of considerable debate (Darder, Torres, & Gutierrez, 1997). Still, at least 30 years of research on Latino underachievement has focused attention on cultural disjuncture, noting that youth of Mexican descent often attend schools where teachers have little knowledge of their cultural backgrounds (Gibson et al., 2004), which has led to widespread student alienation and disengagement from school (Trueba, 1988). Yet first-generation immigrant students exhibit often quite optimistic perceptions of their schooling experiences and educational future (Buriel, 1984; Suarez-Orozco, 1991). Indeed, researchers are beginning to question "cultural difference" perspectives most associated with John Ogbu (1992) by showing that many minority students—regardless of the terms of their incorporation or length of residence in the U.S.—maintain sanguine perceptions about their schooling (Ainsworth-Darnell & Downey, 1998). In short, low average levels of educational achievement and attainment among U.S. Latinos, and Mexican origin youth in particular, remains a persistent and complex problem that demands more exacting theoretical explanations.

5.2. Functional and Critical Interpretations of Social Capital

Given these limitations, social scientists continue to investigate alternative perspectives that can inform our understanding of Mexican American educational performance (Valencia, 2002). One alternative view, based on theories of social capital,[2] calls for researchers and educators to more carefully consider the resources and forms of support found in young people's social networks (e.g., expert knowledge about the complexities of college admission). What this perspective offers is not only a focus on network resources critical to school success, but also a focus on those complex institutional processes that can either facilitate or inhibit the trust necessary for *help giving* and *help seeking*—two forms of agency associated with social capital.

Over the years, researchers have shown how the ideological emphasis on rapid cultural assimilation tends to undermine the utility of social capital among Latino youth (Valenzuela, 1999; Stanton-Salazar, 1997). One specific example is how the devaluation of bicultural identities and of bilingualism, in conjunction with stigma often attached to membership in high school ESL (English as a Second Language) programs, undermines not only the potential for feelings of social integration and "we-ness" between ESL students and their more acculturated peers, but also the possibilities for the latter group to aid the former with resources and forms of support that could facilitate their integration into the school, their

---

[2] Reflected in the ability of individuals to command limited resources by virtue of their relationships or membership in broader social structures (Portes, 1998), social capital is made up of resources that may be converted into material capital (Bourdieu, 1986), human capital (Coleman, 1988) and healthy civic participation and community cohesion (Putnam, 2000). Moreover, the fungibility of social capital bridges the economic and sociological perspectives, thus capturing the attention of policymakers who are seeking creative solutions to social problems.

accommodation of English, and their academic achievement (Conchas, 2001; Flores-González, 2002).

Researchers such as Coleman (1988) and Putnam (2000) have underscored the rather axiomatic notion that social networks have the potential to improve quality of life for individuals and the broader community. Bourdieu (1986) and more recent work by Stanton-Salazar (2001), in contrast, emphasize how social capital processes are embedded in racial, class, and gender inequalities in society. Building upon Bourdieu's work that social capital is a form of wealth that arises out of economic and political stratification, Stanton-Salazar, (2001) argues that social capital among working-class youth (i.e., access, *via* social exchange, to middle-class educational resources) is never the norm. When it does occur, however, it usually requires extraordinary interventions within the household, the school, and the community. For disadvantaged youth, the existence of structural conditions that simultaneously operate to undermine resources and support is the norm, and falls within the purview of research on social capital and educational outcomes (see Dika and Singh, 2002).

5.3.   The Mobility/Social Capital Dynamic

In this chapter we focus our attention on one such condition. Specifically, we argue that for a significant segment of the Mexican origin student population, *academic achievement is adversely impacted by the instability in social relationships that accompanies particularly high rates of student transience and residential mobility of their families.* Like the frequent re-potting of plants, such mobility disrupts social root systems and the social context for interaction (Putnam, 2000). It follows that the *mobility/social capital dynamic* whereby mobility impacts the resources inherent in students' social networks merits attention on the basis of its influence over relationship stability and academic achievement (Ream, 2005b). We elaborate here on this important problem.

5.3.1.   The Incidence of Mobility

High rates of residential and student mobility (non-promotional school changes that may or may not be associated with a change of residence) tend to harm students who change schools and usually present themselves as administrative and pedagogical challenges for teachers and school administrators (Rumberger et al., 1999; Ream, 2005a). Were mobility not so commonplace, it might not warrant the attention of educators and policymakers. A growing body of research shows, however, that student mobility is widespread in many schools and districts throughout the United States. In fact, *most* children make at least one school change without being promoted to the next grade level, and many change schools even more frequently (Rumberger, 2003). Mobility is particularly pronounced within large, predominantly minority, urban school districts with high concentrations of students from low socioeconomic backgrounds

(McDonnell & Hill, 1993). One in every five urban and suburban high schools in California has a mobility rate in excess of 30 percent (Rumberger et al., 1999). Los Angeles Unified School District, for example, reported a high school "transience rate" (measured as the proportion of students who entered after school started or left before school ended) exceeding 35 percent across the district for the 2001–2002 school year (LAUSD, 2004).

Mobility Among U.S. Latinos. Latinos change residence more often than any other racial/ethnic group in the U.S. (U.S. Census Bureau News, January, 2000). Between 2002 and 2003 Latinos were found to have moved at considerably higher rates (18 percent) than non-Latino Whites (12.4 percent) (U.S. Census Bureau, 2004). Moreover, data from the 1998 National Assessment of Educational Progress (NAEP) show that 41 percent of Latino 4th grade students changed schools in the previous 2 years, compared with 33 percent of Asian American students and 27 percent of non-Latino Whites in the same grade cohort (Rumberger, 2003). The Mexican American majority of U.S. Latinos are also highly mobile, particularly at the secondary school level. Excluding dropouts, 37 percent of Mexican American adolescents moved residences at least once between 1988 and 1992 compared to 31 percent of their White counterparts. In terms of student mobility, 30 percent of Mexican Americans made at least one non-promotional school change between 8th and 12th grade, compared to approximately 20 percent of Whites. What's more, the mobility rate for highly mobile students (those with two or more non-promotional school changes between 8th and 12th grade) is nearly twice as high for Mexican Americans as it is for Whites.[3]

The incidence of mobility is also associated with socioeconomic status (SES) and nativity status (i.e., immigrants *vs.* U.S.-born) among Mexican origin youth. For those whose family SES is below the national average, rates of student mobility are considerably *higher* than they are for their Mexican-origin peers whose SES is above the national mean (32 percent compared to 22 percent, respectively). For White adolescents, the incidence of student mobility remains consistent across lower and upper SES groups, at approximately 22 percent. Thus, we can deduce a negative association between SES and student mobility among youth of Mexican descent; whereas SES and student mobility do not reveal associational patterns among Whites. We also consider the data according to nativity status. Mexican immigrants are particularly mobile—with 32 percent changing schools between grades 8 and 12, compared to only 14 percent of non-Latino White immigrants. In comparison, 29 percent of second generation and 24 percent of third+ generation Mexican origin youth changed schools.

---

[3] We use weighted panel data from the National Education Longitudinal Study of 1988 (NELS:88) to illustrate mobility rates (excluding dropouts) among Mexican origin youth. NELS:88 is a nationally representative longitudinal panel study of a cohort of approximately 25,000 8th graders who were re-surveyed in 10th grade (1990), in 12th grade (1992), and then again in 1994 and 2000. For further information on NELS:88, see *http://nces.ed.gov/surveys/nels88*.

The trend moves in the opposite direction among Whites who become slightly *more* mobile with acculturation. Yet even the most stable generation of Mexican Americans changes schools at higher rates than the most mobile generation of Whites, per Figure 5.2.

Historical Perspective and Demographics. It may be illuminating to situate our treatment of the *mobility/social capital dynamic* in a historical context. During the 1960s, more acculturated second and third+ generation Chicanos constituted the majority in many Mexican communities throughout the southwestern United States. In 1960, only 20 percent of California's Latino population was foreign-born; three quarters of all working-age Latinos were U.S. natives, and two-thirds of Latino children were third generation (López & Stanton-Salazar, 2001). The manufacturing sector of our national economy had yet to begin its flight to the "third world," and union membership was still strong. Occupational stability (and unrepentant racial segregation) made student mobility a rather mute issue, except for the children of migrant agricultural laborers. Much has changed in the last 30 years to alter the demographic landscape of urban America in particular; we attempt here only a succinct delineation of the most salient trends.

Although Latino immigration nationwide has been on the rise in the past two decades, the current percentage of immigrants from Spanish speaking nations like Mexico is only slightly higher than historical levels (Moore, 2001). What has

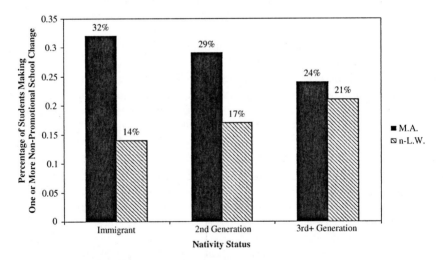

FIGURE 5.2. Student Mobility by Nativity Status, Grades 8–12.
Note: M.A. = Mexican Americans; n-L.W. = non-Latino Whites. Student mobility from grades 8–12 based on data from 12th grade student questionnaire. Student mobility excludes school changes due to promotion from elementary to middle school and from middle school to high school.
Source: National Education Longitudinal Study of 1988, panel of 1988 eighth-grade students resurveyed in 1990 and 1992, excluding dropouts. Statistics weighted (*f2pnlwt/mean f2pnlwt*).

made Mexican immigrants considerably more visible has been the consistency of their immigration combined with their cumulative representation, both of which have paralleled the concomitant decline in the percentage of non-Latino White children, especially in places like California and Texas. Particularly salient has been the demise of the manufacturing sector, the concurrent rise of a low-wage service sector, and the increasing representation of Latino undocumented workers who come to fill many of these jobs. Finally, adult immigrants in the low-wage service sector are concentrated in central cities and in the older suburbs of metro America; better-off third+ generation Latinos have scattered throughout the new suburban American landscape, along with everyone else (Jensen, 2001). Comparably high rates of transience among impoverished Mexican immigrant families must be seen in this economic and historical context. While previous generations (e.g., 1960s) were able to root themselves in cities that still sustained stable manufacturing industries, today's Latino immigrants must contend with a highly exploitative labor sector that forces families to chase better-paying jobs and find affordable housing, moving from neighborhoods that are highly *transitory* and *anomic* to other locales plagued by similar challenging conditions (see Stanton-Salazar, 2001, pp. 52–54).

5.4.   The Impact of Mobility on Students and Schools

Reminiscent of French sociologist Emile Durkheim's seminal research on mobility and large-scale *anomie*,[4] mounting research shows that mobility is detrimental to students' psychological, academic, and social well-being. Coping with a new school environment in the wake of a school change can be psychologically challenging. The following comments from a high school student, published in a comprehensive study of student mobility in California, places that challenge in high relief:

Moving and changing schools really shattered my personality. I feel like there's all these little things I picked up from all the different schools and I feel all disoriented all the time. There's no grounding. I always just feel like I'm floating. It's psychological damage, really...Because you never feel like a complete person. That's how I feel—I feel fragmented. Every time I moved I felt less and less important. (Rumberger et al., 1999, p. 37)

Numerous studies also document the negative impact of mobility on student performance in the primary grades (U.S. General Accounting Office, 1994; Heinlein & Shinn, 2000). Of the achievement-related research at the secondary school level, one study of 643 ninth graders found that mobility negatively

---

[4] Durkheim coined the term *anomie* to describe a state of isolation that typically exists in times of upheaval and social change. Anomie is associated with the loss of a particular way of life—a state of "normlessness" that emerges when rules, habits, and beliefs no longer hold and alternatives have yet to arise.

impacts student performance in mathematics (Benson & Weigel, 1981). But mobility-related studies that take into account background characteristics, such as family structure and socioeconomic status, offer mixed results, at least at the secondary school level (Rumberger, 2003). One such study found that changing both schools and residences during high school reduced 12th grade test scores in reading and mathematics, but that changing schools alone had no significant impact (Pribesh & Downey, 1999). Another found that despite some negative short-term consequences, the incidence of student mobility early in high school does not deter modest gains in mathematics achievement for students who thereafter remain in school through the twelfth grade (Swanson & Schneider, 1999). Thus, the impact of student mobility may have something to do with its timing, and timing might be associated with the *reasons* students change schools (Ream 2005a).

The strongest and most consistent impact of mobility is on students' prospects for graduation from high school (Rumberger, 2003). There is clear evidence that mobility during high school diminishes the likelihood of completing school on time (Haveman, Wolfe, & Spaulding, 1991). One longitudinal study that examined the relationship between residential mobility and high school completion found that, even after controlling for a variety of family background variables, residential mobility reduced the odds of graduation (Haveman & Wolfe, 1994). Another study shows that students who made just one non-promotional school change between the 8th and 12th grades were less than half as likely to graduate from high school compared to students who did not make a non-promotional school change (Rumberger et al., 1999).

There are several reasons as to why student mobility may negatively impact educational attainment. Adapting to a new school environment can be a challenging proposition for anyone. This is particularly so for adolescent youth who are in the midst of a difficult developmental life stage characterized by increased peer orientation, invidious social comparison, dissonant identities, and gradual autonomy from family control (Hartup & Stevens, 1997). New class-mates and teachers as well as changing academic standards and behavioral expectations must be adjusted to in an often compressed time-frame (Jason et al., 1992). The lack of an adequate administrative system responsive to transient families plays a prominent role. Such a system would entail a sort of safety net or support system designed to socially integrate new students in an efficient, intensive, and compassionate manner. In the absence of such a system, we often find a syndrome of misplaced transcripts, misdirected classroom placements, and curricular incoherence between sending and receiving schools that typically exacerbate already difficult transitions for mobile students. Mid-year school changes in particular are nearly synonymous with awkward transitions during which students may be mistakenly transplanted into classes they have already taken, or re-situated in classrooms where they are ill prepared to succeed.

Mobile students are not the only ones who suffer the consequences of student mobility: students with stable attendance records may also be academ-ically impaired if they attend schools with highly mobile student populations

(Hanushek, Kain, & Rivkin, 2001). To illustrate, students who attended high schools with overall mobility rates of 40 percent scored significantly lower on 10th grade standardized mathematics tests than students who attended high schools with mobility rates of 10 percent (Rumberger et al., 1999). Furthermore, mobility can have a negative effect on classrooms and schools. It is not only administrative costs—and added expenses due to students who, upon their departure, fail to return textbooks—that tax schools when dealing with transient student populations. Developing and sustaining a cohesive student body and a school-wide *esprit de corps* in a chaotic and ever-changing school environment can also present a Herculean challenge that under-resourced schools may be ill-prepared to overcome.

Disconnect Between Mobile Students and School Personnel. Informal family bonds can act to moderate or lessen the negative impact of mobility on transient youth (Hagan, Macmillan, & Wheaton, 1996). Latinos are known to rely heavily on their parents and other family members for emotional and psychological support (Vélez-Ibañez, 1997; Stanton-Salazar, 2001). Immigrant parents' investments in their children's well being can be limited, however, by the demands and stressors parents confront as immigrants in the low-wage labor force (Trejo, 1996), and by the language barriers that distance parents from the schools their children attend (Delgado-Gaitan, 1991; Romo & Falbo, 1996). Thus, relative to many other student groups, scholastic success among many Latino youth from immigrant households is much more dependent upon resource-full relationships with *nonfamilial* adults *outside the home*. More specifically, school personnel, who possess valuable information about educational programs, academic tutoring, college admission and the like, have been identified as critical institutional agents who can be particularly helpful to second-generation Latino students living in working-class homes embedded in stressful ecological conditions (Stanton-Salazar, 2001; Ream, 2005a).

At the same time, however, Latino and other minority students routinely confront institutional conditions and social forces that are quite difficult. Many of these forces have been elaborated in our previous work (Stanton-Salazar, 1997, 2001; Ream, 2003, 2005a). Most important, we believe, is that the development of supportive ties with school personnel is difficult due to cultural and language differences, racialized identities, and social class distinctions, which create infertile ground for developing trust, positive affect, and mutual emotional investment. Such conditions, particularly when combined with the added problem of mobility, can (a) inhibit help-seeking behaviors among Mexican origin youth, and (b) dissuade school personnel from conscientiously investing in the academic success of minorities. What we find, then, is a paradox where students, although embedded in an environment replete with human and institutional resources, and socially engaged within a network of school administrators, teachers and counselors, are nevertheless unable to position themselves within a genuine system of social support.

Here we focus our attention on the vexing problem of student mobility and less on the consequences of racialized interactions between students and school personnel. An excerpt from Ream's (2005a) study, clarifies just how mobility diminishes the necessary ingredients for the formation of social capital. One teacher declared with confidence that "The connection to success is the connection children feel to the teacher." She followed this insight, however, with the following lament: "It takes awhile for teachers and students to feel comfortable with one another, to take risks and all those wonderful mysterious factors of learning—student mobility keeps interrupting that process" (Ream, 2005a, p. 142). Indeed, her view reflects the perspectives of many other educators serving highly transient student populations (Rumberger et al., 1999).

Social scientists have long understood that the norm of "reciprocity" is one fundamental ingredient in the development of social capital (i.e., access to resources via cooperative, mutually beneficial relationships). Neither mobile students nor school personnel are particularly motivated to invest in relationships lacking time-earned trust. Teachers know that newly arriving students, especially mid-year school changers, are often here today and gone tomorrow. Under such conditions, teachers may be less inclined to invest in mobile students when they seem unlikely to fulfill the implicit reciprocal contract (Wehlage et al., 1989). And with repeated experiences of mobility, transient students often become resigned to developing a coping strategy of self-reliance and lowered expectations of support from school-based agents.

The phenomenon of mass teacher "burn-out" can arise from the repetitive loss of students they emotionally invest in and can result in disinclination to work with transient students. The comments of one frustrated second-year English instructor in a high school with particularly high rates of mobility illustrates the point:

Teachers put effort into teaching and the kids leave. So we don't have that sense of continuity and accomplishment with the transient students—and that affects morale. (Ream, 2005a, p. 142)

The notion that student learning most effectively occurs in the context of stable and caring pedagogical relationships is well-documented in the education field. Paradoxically, it has also been long recognized that even when schools serving minority student populations do put in place empowering pedagogical practices and curriculum, social forces outside the school, particularly those rooted in the local and regional economies, often undermine the best of educational reforms (Feagin, 1980).

5.5.   The Causes of Student Mobility

Residential mobility is often associated with a school change—particularly among elementary school children. One national study found that students who moved were five times more likely to change schools than students who did not move (Rumberger & Larson, 1998). Changing residences, however, does not always result in changing schools. Some states, such as California, have policies allowing students whose family has moved into a different school district to remain in their initial school placement. Just as students may move without changing schools, some students change schools without moving. About one-third of all school changes among Mexican American adolescents are *not* associated with a change of residence (27% among Whites). These numbers distinguish residential from student mobility, and suggest that Mexican American students are *less* likely to make a residential change without changing schools and are *more* likely to change schools without changing residences than their non-Latino White peers (Ream, 2005a).

At the secondary school level, parents, students, and school personnel all make decisions contributing to high rates of student mobility. Under the best of circumstances, mobility is the product of aspiration, opportunity, and rational action. The reality, however, is that adolescents often change schools suddenly and *reactively*—when an unpredictable job market causes working-class parents to scramble after insecure employment opportunities, or when parents split up and a custodial parent leaves town. Under optimal conditions there is genuine strategy underlying a planned school change, with parents and students acting as rational actors and informed consumers in the educational "marketplace." Frequently, however, students change schools for reasons that are neither entirely beyond their control, nor exclusively the result of strategic forethought.

Family-Initiated Mobility. Family-initiated mobility among Mexican Americans is often *reactive* in nature. One student, Ivan, recalled being whipsawed from school-to-school as a result of his father's demanding work-related responsibilities. "I do maintenance and I used to work for Z-Property Management," his immigrant father explained, "and so the company forced me to move to different cities." (Ream, 2005a, p. 77). Each time the family moved residences, Iván was forced to change schools, often in the middle of the school year. In Iván's case, however, school changes were at times *reactive* and on one occasion, somewhat more *strategic*. His parents initiated a slew of reactive school changes in response to his father's demanding mainte-nance job, but on one occasion the family changed residences for the explicit purpose of helping their son escape an especially poor school and enroll in a markedly better one. "When we moved to San Roque, Iván suffered a lot because that technical school there is one of the worst high schools. That's why I quit my last job. We moved right away, this time because of the schools." (Ream, 2005a, p. 79)

Student-Initiated Mobility. Given the increased autonomy that coincides with adolescent development, it is not surprising that high school students sometimes make independent decisions to change schools. In fact, a large percentage of student mobility at the secondary level—nearly 50 percent in the state of California—is the result of student-initiated requests to change schools (Rumberger et al., 1999). Among transient Latinos who make their own decision to change high schools, reactive mobility may be the norm (Ream, 2005a). Unful-filled reciprocity expectations, a breakdown in trust, or cultural and normative differences between minority students and mainstream school personnel can contribute to sudden and often mid-year school changes. Intimidation or overt racism also may cause some kids to change schools, but still others are motivated by loneliness, finding themselves bereft of a committed peer group, or feeling trapped in an uncaring school environment that can cause despairing adolescents to look elsewhere for a sense of belonging. Although the causes of student alienation and subsequent transience are not always so obviously measurable, school ethnographies have identified a superficial notion of caring deployed by at least some school personnel that stands in stark contrast to students' ideas about what a more authentic notion of caring should be (Courtney & Nobilit, 1994). Angela Valenzuela's (1999) research among adolescent Mexican Americans is informative:

When Mexican American youth reject schooling, they do so because their teachers do not fully apprehend their ethnic, social-class and peer-group realities, including their culture of caring. (Valenzuela, 1999, pp. 324–325)

Valenzuela suggests that different conceptions of caring can lead to a breach of trust between mainstream school personnel and non-mainstream students. Other studies demonstrate similar patterns of distrust and social distance between mainstream school personnel and minority youth (Sánchez-Jankowski, 1991), which may result in part from a lack of overlap in sub-cultural values and norms (Gibson et al., 2004). As a consequence, many students do not believe teachers are highly interested in their well-being, and this perception promotes their disengagement from school.

School-Initiated Mobility. Besides family- and student-initiated types of mobility, there is the growing phenomenon of mobility as precipitated by the schools themselves (Gotbaum, 2002), known as an *Opportunity Transfer* or "OT." Although *OTs* are sometimes employed to address problems such as misbehavior or fighting in school, students are often transferred out for less egregious reasons, such as poor attendance or flagging grades. The latter comes in the context of policy changes that simultaneously demand greater school-level accountability and higher graduation standards for students. Some teachers contend that the children of working class Latinos are particularly vulnerable to being transferred, involuntarily, to another school:

My experience as a teacher—and I have a lot of it—is that schools transfer Hispanic kids because the parents will not protest…Hispanic parents are more fearful and more respectful. The middle class White parents would say, 'You're not transferring *my* kid!' (Ream, 2005a, p. 85)

Case studies of urban high schools document that school officials do actively try to get rid of "troublemakers" by forcing them to leave or telling them they must leave (Fine, 1991). As emergent federal and state accountability schemes are putting increasing pressure on schools to demonstrate test-score improvement, the *OT* option seems likely to become an even more attractive tool both for removing troublemakers and for shuffling under-performing students elsewhere, so as not to tarnish schools' educational performance statistics.

Finally, the increasingly intense focus on accountability for test scores and graduation rates at the school level may inadvertently encourage administrators and other institutional agents to cast a blind eye to the needs of highly mobile student populations. If schools cannot, and are not encouraged to exemplify the sort of institutional staying power that helps keep students from changing schools, we may continue, instead, to exacerbate the "card-shuffling" process to the detriment of those students in our schools who face the most explicit educational challenges.

5.6.   Discussion of Policy Implications

In a landmark study of Congressional agenda-setting, John Kingdon (1995) suggests that three factors must converge in order for an issue, such as the underachievement of Mexican origin youth, to be placed front-and-center on the policy agenda. First, the issue—in this case, low average levels of Mexican American educational achievement and attainment—must be broadly recognized as a problem with clear social implications. Second, the political winds must blow in a direction giving elected officials practical reasons to believe the issue may be relevant to concerns about their own career viability before the issue will get incorporated as an important item in her/his political platform. Third, there must be policy solutions available to address the problem. When considering the contributions of teachers and school personnel, we agree with the importance of focusing on alterable variables as emphasized by Waxman, Padron, & Garcia (Ch. 8, this volume). We also echo Thompson's strategy (Ch. 9, this volume) of distinguishing between "alterable variables," or what educators *can* change (e.g., reading instruction, administrative practices) and those structural conditions outside the immediate control of educators and the school (e.g., concentrated neighborhood poverty). In the following section of this chapter, then, we consider a number of *alterable variables* that educators and policymakers can consider as they address the *mobility/social capital dynamic*, specifically in terms of its adverse effects on frequently mobile Latino students from low-income immigrant families.

5.7.   Accountability Mechanisms

Although some instances of student mobility are the result of strategic relocation (i.e., a carefully-considered move to a better school), many other instances are reactive in nature. Case studies have shown, however, that schools undertaking substantial and meaningful reforms can reduce unnecessary student transience. In a three-year period from 1987 to 1990, Hollibrook Accelerated School, in Houston, Texas, reduced its student mobility rate from 104 to 47 percent (McCarthy & Still, 1993, p. 80). Programs that target high-risk students have also been shown to reduce student mobility dramatically. For instance, a successful dropout prevention program in Southern California reduced student turnover by one half among the most at-risk Latino students in a Los Angeles area middle school (Larson & Rumberger, 1995).

In today's accountability-oriented environment, however, there may actually exist inherent disincentives for schools to work toward the retention of transient youth and families. By enrolling higher performing students while encouraging academically challenged students to head elsewhere, schools can boost overall test score performance and reduce dropout rates. Working-class immigrant Latinos may be particularly vulnerable to the "card shuffling" that results when school administrators push underperforming students out their doors, often by employing practices under such euphemistic names as *Opportunity Transfers*, or *OTs*. Certainly, this is a disturbing shortcut to "success"—and one that has been thoroughly reported in a recent series of articles in *The New York Times* (Medina & Lewin, 2003; Lewin, 2004). Education policymakers must grapple honestly and schools must wrestle self-critically with account-ability incentives that implicitly encourage the removal of under-performing students.

- *Hold School Districts Accountable*. Beyond examining aggregate test scores of individual schools in isolation (a method that might reward schools for using *OTs* to distribute at least some of their charges elsewhere), we should also measure accountability more broadly, at the school district level. Indeed, student mobility is best understood as an intra-district phenomenon that occurs within a localized geographic area.[5] If *Adequate Yearly Progress* (AYP) was redefined in such a way that it could function as a district *and* a school performance standard, such a policy might encourage (a) effective district-level strategies to counter reactive student mobility, and (b) a greater degree of between-school coordination and collaboration to assist mobile students with the school-to-school transition process. Thus, high rates of non-promotional student transience could be seen for what they really are, and schools could rightly see themselves as part of the solution to the wider problems within a district. In short, accountability mechanisms should be adjusted to draw district- and school-level distinctions regarding student mobility in order to develop a more thoughtful incentive structure behind systemic educational reforms (Offenberg, 2004).
- *Report cohort mobility rates*. What specific forms of accountability might be established so as to encourage districts and secondary schools in particular to undertake efforts to reduce reactive student mobility? Extra funding to document cohort graduation rates (the proportion of students who graduate from a specific entering class or cohort of students) would also reveal

---

[5] Rumberger & Larson (1998) found that 80 percent of non-promotional school changes for a cohort of urban Los Angeles area Latino students were within the same district.

the number of students from each cohort who left before completion—the cohort mobility rate (Rumberger et al., 1999). Measuring mobility rates in this way would at least provide a partial reflection of a schools' "holding power"—by which we mean schools' capacity to engage students in the educational process so as to assure more stable student populations. Schools could be evaluated over set periods to measure increase or decrease in overall rates of student transience in comparison to base year figures. Those schools that succeed in reducing the incidence of *reactive* mobility across time could be rewarded for promoting a more stable educational environment precisely because it is likely to have direct bearing on the standards of educational achievement for *all* students who participate in the system.

5.8.   Schools at the Center of Social Capital Development

We assert here that secondary schools can be better designed to act as the fulcrum for social capital development among working-class minority youth across family, peer, school, and community domains. Current educational experiments and model intervention programs—particularly those that tap into the value of healthy and reciprocal social relationships—are improving the lives of students from low-income households and communities (Maeroff, 1998; Stanton-Salazar, Vásquez, & Mehan, 2000). We propose that such programs offer helpful guidelines as to how we can re-design schools serving frequently transient immigrant populations. In the remaining pages we call attention to innovative programs that deserve attention by researchers, school reformers, and policy-makers. A close examination of these programs—each of which draws upon the power of relationships and the resources that inhere within social networks—reveals four essential components that are given brief consideration below.

(1) The School Component

- *Newcomer Clubs*: Many schools have responded to the regular entrée of new immigrant students by instituting programs designed to smooth the transition process. One southern California high school, for example, implemented a comprehensive plan to reduce mobility and mitigate its negative effects by encouraging new arrivals to join the "Newcomers Club," which meets weekly with school counselors. Parents of transient youth are also provided extra opportunities to meet with school counselors in order to fortify a home-school connection. A Maryland suburban high school implemented a similar program, initiating a "New Student Support Group" where counselors meet weekly with new students to provide information about the school and to discuss students' concerns about relocating (Wilson, 1993).

- *Student-counselor relations*: Shoring up student-counselor relations appears as an essential part of the most effective interventions.[6] The *Puente Project*, another well-studied program, is designed to enhance the resource exchange potential inherent in students' social networks, and targets Latino freshmen and sophomores across a wide achievement spectrum, offering to help them graduate and go on to college (Gándara, 2002). The *counseling component* is largely designed to ensure that *Puente* students are placed in college preparatory classes and offered the information necessary to prepare themselves for college eligibility. Counselors supervise college visits, initiate meetings between parents and *Puente* personnel, and even oversee the extramural *Puente Club* through which students socialize in structured extracurricular environments.

- *Teachers-counselor networks*: The fortification of collaborative ties between teachers and counselors is another key component found in many educational reform efforts. The *ALAS* program—*Achievement for Latinos through Academic Success*— is a dropout prevention program targeting high-risk middle-school Latino youth who live in impoverished urban neighborhoods. *ALAS* counselors work with middle school teachers to initiate more regular feedback to students and parents regarding students' educational progress and needs. One study evaluating *ALAS* concluded that the program had a practical impact on students directly affected by its interventions, reducing student turnover by one half among at-risk Latino students in a Los Angeles area middle school (Larson & Rumberger, 1995).

(2) The Peer Group Component

Recent scholarship has strongly emphasized the essential role of peers in both child and adolescent development (Harris, 1998) and school achievement (Gibson et al., 2004). So it is hardly surprising that peer group support is another key aspect of many successful programs, including the *Advancement Via Individual Determination (AVID)* program now with many sites across the U.S. *AVID* seems to us outstanding for its particular sensitivity to the notion that underachieving ethnic or linguistic minority students from highly transient low-income families might benefit from the thoughtful re-organization of social life in and beyond the school. *AVID* taps the resources that inhere in students' social networks by valuing the role and simultaneous (if not collaborative) social support of all key parties: parents, the peer group, school personnel, and community agents. By

---

[6] Since school counselors are largely responsible for guiding mobile students on both the departure and arrival ends of the school transfer process, bolstering the bi-lingual and bi-cultural counseling staffs at schools serving an especially transient immigrant second generation would undoubtedly help mitigate the potential negative impacts of student mobility. Yet even the most optimistic estimates of the current national average of one guidance counselor to 600 students paint a less than rosy picture of what appears quite literally to be a lonely profession.

helping students become part of a trusting, school-oriented network of peers that share common educational goals, *AVID* reframes achievement as a collective experience rather than as an individual one. This is done by bringing mid-performing adolescents together in collaborative learning environments—study groups, reader-writer workshops, and a special elective class that meets for one academic period a day, 180 days a year, for 3 or 4 years (Mehan et al., 1996; Gándara et al., 1998).

(3) *Home-School Connections*

There is by now a substantial literature on the educational value of parents' informal relations with their own children (Steinberg, 2001), as well as their more formal relationships with other parents (Carbonaro, 1998) and with school personnel (Chrispeels & Rivero, 2001). Indeed, fortifying home-school connections is another essential component of the most effective programs, as suggested in those schools that set up "Newcomer Clubs." *AVID*'s success is also partly contingent upon its empowerment of parents. Parent advisory boards, family study skills gatherings, and college awareness meetings are among the *AVID* activities facilitating parent involvement in schools. Family Night Dinners are another way that *AVID* bridges the family-school divide.

(4) *Community-Component & Student Mentoring*

The *Puente Project* and *AVID* also stand by the notion that the broader community must be woven into the fabric of the school experience. A community mentor liaison is responsible for the mentoring component of the *Puente Project*, which is fashioned so as to harness the power of community social capital by identifying, training, and then matching Latino community mentors with 9th graders. By this process, the mentoring component facilitates capital-rich and mutually rewarding relationships between students and community mentors (Gándara et al., 1998). *AVID* further expects colleges, universities, and area businesses to share in the task of preparing and motivating underserved students who are willing to work hard to get into college.

5.9.   Conclusion and Recommendations

The lesson we can derive from the various programs noted above is the paradigmatic approach they take in working with students from groups that have historically been most underserved by our school system. Foremost is the operating assumption that these students can indeed succeed in school, in spite of the many economic and ecological hardships they and their families endure. Secondly, such success is predicated upon the very intentional design of a *social support system* around each student—a system that functions across family, peer, school, and community domains as a *countervailing* force in their lives.[7] Students, thus, are embedded in inter-connected networks of agents already existing in their social world, or within close proximity. Most importantly, these programs take on the charge of training and mobilizing all network participants to work together on behalf of targeted students, in great part, by guiding them in how to utilize most effectively the resources and support they have at their disposal (e.g., knowledge funds, institutional networks, and affiliations across sociocultural domains). To recap, the following recommendations emerge from our collaborative research effort:

5.9.1. Reduce Unnecessary Student Mobility

*Accountability mechanisms should be adjusted to take into account mobile youth.

1) Hold schools and districts accountable for students who make non-promotional school changes
2) Report school-level cohort mobility rates

5.9.2. Develop Social Capital

*Effective school reform programs must be predicated on a *social paradigm*, one in which it is understood that *social relationships* are dramatically important to low-status Latinos.

1) Build upon relationally driven programs including *Alas*, the *Puente Project*, and *AVID*
2) Bolster school guidance counseling by reducing the student/counselor ratio
3) Facilitate home-school connections
4) Foster peer relations that *bridge* nativity status and social class barriers
5) Develop teacher-counselor networks
6) Weave the broader community into the fabric of the school experience

The growing prosperity gap within the U.S., accompanied by global labor market changes, make the consequences of school failure and persistent underachievement an increasingly serious problem in the age of information-technology. As the U.S. economy has shifted from producing goods to service employment and high-tech information processing, well-paying jobs for the under-skilled have largely disappeared. The negative consequences will not only

---

[7] See Stanton-Salazar's discussion of "counterstratification" influences (with the student, the family, school, and community) that act to both 'buffer' the student from negative ecological forces (e.g., gang violence) and to cultivate key forms of resiliency among low-status youth (2001, p. 22). See also Stanton-Salazar and Spina (2000) for an extended critical review on existing research on resiliency.

be felt among minorities for whom the U.S. educational and political economy has proven to be especially marginalizing, but also by the nation as a whole—particularly in terms of loss of human resources and erosion of democratic participation. The *mobility/social capital dynamic* is both a symptom of a "nation at risk," and an opportune point of departure for serious school reform.

In this chapter, we have emphasized the importance of changing basic features of school accountability schemes to better address the problematic incidence of student transience among adolescent Latinos. And we have also recommended an intervention approach oriented toward increasing their stocks of empowering forms of social capital. However, we must also assert that these reform efforts will not alone solve the inter-connected problems of student mobility, social *de*-capitalization, and academic underperformance among Latino youth. Social reforms that address working-class income and wealth disparities must accompany more direct school reform efforts (Anyon, 2005). Broad economic indicators suggest, however, that market forces and domestic social policy have been marching, for some time, in just the opposite direction (Congressional Budget Office, 2003). Without a renewed commitment to economic and political reforms designed to stymie growing resource inequality,[8] Latino youth will continue to demonstrate high mobility patterns and suffer its attendant adverse effects in spite of thoughtful strategies designed to augment students' social capital and promote their school success.

References

Aguirre, A. & Martinez, R. (2000). *Chicanos in Higher Education: Issues and Dilemmas for the 21st Century*. Washington, DC: John Wiley & Sons.

Ainsworth-Darnell, J. & Downey, D. (1998). Assessing the oppositional culture explanation for racial/ethnic differences in school performance. *American Sociological Review*, 63, 536–553.

Anyon, J. (2005) *Radical Possibilities: Public Policy, Urban Education, and a New Social Movement*. New York: Routledge.

Benson, C. & Weigel, D. (1981). Ninth-grade adjustments and achievement as related to mobility. *Educational Research Quarterly*, 5, 15–19.

Bourdieu, P. (1986). The forms of capital. In Richardson, J. (ed.), *Handbook of Theory and Research on the Sociology of Education*. New York: Greenwood Press.

Brooks-Gunn, J. & Duncan, G. (1997). The effects of poverty on children. *The Future of Children*, 7, 55–71.

Buriel, R. (1984). Integration with traditional Mexican-American culture and sociocultural adjustment. In Martinez, J. Jr & Mendoza, R. (eds), *Chicano/a Psychology* (2nd edn). Orlando, FL: Academic Press.

Carbonaro, W. (1998). A little help from my friend's parents: Intergenerational closure and educational outcomes. *Sociology of Education*, 71, 295–313.

---

[8] See Richard Rothstein (2004) for recommended social and economic reforms geared toward forging a more effective and meritocratic system of education.

Congressional Budget Office (2003). *Effective Federal Tax Rates For All Households By Household Income Category, 1979–2000*. Washington, DC: Author.

Chrispeels, J. & Rivero, E. (2001). Engaging Latino families for student success: How parent education can reshape parents' sense of place in the education of their children. *Peabody Journal of Education*, 76, 119–169.

Coleman, J. (1988). Social capital in the creation of human capital. *American Journal of Sociology*, 94, S95–S120.

College Entrance Examination Board. (1999). *Reaching the Top: A Report of the National Task Force of Minority High Achievement*. New York: The College Board.

Conchas, G. (2001). Structuring failure and success: Understanding the variability in Latino school engagement. *Harvard Educational Review*, 71, 475–504.

Courtney, M. & Nobilit, G. (1994). The principal as caregiver. In Prillaman, A., Eaker, D. & Kendrick, D. (eds), *The Tapestry of Caring: Education as Nurturance*. Norwood, NJ: Ablex Publishing.

Darder, A., Torres, R., & Gutierrez, H. (eds). (1997). *Latinos and Education: A Critical Reader*. New York: Routledge.

Delgado-Gaitan, C. (1991). Involving parents in the schools: A process of empowerment. *American Journal of Education*, 100, 20–46.

Dika, S. & Singh, K. (2002). Applications of social capital in educational literature: A critical synthesis. *Review of Educational Research*, 72, 31–60.

Feagin, J. (1980). School desegregation: A political-economic perspective. In Stephan, W. & Feagin, J. (eds), *School Desegregation*. New York: Pleum Press.

Fine, M. (1991). *Framing dropouts: Notes on the Politics of an Urban Public High School*. Albany, NY: State University of New York Press.

Flores-González, N. (2002). *School Kids/Street Kids: Identity Development in Latino Students*. New York: Teachers College Press.

Gándara, P. (1994). Language and ethnicity as factors in school failure: The case of Mexican Americans. In Wollons, R. (ed.), *Children at Risk in America: History, Concepts and Public Policy*. Albany, NY: State University of New York Press.

Gándara, P. (2002). A study of high school Puente: What we have learned about preparing Latino youth for postsecondary education. *Educational Policy*, 16, 474–495.

Gándara, P., Larson, K., Mehan, H. & Rumberger, R. (1998). *Capturing Latino Students in the Academic Pipeline* (Chicago/Latino Policy Project, Policy Report Vol. 1, No. 1). Berkeley, CA: University of California.

Gibson, M., Gándara, P., & Koyama, J. (eds). (2004). *School Connections: U.S. Mexican Youth, Peers and School Achievement*. New York: Teachers College Press.

Gotbaum, B. (2002). *Pushing Out at-risk Students: An Analysis of High School Discharge Figures*. New York: The Public Advocate for the City of New York and Advocates for Children.

Hagan, J., Macmillan, R., & Wheaton, B. (1996). New kid in town: Social capital and the life course effects of family migration on children. *American Sociological Review*, 61, 368–385.

Hanushek, E., Kain, J., & Rivkin, S. (2001). *Disruption Versus Tiebout Improvement: The Costs and Benefits of Switching Schools* (NBER Working Paper No. W8479). Cambridge, MA: National Bureau of Economic Research.

Harris, J. (1998). *The Nurture Assumption*. New York: The Free Press.

Hartup, W. & Stevens, N. (1997). Friendships and adaptation in the life course. *Psychological Bulletin*, 121, 355–370.

Haveman, R. & Wolfe, B. (1994). *Succeeding Generations: On the Effects of Investments in Children.* New York: Russell Sage Foundation.

Haveman, R., Wolfe, B., & Spaulding, J. (1991). Childhood events and circumstances influencing high school completion. *Demography*, 28, 133–157.

Heinlein, L. & Shinn, M. (2000). School mobility and student achievement in an urban setting. *Psychology in the Schools*, 37, 349–357.

Jason, A., Weine, A., Johnson, J., Warren-Sohlberg, L., Filippelli, L., & Turner, E. et al. (1992). *Helping Transfer Students: Strategies For Educational and Social Readjustment.* San Francisco: Jossey-Bass.

Jencks, C. & Phillips, M. (eds). (1998). *The Black-White Test Score Gap.* Washington, DC: Brookings Institution Press.

Jensen, L. (2001). The demographic diversity of immigrants and their children. In Rumbaut, R. & Portes, A. (eds), *Ethnicities: Coming of Age in Immigrant America.* Berkeley and New York: University of California Press and Russell Sage Foundation.

Kingdon, J. (1995). *Agendas, Alternatives and Public Policies* (2nd edn). New York: Harper Collins College Publishers.

Larson, K. & Rumberger, R. (1995). ALAS: Achievement for Hispanic Americans through academic success. *Staying in School: A Technical Report of Three Dropout Prevention Projects for Middle School Students With Learning and Emotional Disabilities.* Minneapolis, MN: Institute on Community Integration, pp. A1–A71.

Latinos in Education. (1998). *Early Childhood, Elementary, Secondary, Undergraduate, Graduate.* Washington, DC: White House Initiative on Educational Excellence for Hispanic Americans.

Lewin, T. (2004, June 19) *City Resolves Legal Battle Over Forcing Students Out.* New York Times.

López, D. & Stanton-Salazar, R. (2001). The Mexican American second generation: Yesterday, today, and tomorrow. In Rumbaut, R. & Portes, A. (eds), *Ethnicities: Coming of Age In Immigrant America.* Berkeley and New York: University of California Press and Russell Sage Foundation.

Los Angeles Unified School District (LAUSD) (2004). Robert Ream's Correspondence With Shirley Kouffman, Director of the Planning Assessment and Research ED vision, School Information Branch (June, 2004). Los Angeles: Los Angeles Unified School Transience and stability in the Los Angeles Unified School District (Publication 580). Los Angeles: Author.

Maeroff, G. (1998). *Altered Destinies: Making Life Better for Schoolchildren in Need.* New York: St. Martin's Press.

McCarthy, J. & Still, S. (1993). Hollibrook accelerated elementary school. In Murphy, J. & Hallinger, P. (eds), *Restructuring Schooling: Learning From Ongoing Efforts.* Newbury Park, CA; Corwin Press, pp. 63–83.

McDonnell, L. & Hill, P. (1993). *Newcomers in American Schools: Meeting the Educational Needs of Immigrant Youth.* Santa Monica: RAND Corporation.

Medina, J. & Lewin, T. (2003, August 1). High school under scrutiny for giving up on its students, *Pushed Out*, Part 2. New York Times.

Mehan, H., Villanueva I., Hubbard, L., & Lintz, A. (1996). *Constructing School Success: The Consequences of Untracking Low-Achieving Students.* Cambridge: Cambridge University Press.

Miller, S. (1995). *An American Imperative: Accelerating Minority Educational Advancement.* New Haven, CT: Yale University Press.

Moore, S. (2001). *U.S.-Mexico Migration Issues: Testimony Before the Senate Judiciary Committee Subcommittee on Immigration.* http://judiciary.senate.gov/oldsite/te090701si-moore.htm. September 7.

Offenberg, R. (2004). Inferring adequate yearly progress of schools from student achievement in highly mobile communities. *Journal of Education for Students Placed at Risk,* 9, 337–355.

Ogbu, J. (1992). Understanding cultural diversity and learning. *Educational Researcher,* 21, 5–14.

Portes, A. (1998). Social capital: Its origin and applications in modern sociology. *Annual Review of Sociology,* 24, 1–24.

Portes, A. & Rumbaut, R. (2001). *Legacies: The Story of the Immigrant Second Generation.* University of California Press.

Pribesh, S. & Downey, D. (1999). Why are residential and school moves associated with poor school performance? *Demography,* 36, 521–534.

Putnam, R. (2000). *Bowling alone: The Collapse and Revival of American Community.* New York: Simon & Schuster.

Ream, R. (2003). Counterfeit social capital and Mexican-American underachievement. *Education Evaluation and Policy Analysis,* 25, 237–262.

Ream, R. (2005a). *Uprooting Children: Mobility, social capital and Mexican American underachievement.* New York: LFB Scholarly Publishing, LLC.

Ream, R. (2005b). Toward understanding how social capital mediates the impact of student mobility on Mexican American achievement. *Social Forces,* 84, 201–224.

Romo, H. & T. Falbo. (1996). *Latino High School Graduation: Defying the Odds.* Austin, TX: University of Texas Press.

Rothstein, R. (2004). *Class and Schools: Using Social, Economic, and Educational Reform to Close the Black-White Achievement Gap.* NY: Columbia University, Teachers College, Economic Policy Institute.

Rumberger, R. (2003). The causes and consequences of student mobility. *Journal of Negro Education,* 72, 6–21.

Rumberger, R. & Larson, K. (1998). Student mobility and the increased risk of high school dropout. *American Journal of Education,* 107, 1–35.

Rumberger, R., Larson, K., Ream, R., & Palardy, G. (1999). *The Educational Consequences of Mobility for California Students and Schools.* Berkeley, CA: University of California, Policy Analysis for California Education.

Sánchez-Jankowski, M. (1991). *Island in the Street: Gangs and American Urban Society.* Berkeley, CA: University of California Press.

Suarez-Orozco, M. (1991). Immigrant adaptation to schooling: A Hispanic case. In Gibson, M. & Ogbu, J.U. (eds), *Minority Status & Schooling: A Comparative Study of Immigrant and Involuntary Minorities.* New York. Garland Press.

Smith, J. (2003). Assimilation across the Latino generations. Proceedings of the AEA, USA, 93, 315–319.

Stanton-Salazar, R. (1997). A social capital framework for understanding the socialization of racial minority children and youths. *Harvard Educational Review,* 67, 1–40.

Stanton-Salazar, R. (2001). *Manufacturing Hope and Despair: The School and Kin Support Networks of U.S.- Mexican Youth.* New York: Teachers College Press.

Stanton-Salazar, R. & Spina, S. (2000). The network orientations of highly resilient urban minority youth. *The Urban Review: Issues and Ideas in Public Education,* 32, 227–262.

Stanton-Salazar, R., Vásquez, O., & Mehan, H. (2000). Engineering success through institutional support. In Gregory, S. (ed.), *The Academic Achievement of Minority Students:*

Comparative Perspectives, Practices, and Prescriptions. New York: University Press of America.

Steinberg, L. (2001). We know some things: Parent-adolescent relationships in retrospect and prospect. *Journal of Research on Adolescence*, 11, 1–19.

Swanson, C. & B. Schneider. (1999). Students on the move: Residential and educational mobility in America's schools. *Sociology of Education*, 72, 54–67.

Tienda, M. (2001). College admissions policies and the educational pipeline: Implications for medical and health professions. In Smedley, B., Stith, A., Colburn, L., & Evans, C. (eds), *The Right Thing To Do, the Smart Thing To Do: Enhancing Diversity in the Health Professions*. Washington, DC: The National Academy of Sciences.

Trejo, S. (1996). *Obstacles to Labor Market Progress of California's Mexican Origin Workers*. Berkeley, CA: University of California, Chicano/Latino Policy Project.

Trueba, H. (1988). Culturally based explanations of minority students' academic achievement. *Anthropology and Education Quarterly*, 19, 270–287.

U.S. Department of Commerce, Bureau of the Census. (2000a). *Hispanic Population of the United States: March 1999* (Current Population Reports, series P-20, No. 527). Washington, DC: U.S. Government Printing Office.

U.S. Department of Commerce, Bureau of the Census. (2000b). *Census 2000 Brief: Overview of Race and Hispanic Origin*. Washington, DC: U.S. Government Printing Office.

U.S. Department of Commerce, Bureau of the Census. (2004). *Geographic Mobility: 2002 to 2003 population Characteristics*. (Current Population Reports, series P-20, no. 549). Washington, DC: U.S. Government Printing Office.

U.S. Department of Commerce, Census Bureau News. (2000). *Moving Rate Among Americans Declines*, Census Bureau Says. Press Release 19 January 2000. Washington, DC: U.S. Government Printing Office.

U.S. Department of Education, National Center for Education Statistics (NCES). (2002). *Dropout Rates in the United States: 2002*. Washington, DC: U.S. Government Printing Office.

U.S. General Accounting Office. (1994). *Elementary School Children: Many Change Schools Frequently, Harming Their Education*. Washington, DC: U.S. Government Printing Office.

Valencia, R. (ed.). (2002). *Chicano School Failure and Success: Past, Present and Future* (2nd edn). London: Routledge Falmer.

Valenzuela, A. (1999). *Subtractive Schooling: U.S.-Mexican Youth and the Politics of Caring*. Albany, NY: State University of New York Press.

Vélez-Ibañez, C. (1997). *Border Visions: Mexican Cultures of the Southwest United States*. Tucson, AZ: University of Arizona Press.

Vernez, G. & Mizell, L. (2002). *Goal: To Double the Rate of Hispanics Earning a Bachelor's Degree*. Santa Monica, CA: RAND Corporation, Center for Research on Immigration Policy.

Wehlage, G., Rutter, R., Smith, G., Lesko, N., & Fernandez, R. (1989). *Reducing the Risk: Schools as Communities of Support*. Philadelphia: Falmer Press.

Wilson, C. (1993). Providing support for high school transfer students. *The School Counselor*, 40, 223–227.

6
Educational Attainment of Immigrant and Non-Immigrant Young Blacks

Xue Lan Rong and Frank Brown

The United States has experienced resurgence in immigration over the last three decades and the U.S. Black population has been affected by the current immigration patterns. The number of immigrants from Caribbean and African countries to the United States has grown noticeably since the 1970s. Despite this increase and a growing interest in other immigrant populations, little has been written about the educational conditions and attainment of Black immigrant children. To promote academic success for Black students, our society and educators must acknowledge the presence of the immigrant segment in the Black population, be aware of their socioeconomic status and cultural patterns, and further recognize the complexities within the Black population.

The purpose of this chapter is to identify and differentiate the causes of variations in educational attainment among different groups of Black children. The chapter starts with a brief review of the historical significance of the presence of African and Caribbean Black immigrants in the U.S., and provides information about their demographic characteristics and geographic distribution. Based on a synthesis of research and earlier work by the author (Rong, 2005), the chapter discusses educational achievement and attainment patterns, including cultural patterns and schooling behaviors based on self-defined identities for Black students. Then, based on Census 2000 data, we illustrate these variations in educational attainment by discussing socioeconomic, demographic, and parental variables related to Black children's life conditions and their environment. The chapter concludes with recommendations for policy and practice.

6.1. Black Historical Presence

The Black presence in North America has a history of over 400 years, and from the outset this population has been heterogeneous. Different groups of Blacks came to the United States from different origins, at different times, for different reasons, and by different means. Among the people of North America, about

500,000 African Blacks were brought to North America as slaves between 1619 and 1800 before slave importation into the United States was banned in 1808. At present, approximately 90% of the 34 million Black people currently living in the United States are descendants of the 500,000 slaves brought forcibly to the United States before 1808.

Although the Black population has the smallest proportion of the post-1900 immigrants to the United States, the Black immigrant population has increased significantly in the last four decades (especially in the 1980s and 1990s). The foreign-born Black population in 1960 was only slightly more than 100,000, but by the year 2000, over 2 million foreign-born Black immigrants were living in the United States, an increase of about 2000%. The proportion of immigrants among the total U.S. Black population increased from 0.7% in 1960 to 1.1% in 1970, 3% in 1980, 4% in 1990, and 7% in 2000. The U.S. Census Bureau projects a further increase in the foreign-born Black population and their offspring over the coming decades.

Among Black immigrants, non-Hispanic Caribbean natives (mostly Barbadians, Grenadians, Haitians, Jamaicans, Trinidadians and Tobagonians) and Africans (mostly Ethiopians, Ghanaians, Kenyans, Nigerians, Somalis and South Africans) made up the majority of the two million foreign-born people of African origin in the 2000 U.S. Census. According to the U.S. Bureau of the Census (2003), the Caribbean Black population is composed of approximately 450,000 Haitians and 600,000 Jamaicans, and they are concentrated in a few states. About half live in New York and approximately 20% live in Florida, primarily in the Miami area. Moreover, virtually all Haitians and Jamaicans live in large cities.

In comparison to the Caribbean immigrant population, only a small number of African Black immigrants (approximately 540,000) were able to come to the United States between 1820 and 2000, although the rate has increased sharply in recent years with more Blacks migrating to the United States from Africa between 1990 and 2003 than in nearly the entire preceding two centuries. As a result, for the first time in U.S. history, more Blacks (50,000 annually) now come to the United States from Africa than those who came during the years of slave trade (Roberts, 2005). Nigerians constitute the largest number at about 100,000 persons. Many African immigrants choose New York City as their place of residence. However, no large ethnic community of Black immigrants from a single African country currently exists in the United States.

6.2.   Socialization, Identity, and Achievement of Black Students

Researchers and commentators of the past and present reported adverse living situations, residential segregation, and social isolation as prevalent among the Black American population in the United States and attributed these problems to the combined effects of classism and racism (Du Bois, 1989). Researchers generally agree that children from families with low socioeconomic status are more likely to experience difficulties in school and attain lower levels of overall academic achievement than their middle-class counterparts in the United States and that, racism has played a significant historical role in the disproportionate numbers of Black and Hispanic children living in poverty relative to White children. The lack of familial resources and unconcerned or ambivalent educational institutions are largely responsible for the historical failure of minority children in schools. However, psycho-cultural factors may also play a role. Research indicates that a low level of academic attainment by Black children is also related to their self-prophecy, in which social-historical negative images and low expectations have a psychological impact on Black children's self-esteem and confidence. This, in turn, affects levels of academic attainment. This could be ascribed to the influence of the peer group and a defensive anti-school culture, which are particularly prevalent among Black students in middle and high school years (Fordham & Ogbu, 1989)

6.2.1.   Impact of Socioeconomic Conditions

Researchers generally agree that socioeconomic conditions influence children's level of educational attainment. Race is highly correlated with class and it is, therefore, difficult to disentangle their influences on educational processes and outcomes (Mickelson & Dubois, 2002). In spite of the fact that a considerable portion of the Black American population has moved steadily into the middle class since the Civil Rights movement in the 1960s, a higher percentage of the Black population has remained at or under the poverty level than any other racial group. A significant number of studies have addressed the low socioeconomic status, adverse living conditions, and single parent family structures among certain segments of the Black population in the United States, and the impact of these factors on Black children's education. For example, Lara-Cinisomo, Pebley, Variana, Maggio, Berends and Lucas (2004) found that the most important factors associated with the educational achievement of children were socioeconomic factors, broadly defined (e.g., parental education levels, family and neighborhood income and poverty, etc.). Therefore, it is necessary to evaluate the impact of socioeconomic and social factors on children's education.

6.2.2.   Impact of Socialization in School

Research studies of the socialization process for children in school indicate the powerful influences on children from peer pressure and popular culture. The influences divert children's attention from understanding the important link between their academic studies and their future. American teenagers who experience more peer pressure, and who are more influenced by popular culture, relative to their peers tend to do poorly in school. Furthermore, researchers report an interesting phenomenon in which working-class White teens (e.g., Weis, 1985) and oppressed minority children of all classes are affected by an anti-school culture, resulting in disrespect for authority and an increased emphasis on peer solidarity. To some extent, this phenomenon results in a collectively defensive identity, whereby underprivileged children resist feelings of subordination by intentionally ignoring social customs and school rules in order to protect their self-esteem. Researchers report that black students who pursue academic advancement in school are sometimes viewed as "acting White" and as being less loyal to their peers. These stereotypes among some Black American students can result in negative and counterproductive consequences (Fordham & Ogbu, 1989).

Immigrant children from countries where schools teach values and practice socialization patterns differently from schools in the United States may struggle with different interpretations of, and psychological reactions to, the socialization process in US schools. Such children may also face problems developing effective coping strategies for the difficulties they encounter in the United States. For example, many immigrant teenagers are viewed as strangers and outsiders by their native-born peers, and suffer from social exclusion, and thus may not be as readily influenced by popular culture as native-born children. Many immigrant teenagers also have parents who strongly deny the legitimacy of youth popular culture in the home and community, thus guarding them from being overwhelmed by its influence (Gibson, 1988).

6.3.   Cultural Patterns and Identities

Empirical studies indicate that different Black groups developed distinct forms, ways and rates of cultural adaptation, with various and sometimes contradictory strategies. Adaptation strategies are influenced by the structural context of the receiving societies, the immigrant communities, and their interactions. Parents and children developed and applied a variety of adaptive strategies derived from how different groups perceived their vulnerabilities and resources, and how the results of these strategies played out in the specific social and cultural contexts in their home countries and in the United States. One of the adaptation strategies relates to self-perceived identity. Black immigrants may perceive the possibility of renegotiating the meanings of their racial identity with mainstream society in an attempt to change their racial label by reserving their status as immigrants who maintain an ethnic/nationality identity reflecting their parents' national origins.

It is important for researchers to explore the issues related to the perceptions of Black immigrants and their strategies to cope with difficulties when we examine the role of their identity deconstruction and reconstruction. For example, an increasing number of studies have reported that many Caribbean immigrants want mainstream society to identify them as Caribbean or West Indian, and not as Black Americans, in order to help them cope with issues of racism, classism, and assimilationism. Since most research focusing on Black immigrant identity issues has studied West Indians rather than immigrants from Africa (see Kamya, 1997), the research here uses Caribbean Blacks as examples for the theoretical framework presented.

Recent studies of identity formation among Black immigrants may elucidate implications of studies of identity and educational performance. Scholars (e.g., Foner, 1987; Gibson, 1991; Waters, 1999) have observed a cultural division between Caribbean Blacks and Black Americans. Dodoo (1997) and Woldemikael (1989) identify several major differences between Black immigrant communities and Black American communities that may partially explain their different perceptions of reality and their reactions to societal discrimination. First, the migration ideology of most Caribbean immigrants may be the reason not only for their optimistic perception of the possibility of upward mobility for Black immigrants but also for their motivation to endure hardship and discriminatory treatment. Ogbu (1991, 1994) argues that immigrants who come to the United States voluntarily for economic reasons tend to downplay discriminatory treatment and emphasize progress made in their economic condition and their children's education opportunities because they do not compare themselves to the more affluent White Americans, but rather to the poorer folks back in their home countries.

Secondly, the recallable life experiences of Black immigrants from most Caribbean and African countries are different from those of native-born Black Americans, which is due in large part to different sociocultural histories in the countries from which they emigrated. Most West Indian immigrants were socialized in the more favorable racial and cultural climate of the Caribbean, where they have always been a racial majority and have had more positive role models in all walks of life. This situation may promote self-confidence, leading to high expectations and a more optimistic attitude about the future, which may manifest in higher educational and occupational achievement (Dodoo, 1997).

Thirdly, Ainsworth-Darnel and Downey (1998) suggest that Black Americans and Black immigrants have different interpretations and solutions for the "Black problem" in contemporary America due to segregated occupations and housing situations, lack of knowledge regarding racial history, and inexperience with discriminatory realities in the United States. While many Black Americans may applaud the progress made in the last several decades, they also blame their continuing difficulties on social and economic inequality and racial discrimination. Many Black Americans advocate government efforts, such as affirmative action, to eliminate historical and current barriers for Black people. In contrast, immigrant Blacks may perceive that Black Americans overemphasize their own vulnerability and discount the power of individual initiative and determination. Although some of these perceptions may be due to different sociocultural experiences, they may also be due to the segregated occupational and housing situations of most recent Caribbean immigrants in larger cities. Many Caribbean immigrants living in inner-city areas tend to have more contact with the most vulnerable segments of the Black American population. They may misinterpret their experiences with poor, undereducated, and unemployed inner city Black residents as the typical characteristics of the Black American population as a whole.

These different perceptions and understandings may have produced survival and success strategies for Black immigrants and their children that differ from those of non-immigrant Black Americans. Kasinitz (1992) reports that Black immigrants attempt to escape the negative racial label attached to Black Americans by holding on to their native culture and national identity. Waters (1999) pointed out that the formation of identity among young Caribbean Blacks allows them to negotiate the meaning of their racial identity, replacing the racial label with their preferred ethnicity or nationality. In Waters' findings, youngsters who identified themselves as Caribbean Blacks were more likely to live in a Caribbean immigrant community where subcultures are built on optimism, self-defined identity, and social networks. Many youngsters and their parents tended to see more opportunities and rewards for their efforts and initiative. Waters also found that immigrant youngsters who identified themselves as Black Americans were more likely to perceive their future less optimistically and see less economic return on their educational investment. Relative to youngsters who chose a Caribbean Black identity, these youngsters were more likely to associate with low-motivation peer groups and tended to do poorly in school (Fordham, 1996).

Related to the above, the strength of the immigrant community is a powerful predictor of the outcomes of children's socialization (Stanton-Salazar, 1997). Waters (1999) points out differences in children's behavior result from what children hear from their parents and how they share their interpretation of these messages with their peers. Many Caribbean parents work hard to make rapid economic progress and to achieve middle class status while preserving their immigrant homeland culture, pride, values, and solidarity. They pass on these beliefs and behaviors to their children, individually as well as collectively. As observed by Vickerman (1999), of great importance to the Caribbean Black community is that all parents of second-generation Caribbean immigrant children pass on the same message and values to their children.

6.4.   Immigration, Assimilation Models, and Educational Attainment

Although there have been some research studies on Black adults (Bryce-Laoirte, 1972), very little comparative work exists on the educational attainment of Black immigrant and Black American children. In this section, we begin by briefly describing the relationship between immigration-related assimilation patterns and educational attainment in terms of classic assimilation and segmented assimilation.

6.4.1.   Classic and Segmented Assimilation

Past studies were more likely to apply classic assimilation, which assumes quick and complete Americanization and integration into the middle classes. However, this straight-line assimilation model, usually associated in the past with White immigrant ethnic groups, is inconsistent with actual educational and occupational attainment of third-generation Black immigrants (e.g., Schlesinger, 2002). This model has also been challenged by the persistent educational and economic gaps among minority groups and between minorities and majority Whites. The economic and social outlook for many Blacks and Latinos whose families have lived in the United States for generations may veer in a direction opposite to their immigration dream, resulting in an entry into the economic underclass.

Focusing their research on Hispanic and Asian immigrants, some scholars (e.g., Portes & Zhou, 1993) have proposed a segmented assimilation model that emphasizes the multiple and contradictory paths various immigrant groups take and that predicts complex outcomes as a result of these variations. The earlier segmented assimilation model characterized the immigrants' new home, the United States, as the home of multiple stratification systems with economic, racial and gender hierarchies. When immigrants were absorbed into U.S. society, they were incorporated into these stratified configurations (Ogbu, 1994). The concentration of Black immigrants in central cities made for their easy entrance into the lowest stratum of society. Scholars have argued that central city residency exposed immigrant minority children to the poverty subculture developed by marginalized native youths to cope with their own difficult situation (Portes, 1995).

6.5.   Generational Effects

The recent experiences of Black immigrants and those of other immigrant groups have invalidated the theories of the classic assimilation model. Recent quantitative studies have indicated that the segmented/selective assimilation framework is more viable for predicting and interpreting immigrant children's level of educational attainment when examining the gaps among race and generation status (Rumbaut & Portes, 2001). Many studies have reported an intergenerational decline in education and incomes for some groups, as well as persistent educational and income gaps between Whites and non-Whites across generations. Without considering the generational effect, previous research involving cross-racial and ethnic-group comparisons show that Black students generally do not do as well as either White or Asian students in school, but do better than Mexican and Puerto Rican students in terms of number of school years completed, percentage of high school graduates, percentage of college graduates, and most other indicators of educational attainment (Arias, 1986; Grant and Rong, 1999; Matute-Bianchi, 1986).

When the immigrant generation effect is taken into consideration, some studies show a curvilinear pattern for student achievement across generations. The second-generation students (American-born children with immigrant parents) do better educationally than immigrant or native-born groups, though immigrant youths who arrive at a young age may perform at an equivalent level to second-generation students (e.g., Rong and Grant, 1992; Kao & Tienda, 1995). Rong & Brown (2001) reported that second-generation Caribbean Black immigrant youth have higher levels of educational attainment than Black children without an immigration background.

More recent studies, however, reported a downward trend associated with time of residency, with newcomers attaining higher grade point averages than students whose families have lived in the U.S. longer (Porte & Rumbaut, 2001; Rumbaut & Portes, 2001). Using NELS 1988 data, Kao & Tienda (1995) reported that first-generation (foreign-born) Black children achieved the highest scholastic outcomes on two out of four achievement measures. The John Harvard Journal (2004) found that over 50% of the Black undergraduate students at Harvard University are first-or second-generation immigrant youths, though these two generations make up less than 10% of the Black American population. Rong and Preissle (1998) have also reported that Black immigrant children are ahead in schools and are more likely to be ahead of other children in educational measures (e.g., persistence in school, satisfactory academic progress). Black immigrant youth are also more likely than their Black American peers to stay in school until receiving their high school diplomas. All these studies considered the intertwining effects of race, ethnicity, generation, gender, social class, and other important socio-demographic and cultural variables. These findings are also consistent with the higher educational achievement and aspirations among first- and second-generation Black immigrant children in Gibson's qualitative studies (1991).

6.6.   Other Factors

Gender is another under-studied pertinent factor that influences the schooling of immigrant students. It has been an established pattern that U.S. female students generally outperform male students (Spring, 1994; U.S. Department of Education, 2003). This includes Black female students who on average achieve higher levels of educational attainment than Black male students at almost all levels of education (Grant and Rong, 2002). Gibson's (1991) ethnographic study focused on the schooling of Black immigrant children in relation to their immigrant generation, gender, ethnicity, and nationality. Gibson found that female students did better than male students, regardless of immigrant status. However, gender proved to be more significant for native-born youths than for immigrants.

Caribbean Black immigrant students performed better than native students, but the differences between females in both groups were minimal, while differences between the immigrant and non-immigrant boys were substantial. Gibson's study also revealed a relationship between gender and immigrant status. In spite of the fact that West Indian immigrants outperformed indigenous students, indigenous female students actually did better in school than immigrant male students, though the gap was fairly small. A similar gender pattern appeared in British schools where, in general, West Indian females outperformed West Indian males in academics, school persistence, and in overall school behavior (Fuller, 1980).

6.7.   Findings from U.S. 2000 Census Data

In light of our discussion on the variation of Black educational attainment patterns and assimilation models, we highlight our findings of Black children's educational attainment patterns. Based on the U.S. 2000 Census data, we conducted a demographic study to analyze the factors contributing to attainment variations.[1] The research also involved data from the Public Used Microdata Samples[2] (PUMS 5%, U.S. Bureau of the Census, 2003), which represented the largest population sample ever used in educational research[3].

Our research project first examined the reality of children's lives and their schooling, and compared and contrasted the individual characteristics, family types, and community environments across generations of U.S. residence, race/ethnicity and gender. This project, then, explored levels of educational attainment for each subgroup and conducted comparisons across these subgroups, which examined the relationships between socio-economic and demographic factors and young people's educational attainment.

The variables used in the research related to children's surroundings, the social and physical environments in which children live, related information on immigrant parents, the types of families of the children live, residential areas, local communities, and the states and regions in which they live. Since children are compared based on their residential generations, the following variables were included in the data analysis: language resources, the attrition and retention of their native tongues, and English acquisition.

Socioeconomic Conditions, Generation Effects, and Ethnic Differences. Although many studies have addressed the relationship between the socioeconomic status of the family and children's levels of educational attainment, few studies have compared the socioeconomic condition of a Black population by immigrant generation and ethnic group simultaneously. The findings of this research project were consistent with the reviewed literature. As stated earlier, being Black is likely to be a disadvantage regarding socioeconomic status, family situation, and structure. By contrast, being a member of the Second-Generation

---

[1] For the purposes of this chapter, we did not elaborate on our research methods and design. Please note, however, that "ordinary least squares regressions" were conducted to examine the simultaneous effects of generation of residence, gender, and race and ethnicity on educational attainment along with other socio-economic and demographic variables. Since the primary data analysis revealed interaction between race and ethnicity and generation of residence; therefore, regressions were conducted separately for African Blacks, Caribbean Blacks, and Non-Hispanic European Whites.

[2] PUMS 5% (U.S. Bureau of the Census (2003)) represents 5% of the total housing units in the United States and 14 million persons residing in them.

[3] The population was a stratified sub-sample of the full decennial U.S. Censuses of Population and Housing, approximately 16% of all housing units that received the long-form census questionnaires in 2000. The project used the data of approximately three million children and youth between the ages of 5 and 24 years old who were living with parent(s) or guardian(s) in 2000.

is likely to put that person at an advantage regarding the same set of factors. In combining the effects of race and generation, African American long-term residents (the Third-plus Generation and beyond) are the most disadvantaged in most aspects of social, economic, and family life. Second-Generation Whites are the most advantaged in most of the same respects.

For example, three observations can be made here. First, American-born children of immigrant parents are less likely to be in families under the poverty level and more likely to be in families whose incomes are equal to or higher than 95% of the U.S. population. This observation is consistent for White, Caribbean Black, and African Black children alike. Secondly, the effects of being third-generation on family economic status are varied. At the poorest end of Americans, First-Generation Caribbean Blacks and African Blacks are less likely to live in families at or under the poverty level than those in the Third-Plus Generations. For Whites, the First-Generation is worse off financially than the Third-Plus Generation, as more First-Generation than Third-Plus Generation Whites live at or under the poverty level. At the richest end of Americans, first Generation Whites and African Blacks are more likely to live in families whose incomes are at or higher than the 95th percentile, although First-Generation Caribbean Blacks are less likely to live in families with income levels at or higher than 95% of the U.S. population. Thirdly, race is clearly correlated with family economic conditions. White children are less likely to live in families at or under poverty level, but are more likely to live in families at the top 5% of the population in terms of income than either Caribbean Black children or African Black children across all generations.

Educational Attainment and Other Factors. The educational attainment data suggest complex patterns varied with race or nationality and generation. Several general patterns emerge. The descriptive data indicate that children's educational attainment clearly varies with race and ethnicity as well as with generation of residence. Descriptive statistics also indicate that, for all groups, the cross-generational gender patterns conform to the current U.S. pattern of women attaining more years of school than men for each generation. The examination of the combined effects of race/ethnicity, generation and gender revealed that the African Black males were disadvantaged for each generational phase compared with White and Caribbean Black males. However, Caribbean Black males in the Second-Generation and Third-Plus Generation had more years of school than co-generation White males, and Caribbean Black females in the Second Generation and Third-Plus Generations also compared favorably to co-generation White females measured by the mean years of school. African Black males of the Third-Plus Generation have the lowest years of school, and higher school graduation rates and college graduation rates than any other subgroup.

In examining the simultaneous effects of generation of residence, gender, and race or ethnicity on educational attainment, the socio-economic and demographic variables[4] were considered the most significant. Assuming that demographic and

---

[4] the inferential statistics reveal the significant effects of most socioeconomic variables included in the model.

socioeconomic factors are equalized, the impact of being Second-Generation on years of school attainment is consistent across race or pan-nationality and gender groups. Children of the Second-Generation attain significantly more years of school than members of the First-Generation for all race or ethnic groups.

The greatest increase at this generational phase occurs for Caribbean Blacks, for whom being Second-Generation rather than First-Generation has the most powerful impact on educational attainment. The effects of being Third-Plus Generation on educational attainment reveal two patterns for the three groups. For African Blacks and Whites, educational attainment peaks in the Second-Generation and declines thereafter; for Caribbean Blacks, attainment peaks in the Second-Generation and levels off from the Second-Generation to the Third-Plus Generation.

When levels of educational attainment are compared between the First-Generation and the Third- Plus Generation, it is found that being born of immigrant parents in the United States results in definite educational benefits for a child. Longer residence in the United States, however, may not produce further gains and, in some cases, is even associated with steep declines in levels of educational attainment. White children of the Third-Plus Generation have much fewer years of school than do White children of the First-Generation. For Caribbean Blacks and African Blacks, being born and living in the United States for more generations provides no gains in comparison to being an immigrant.

6.8.   Discussion of Findings

The combination of the classic assimilation model and the segmented assimilation model provides a suitable basis for interpreting the empirical findings. The results for our research project indicate that the barriers for Blacks are both socioeconomic and racial. Caribbean and Black youth are more likely to live in families with fewer resources than White children, and difficult family situations jeopardize Black children's educational advancement. Length of residency of generations in the United States exacerbates the difficulties faced by Black Americans and does not necessarily alleviate them. One of the explanations for why the Non-Hispanic White youth in the first generation can move forward more quickly economically and educationally than any other group is that White immigrants may face fewer barriers in a racially stratified society.

In addition to the structural explanation, intergenerational progression acculturation theories also provide valid explanations for the research findings. This acculturation theory illuminates the psychological coping strategies developed from ethnic identity reconstruction as described earlier. In addition, it is important to consider how social/cultural capital can influence community life (e.g., networking, solidarity, transnational and transcultural social space).

The findings also indicate that basic assimilation steps, such as acquiring English proficiency, are significant predictors of higher attainment. More extensive assimilation steps, however, such as abandoning one's heritage language and moving away from ethnic communities in central cities, can have an adverse impact on educational attainment.

The research literature provides a valid explanation for the economic and educational differences in findings between Black immigrants and Black Americans (Vickerman, 1999). Vickerman reported that earlier writers (e.g., Reid, 1939) advanced the notion that cultural factors, both historical and contemporary, are the determinants of the extent to which upwardly mobile Blacks can achieve higher socioeconomic status and levels of educational attainment in the United States. Dodoo (1997) explains that Caribbean immigrants' socialization is strengthened by the more racially supportive climate of the Caribbean, where they have always been a racial majority. From this point of view, Black Americans may be vulnerable relative to Caribbean Blacks because of the legacy of having endured a harsh racism and post-slavery existence as a racial minority in the United States (see also Sowell, 1994). Therefore, Caribbean Blacks, as well as newly emigrated Africans, bring a different cultural history that may support a stronger desire to overcome the challenges of their immigrant status and race (see also Omi & Winant, 1986).

Regarding the differences in the research findings between African and Caribbean groups, it is speculated that the higher levels of educational attainment of second-generation Caribbean Black immigrant youths over African immigrants, and the third-generation decline in comparison to the first generation (characteristic of African youth rather than Caribbean youth), may be partially attributed to the very large concentration of Haitians and Jamaicans in large cities, such as New York and Miami. In contrast to the Caribbean Blacks, recent African immigrants do not have large African neighborhoods or communities that provide strong social networks. Traveling to Caribbean countries has always been easier than traveling to Africa and the exchange of transnational human resources and material goods is a long-established pattern between North America and Caribbean areas (Rong & Brown, 2001).

However, some scholars (Kasinitz, Battle & Miyares, 2001) have argued that all immigrants have tended to move along the continuum from a national identity for their country of origin towards an American identity when the length of their U.S. residency is taken into consideration:

Since their racial socialization takes place in the United States they have little or no direct experience of societies in which people of African descent are the majority. Without a viable ethnic enclave to serve either as a springboard or a safety net, the future of a West Indian middle class is ultimately linked to that of the larger African-American middle class, into which it is, for better or for worse, rapidly merging. (p. 295).

In terms of gender effects, the research findings are consistent with the findings of other studies when the intertwined effects of race, ethnicity, generation, and other important socio-demographic variables are taken into account. To explain the gender gap associated with immigrant generations, Portes (1996) and Pedraza (1991) have concluded that immigrant communities in the U.S do not necessarily replicate native cultures, but rather combine traditional norms and practices with novel responses to unique structural conditions encountered in the United

States. Thus, they speculate that immigration may enhance women's levels of achievement by freeing them from patriarchal norms in their countries of origin. Gibson (1991) has argued that Black male students may experience more racism and, therefore, may be more strongly motivated to become involved with anti-school cultures. Black teenage girls were less likely than their brothers to develop an adversarial relationship with the school system or to view schooling as a threat their identity.

6.9.   Conclusion and Recommendations

In summary, we offer three major categories of recommendations that have emerged based on our chapter (see also Rong & Brown, 2002). These recommendations relate to policymaking, changes in schools, and teacher training and retraining:

6.9.1.   Educational Policies and Children's SES Status

Since researchers have found that improved socioeconomic conditions among Black children correspond strongly to decreases in test score gaps (Lara-Cinisomo et al., 2004), it is important that structural inequalities (such as poverty, adverse living conditions, inferior education, occupational stratification, etc.) are highlighted and taken into account when educational policies are made. Two concrete recommendations emerge from our chapter:

1. SES Components for Educational Policies: Education policy for disad-vantaged families and communities should not be limited to conventional education policy alone; that is, socioeconomic policies that benefit lower-income families and communities should be recognized also as educational policies on behalf of the children in these families and communities.
2. Being Advocates for Children from Disadvantaged Backgrounds: Educators need to pay greater attention to contextual factors promoting or impeding the educational achievement of immigrant and native minority children, as indicated in the findings from our project with census data. Schools and teachers need to be these children's advocates who encourage and urge governments to act affirmatively to promote structural changes and provide equal educational opportunities for all people, especially disadvan-taged minorities (Nieto, 1995).

6.10.   Diversity and School Reform

Recent waves of immigrants have further diversified the U.S. population, and racial and ethnic identities are becoming increasingly complex as American society becomes more heterogeneous. Educators who work with immigrant children need to change their simplistic notion that race relations in America are mostly binary. Although this may still be true in many parts of the country, the flood in immigration over the past three decades has redrawn the map of racial and ethnic composition in many communities, where the polyethnic split is now among Whites, Blacks, Latinos, and Asians. In this context, the following three recommendations emerge from our chapter:

1. *Change of Teachers' Perceptions and Attitudes*: Educators need to move away from the conventional thinking that each racial group is represented by one homogenous culture with a single identity. According to earlier scholarly writings, the intragroup variability in the Black American population has always existed, and the modern period has witnessed examples of these differences among African Americans (see Butler, 1991; Horton, 1993; Lee, 1993). Teachers should avoid simplistic expectations about Black immigrant students' attitudes and behaviors, educational aspirations, and academic performance. They need to recognize and respect the wide range of identities and cultural competencies in Black students – immigrant and nonimmigrant alike.

2. *Changes in Instruction and Instructional Environment*: Teachers should devise instruction appropriate for teaching students from diverse backgrounds. Furthermore, teachers need to reconstruct learning environments in such a way that diverse conditions and resources are acknowledged and accommodated. With this in mind, educators working on intervention programs can focus on established patterns of practice to improve the experiences of all Black students in U.S. schools and to look for alternative practices as well.

3. *Promote Cross-group Interactions*: Schools are excellent arenas in which to promote awareness and exchange of a wide range of identities and cultural competencies available to all Black students. Schools need to conscientiously promote and encourage cultural interaction (such as school-community interaction, parental participation in education policy decision-making processes, etc.) and cross-nurturing among native-born Black Americans and immigrant Blacks. Through cultural exchange, empathetic interactions, and mutual understanding and influence, Black immigrants and native Blacks could together challenge the *status quo* in race relations in the United States and build a broader and more inclusive African American community that may provide resources for all.

6.11. Black Teachers and Black Immigrant Students

Since the majority of Black immigrants live in central cities and other metropolitan areas and study in schools with a mix of many minority groups, they are likely to be taught by educators who are themselves minorities, most of whom are Black Americans. Black American teachers need to recognize within-black diversities and give legitimacy to ethnic, national and cultural claims.

Due to the different racial contexts Black immigrants will encounter in the United States, they may not be well prepared to deal with racism in their daily lives. Black educators can help Black immigrant children close the gap between Black immigrants' knowledge of American society prior to their immigration and the current American reality. Although it is an understandable psychological reaction and sociological tactic for newcomers to resist, reject, and distance themselves from involuntary negative race classifications when they perceive they have the option to do so, it is important for Black educators to caution Black immigrant students not to misconstrue the problems of the most disadvantaged Black Americans as being necessarily characteristic of the experiences of all African Americans (Vickerman, 1999).

References

Ainsworth-Darnell, J.W. & Downey, D.B. (1998). Assessing the oppositional culture explanation for racial/ethnic differences in school performance. *American Sociological Review*, 63, 536–553.

Arias, M.B. (1986). The context of education for Hispanic students: An overview. *American Journal of Education*, 95, 26–57.

Bryce-Laporte, R.S. (1972). Black immigrants; the experience of invisibility and inequality. *Journal of Black Studies*, 3(1), 29–56.

Du Bois, W.E.B. (1989). The study of the Negro problem. *Annals of the American Academy of Political and Social Science*, 1, 1–23.

Butler, J.S. (1991). *Entrepreneurship and Self-help among Black Americans: A Reconsideration of Race and Economics*. New York: State University of New York Press.

Dodoo, F.N. (1997). Among Africans in America. *Social Force*, 76(2), 527–546.

Fordham, S. & Ogbu, J.U. (1989). Black students' school success: Coping with the burden of 'Acting White.' *Urban Review*, 18, 176–206.

Fordham, S. (1996). *Blacked Out: Dilemmas of Race, Identity, and Success at Capital High*. Chicago: University of Chicago Press.

Foner, N. (1987). The Jamaicans: Race and ethnicity among migrants in New York City. In Foner, N. (ed.), *New Immigrants in New York*. New York: Columbia University Press, pp. 131–158.

Fuller, M. (1980). Black girls in a London Comprehensive School. In Deem, R. (ed.), *Schooling for Women's Work*. London: Routledge & Kegan Paul, pp. 52–65.

Gibson, M.A. (1988). *Accommodation without assimilation: Punjabi Sikh Immigrants in American High Schools and Community*. Ithaca, NY: Cornell University Press.

Gibson, M.A. (1991). Ethnicity, gender and social class: The school adaptation patterns of West Indian youths. In Gibson, M.A. & Ogbu, J.U. (eds), *Minority Status and Schooling: A Comparative Study of Immigrant and Involuntary Minorities*. New York: Garland, pp. 169–203.

Grant, L.M. & Rong, X.L. (1999). Gender, immigrant generation, ethnicity and the schooling progress of Youth. *Journal of Research and Development in Education*, 33, 15–26.

Grant, L. & Rong, X.L. (2002). Gender Inequality. In Levinson, D., Cookson, P.W. Jr & Sadovnik, A. (eds) *Education and Sociology: An Encyclopedia, 2002*. New York: Routledge Falmer, pp. 289–295.

Horton, J.O. (1993). *Free People of Color: Inside the African American Community.* Washington, DC: Smithsonian Institution Press.

John Harvard Journal. (2004, September–October). "Roots" and race. *John Harvard's Journal*, 107(1), 69.

Kamya, H.A. (1997). African immigrants in the United States: The challenge for research and practice. *Social Work*, 42(2), 154–165.

Kao, G. & Tienda, M. (1995). Optimism and achievement: The educational performance of immigrant youth. *Social Science Quarterly*, 76(1), 1–19.

Kasinitz, P. (1992). *Caribbean New York: Black Immigrants and the Politics of Race.* Ithaca, NY: Cornell University Press.

Kasinitz, P., Battle, J., & Miyares, I. (2001). Fade to Black? In Rumbaut, R. & Portes, A. (eds), *Children of Immigrants in America.* Berkeley: University of California Press, pp. 267–300.

Lara-Cinisomo, S., Pebley, A.R., Variana, M.E., Maggio, E., Berends, M., & Lucas, S.R. (2004). A matter of Class. *Rand Review*, 28 (3), 10–15.

Lee, C.C. (1993). Psychology and African-Americans: New perspectives for the 1990s. In Ernest. R. Myers (ed.), *Challenges of a Changing America.* San Francisco: Austin & Winfield, pp. 57–64.

Matute-Bianchi, M.E. (1986). Ethnic identities and patterns of success and failure among Mexican-descent and Japanese-American students in a California high school: An ethnographic analysis. *American Journal of Education*, 95, 233–255.

Mickelson, R.A. & Dubois, W.E.B. (2002). Race and education. In Levinson, D., Cookson, P.W. Jr. & Sadovnik, A. (eds), *Education and Sociology: An Encyclopedia*, 2002. New York: Routledge Falmer, pp. 289–295.

Nieto, S. (1995). From brown heroes and holidays to assimilationist agendas: Reconsidering the critiques of multicultural education. In Sleeter, C.E. & Mclaren, P.L. (eds) *Multicultural Education, Critical Pedagogy, and Politics of Difference.* Albany, NY: SUNY Press, pp. 191–220.

Ogbu, J. (1991). Low school performance as an adaptation: the case of blacks in Stockton, California. In Gibson, M.A. & Ogbu. J.U. (eds), *Minority Status and Schooling: A Comparative Study of Immigrant and Involuntary Minorities.* New York: Garland, pp. 249–286.

Ogbu, J. (1994). Racial stratification and education in the United States: Why inequality persists. *Teacher College Record*, 92(2), 264–298.

Omi, M. & Winant, H. (1986). *Racial Formation in the United States from the 1960s to the 1980s.* New York City: Routledge & Kegan Paul.

Pedraza, S. (1991). Women and migration: the social consequences of gender. *Annual Review of Sociology*, 17, 303–325.

Portes, A. (1995). Segmented assimilation among new immigrant youth: A conceptual framework. In Ruben, G. Rumbaur & Wayne, A. Cornelius (eds), *California's Immigrant Children.* San Diego: Center for U.S.-Mexican Studies, pp. 71–76.

Portes, A. (1996). Introduction: Immigration and its aftermath. In Portes, A. (ed.), *The New Second Generation.* New York: Russell Sage Foundation, pp. 1–7.

Portes, A. & Rumbaut, R.G (eds) (2001). *Legacies: The story of the Immigrant Second Generation.* Berkeley, CA: University of California Press.

Portes, A. & Zhou, M. (1993). The new second generation: Segmented assimilation and its variants. *Annals, the American Association of Political and Social Sciences*, 530 (November), 74–96.

Reid, I.D.A. (1939). *The Negro Immigrant.* New York: Columbia University Press.

Roberts, S. (2005, February 21). More Africans enter U.S. than in days of slavery. *New York Times*, February 21.

Rong, X.L. (2005). *Educational Attainment and Socioeconomic Factors* (Unpublished Manuscript).

Rong, X.L. & Brown, F. (2001). The Effects of Immigrant Generation and Ethnicity of Educational Attainment among Young African and Caribbean Blacks in the United States. *Harvard Educational Review*, 71(3), 536–565.

Rong, X.L. & Brown, F. (2002). Socialization, Culture and Identities: What Educators Need to Know and Do. *Education and Urban Society*, 34(2), 247–273.

Rong, X. L. & Grant, L. (1992). Ethnicity, generation, and school attainment of Asians, Hispanics, and non-Hispanic whites. *Sociological Quarterly*, 33(4), 625–636.

Rong, X.L. & Preissle, J. (1998). *Educating Immigrant Student: What We Need to Know to Meet the Challenge*. CA: Sage-Corwin.

Rumbaut, R. & Portes, A. (eds) (2001). *Children of Immigrants in America*. Berkeley: University of California Press.

Schlesinger, A. (2002). The return to the melting pot. In Takaki, R. (ed.), *Debating Diversity*. New York: Oxford University Press, pp. 257–259.

Sowell, T. (1994). *Race and Culture: A World View*. New York: Basic Books.

Spring, J. (1994). *American Education*. New York: McGraw-Hill.

Stanton-Salazar, R.D. (1997). A social capital framework for understanding the socialization of racial minority children and youths. *Harvard Educational Review*, 67, 1–40.

U.S. Bureau of the Census. (2003). *2000 Census of population and housing – Public use Microdata Samples 5%*. Washington, DC: U.S. Government Printing Office.

U.S. Department of Education. (2003). *Condition of Education 2003*. Washington, DC: National Center for Educational Statistics.

Vickerman, M. (1999). *Crosscurrents: West Indian Immigrants and Race*. Oxford: Oxford University Press.

Waters, M.C. (1999). *Black Identities*. Cambridge, MA: Harvard University Press.

Weis, L (1985). Excellence and student class, race, and gender cultures. In Altbach, P.G., Kelly, G.P., & Weis, L. (eds), *Excellence in Education*. Buffalo, NY: Prometheus Books, pp. 217–232.

Woldemikael, T.M (1989). A case Study of Race consciousness among Haitian Immigrants. *Journal of Black Studies*, 20(2), 224–239.

7
Divergent Origins and Destinies: Children of Asian Immigrants

Min Zhou

Americans of Asian origins have family histories in the United States longer than many Americans of Eastern or Southern European origins. However, their numbers have become visible only in recent decades, rising from 1.4 million in 1970 to 11.9 million (or 4% of the total US population) in 2000. Before 1970, the Asian-origin population was largely made up of Japanese, Chinese and Filipinos. Today Americans of Chinese and Filipino origins are the largest subgroups (at 2.8 million and 2.4 million respectively), followed by Indians, Koreans, Vietnamese and Japanese (at more than one million). Some 20 other national-origin or ethnic subgroups, such as Cambodians, Lao, Hmong, Thai, Indonesians, Pakistanis, and Bangladeshis have been officially counted by government statistics only since 1980. Because of the historical circumstances of legal exclusion and contemporary immigration, Asian Americans have just begun to mature into the second generation in large numbers since the late 1980s, and for the Japanese, into the fourth generation.[1] As of 2000, approximately two-thirds of Americans of Asian origins is foreign born (the first and 1.5 generation), another 27% is U.S. born of foreign-born parentage (the second generation), and less than 10% is U.S. born of U.S.-born parentage (the third generation or higher).[2]

There has been relatively little concern with whether or not the children of Asian immigrants can make it into the American mainstream, partly because of their comparatively high socioeconomic status (SES) upon arrival and partly

---

[1] The 1.5 generation includes the foreign born who arrived in the United States as young children, mostly prior to age 13. As of 1990 the third-generation (the children of U.S. born parentage) represented barely 10 percent, of the Asian American child population. Japanese American children were an exception: 54.3 percent of them are members of the third or higher generation, compared with 9.2 percent of Chinese, 10.7 percent of Filipinos, 1.2 percent of Indians, 2.8 percent of Koreans, 1.2 percent of Vietnamese, and 5.3 percent of other Asians.

[2] Based on estimates from the 1998–2002 Current Population Survey of the U.S. Bureau of the Census.

because of their extraordinary educational achievement. The general perception is that a great majority of the children, even those from poor socioeconomic backgrounds, will succeed in school and later in life, and that the "model minority" image represents a reality rather than a myth. This chapter examines the problems and limitations of the homogenized image of Asian Americans based on the analysis of the U.S. census data and my own ethnographic case studies in Asian immigrant communities. I argue that Asian immigrants and their U.S.-born or U.S.-raised children are living in a society that is highly stratified not only by class but also by race. This reality, combined with unique cultures, immigration histories, family and community resources, has shaped and, to an important extent, determined the educational outcomes of the children of Asian immigrants. The chapter starts with a discussion about intragroup diversity impacted by contemporary Asian immigration. It then explains how diversity creates opportunities and constraints to affect the trajectories of second-generation mobility. Finally, the chapter extracts lessons from two ethnographic case studies, Chinese and Vietnamese, to illustrate how culture interacts with structure to affect unique social environments conducive to education.

7.1.   Contemporary Asian Immigration and Intragroup Diversity

The phenomenal growth of Asian Americans in the span of 30 odd years is primarily due to the accelerated immigration and the historic resettlement of Southeast Asian refugees after the Vietnam War. Between 1970 and 2000, nearly 7 million immigrants were legally admitted to the United States as permanent residents from Asia. The share of immigrants from Asia as a proportion of the total foreign-born population to the United States soared from 5% of all arrivals in the 1950s, to 11% in the 1960s, to more than one-third since the 1970s. While the majority of contemporary Asian immigrants are either family-sponsored migrants (more than three quarters) or employer-sponsored skilled workers (nearly 20%), those from Southeast Asia are primarily refugees. Between 1975 and 2000, nearly one million refugees arrived from Vietnam, Laos and Cambodia as a direct result of the failed U.S. intervention in Southeast Asia. Overall, 76% of all foreign-born Asians entered the United States in the past two decades (43% entered between 1990 and 2000) (Reeves & Bennett, 2004). Table 7.1 shows the ethnic composition and pertinent information of these ethnic populations.

7.2.   Diversity in Socioeconomic Backgrounds

Unlike earlier immigrants from Asia or Europe and contemporary immigrants from Latin America, who were mostly low-skilled laborers looking for work, today's immigrants from Asia have come from more diverse backgrounds.

TABLE 7.1. Selected Characteristics of Asian Americans.

	Percent distribution	Percent under 18	Percent foreign born	Percent English Less than very well	Percent bachelor's degree or more	Managerial & Professional occupations	Median family income ($1000)	Percent in poverty
Chinese	23.8	21.4	70.9	49.6	48.1	52.3	60.1	13.5
Filipino	18.3	22.1	67.7	24.1	43.8	38.2	65.2	6.3
Indian	16.2	24.8	75.4	23.1	63.9	59.9	70.7	9.8
Vietnamese	10.9	26.9	76.1	62.4	19.4	26.9	47.1	16.0
Korean	10.5	24.3	77.7	50.5	43.8	38.7	47.6	14.8
Japanese	7.8	12.1	39.5	27.2	41.9	50.7	70.8	9.7
Cambodian	1.8	38.6	65.8	53.5	9.2	17.8	35.6	29.3
Hmong	1.7	55.2	55.6	58.6	7.5	17.1	32.4	37.8
Laotian	1.6	34.4	68.1	52.8	7.7	13.4	43.5	18.5
Pakistani	1.5	32.8	75.5	31.7	54.3	43.5	50.2	16.5
Thai	1.1	15.3	77.8	46.9	38.6	33.4	49.6	14.4
Other Asian	4.7	31.6	56.5	32.7	41.4	39.8	50.7	15.6
All Asian	100.0	25.6	68.9	39.5	44.1	44.6	59.3	12.4
All U.S.	3.9	23.9	11.1	8.1	24.4	33.6	50.5	12.6

Source: U.S. Census of the Population, 2000 (reconstructed from Reeves & Bennett, 2004).

Contemporary immigrants from Asia have arrived in the United States for a variety of reasons: reuniting with families, investing in businesses, fulfilling the demand for highly skilled and low-skilled labor, and escaping war, political or religious persecution, and economic hardship. Chinese, Filipino, and Indian Americans tend to be over-represented among scientists, engineers, physicians and other highly skilled professionals, while Vietnamese, Cambodian, Laotian, and Hmong Americans, most of whom entered the United States as refugees, tend to be disproportionately low-skilled workers. Overall, however, Asian Americans appear to fare better than the general U.S. population on key socioeconomic status (SES) measures.

As shown in Table 7.1, 44% of adult Asians, as opposed to 24% in the total US adult population, had at least a bachelor's degree, and 45% of workers were in managerial or professional occupations, as opposed to 34% among U.S. workers. The median family income for Asian families was $59,000 in 1999, as opposed to $50,000 for average American families. Poverty rates for Asian families were at the same level as that for other American families (12%). These averages, however, mask the vast heterogeneity among Asian-origin groups. While highly skilled and professional Asians boast high SES, Southeast Asians, especially Hmong and Cambodians, trail far behind. Less than 10 percent of Hmong and Cambodian adults had a bachelor's degree. The median family incomes for Hmong and Cambodian families were $32,000 and $36,000, respectively. Poverty rates for Hmong families was 38% and for Cambodian family, 29%.

Asians also suffer from a severe lack of English proficiency even among some relatively high SES subgroups. While 79 percent of Asians spoke a language other than English at home, reflecting the recency of immigration, 40 percent spoke English less than "very well." The sub-groups that had a majority of people who spoke English less than "very well" included Chinese, Koreans, and Thai (50%); Cambodian and Laotian (54%); Hmong (59%), and Vietnamese (62%) (Reeves & Bennett, 2004).

7.3.   Diversity in Settlement Patterns

Despite the geographical concentration in historically gateway cities, settlement patterns among Asian Americans are more diverse than ever before. While Asian Americans have continued to heavily concentrate in the West, they have become more dispersed geographically and suburbanized. Not surprising, California alone accounts for 35 percent of all Asians (4.3 million) in the United States. California is also home to the largest number of each of the six largest national-origin groups—Chinese, Filipino, Japanese, Indian, Korean, and Vietnamese. Second behind California is New York State, which accounts for 10 percent, or 1.2 million, of all Asians. Chinese, Indians, and Koreans are heavily concentrated in New York, but not Filipinos, Japanese, and Vietnamese.

Several other states are home to large populations of specific Asian-origin groups. For example, Texas has the second largest Vietnamese population, next to California. Illinois has the third largest Filipino population, next to California and Hawaii. Washington has the third largest Japanese population, next to California and Hawaii. And New Jersey has the third largest Indian and Korean populations, next to California and New York. Among cities with populations that exceed 100,000, New York City, Los Angeles, and Honolulu have the largest number of Asians, while Daly City, California and Honolulu are Asian-majority cities. Some smaller cities in California such as Monterey Park (the first city in America that reached an Asian majority in 1990 and remained an Asian-majority city in 2000) have also reached Asian majority status.

Traditional urban enclaves such as Chinatown, Little Tokyo, Manilatown, Koreatown, Little Phnom Penh, and Thaitown continue to thrive or have recently emerged in gateway cities. However, they no longer serve as primary centers of initial settlement for the recently arrived since many new immigrants, especially the affluent and highly skilled, bypass central cities altogether and settle in the suburbs immediately after their arrival. For example, as of 2000, only 8% of the Chinese in San Francisco and 12% of the Chinese in New York live in inner-city Chinatowns. Likewise, only 13% of Vietnamese in Orange County, California, live in Little Saigon, a mere 14% of Koreans in Los Angeles live in Koreatown, and only 27% of Cambodians in Los Angeles live in Little Phnom Penh. The majority of the Asian American population has spread to the outer areas or suburbs in traditional gateway cities as well as in new urban centers of Asian settlement across the country (Lai & Arguelles, 2003).

7.4.   Diversity in Language and Religion

Asian American cultures have diverse origins and different ways of incorporating itself into American society. Each of the national-origin or ethnic groups has brought its own respective cultural traditions including language and religion. Linguistically, Chinese, Japanese, Korean, and Vietnamese immigrants came from countries with a single official language, but with many local dialects. Filipino immigrants, in contrast, came from a country where Tagalog and English are both dominant languages, and most of the Filipino immigrants are fluent bilinguals prior to emigration. Most Indian immigrants are proficient in English, but there are also 16 other official languages such as Hindi, Gujarati, Punjabi, Tamil, Telugu, Bengali, Urdu, and others. Moreover, there are many local and regional dialects spoken within each group. For example, immigrants from China, Hong Kong, and Taiwan share the same written Chinese language but speak a variety of dialects—Cantonese, Mandarin, Fujianese, Chaozhounese, and Shanghainese—that are not easily understood within the group.

In the Asian American community, there is no single religion that unifies a pan-ethnic identity, but religion serves as one of the most important ethnic institutions in the community. Chinese, Japanese, Korean and Vietnamese come primarily from non-Judeo Christian backgrounds where Confucianism and/or Buddhism and its variations are widespread in the homelands. Western colonization in the homelands and immigration to the United States have led to a trend of conversion to Christianity prior to or after arrival. For example, only 20% of the population in Korea is Protestant, but the majority of Koreans in the United States is Protestants. Existing research also suggests Protestant Koreans are more likely than others to emigrate (Min and Pyong Gap, 1995). In Vietnam, only 10% of the population is Catholic, but nearly a third in the United States is Catholic. Many Vietnamese refugees were converted to Catholicism after they fled Vietnam as a way to obtain U.S. sponsorship, largely due to the active role the Catholic Charities played in resettling Vietnamese refugees in the United States. Conversion to Christianity is also noticeable among immigrants from Taiwan, but at a smaller scale among those from Mainland China and Japan. Many Filipino Americans are Catholic since 80% of their homeland population practice Catholicism. Indian Americans come from more diverse religious backgrounds with Hindus dominating, followed by smaller numbers of Muslims, Christians, Sikhs, and Buddhists (Zhou, 2004).

7.5.   The Asian American Second Generation Coming of Age: Opportunities and Constraints

Diversity in origins, socioeconomic backgrounds, settlement patterns, and immigrant cultures has profound implications for the educational prospects and identity formation of immigrant offspring. The U.S.-born Asian American population is still disproportionately young and of immigrant parentage. Unlike their immigrant parents, many children of immigrants lack meaningful connections to their parents' homelands. Thus, they are unlikely to consider a foreign country across the Pacific as a point of reference, but are likely to evaluate themselves or to be evaluated by others by the standards of their country of birth or the one in which they are raised. Today, children of Asian immigrants (1.5 or second-generation) encounter a more open America transformed by the civil rights movements and thus aspire to become incorporated as part of mainstream America. However, the outcomes of their incorporation may indicate upward, downward, or horizontal mobility because American society is highly segmented by class and race (Gans, 1992; Portes & Zhou, 1993; Perlmann & Waldinger, 1997; Zhou, 1997).

First, the prospects of social mobility are complicated by divergence along class lines that lead to fragmentation within the Asian American community. Middle-class immigrants are able to start their American life with high-paying professional jobs and secure a comfortable suburban living for their families. Working-class immigrants and refugees, in contrast, often have to endure poverty and low-paying menial jobs and live in economically deprived inner cities. Their children's chances of getting ahead in society are often constrained by residential segregation and other structural disadvantages associated with low SES and inner-city living, such as economic deprivation, inadequate schools, and unsafe neighborhoods.

There are also other possibilities. Some immigrants from high SES backgrounds in their homelands may find themselves living and/or working amongst their working-class counterparts or poor native minorities in underprivileged inner cities in America because they lack transferable job skills or English proficiency. Other immigrants from low SES backgrounds in their homelands, however, may find their way into middle-class suburbs through family, friendship, or co-ethnic employment networks. They may live and work in immigrant "ethnoburbs" with thriving co-ethnic economies and those who work for middle-class families as live-in housekeepers.[3] Also, because of the global movement of people and capital, some ethnic communities develop viable ethnic enclave economies that create tangible and intangible benefits for low-SES co-ethnic members to move ahead in society, while others lack social, cultural, and financial capital to do so. Thus, class bifurcation may not always naturally reproduce itself in the second generation. What is at issue is *how* to ensure desirable educational outcomes normally associated with high SES while countering negative outcomes associated with low SES.

---

[3] "Ethnoburb" is a term developed by the geographer Wei Li to capture the emerging phenomenon of immigrant concentration in middle-class suburbs in the United States, representing a reversed trend of ethnic concentration and succession (the normal trend being suburban dispersion) in predominantly white middle class suburban communities (Li, 1997).

Second, race is likely to interact with class to affect the Asian American second generation more profoundly than their parent generation. Despite a more open host society and the relatively high SES of the group as a whole, racism and racial stereotyping are the long-standing issues relevant to today's Asian American community. Although Asian Americans have made extraordinary achievements and are celebrated as the "model minority" and even the "honorary white," they are still perceived as "foreigners" and are targeted against with derogative terms and racial slurs. Moreover, Asian Americans have continued to receive unequal returns to education. They often find themselves in situations where they have to score exceptionally high in order to get into a good school and work twice or many more times as hard in order to achieve occupational and earnings parity with their non-Hispanic white counterparts. They often feel that doing just as well as everybody else is not enough. They often hear their parents or themselves saying: "you've got to stand out, and you've got to work much harder and do much better." Moreover, professional Asian Americans have constantly faced the glass-ceiling barriers. For example, they are often considered hard workers, competent scientists, engineers, and technicians, but not good managers or executives.

The dual image of the "honorary white" and "forever foreigner" can be a source of frustration; it can also serve as the basis for empowerment in the second generation. Unlike their parents who appear all too ready to appreciate the opportunities in their new country, to swallow the bitter fruit of unfair treatment, and to bear the blunt of racism, the children feel entitled to equal citizenship rights as all other Americans. They may consciously resist the unequal system of racial stratification, but such resistance is often constrained by class. For example, like their native-born minority counterparts in the inner city, US-born children of working-class Asian immigrants may internalize their socially imposed inferiority as part of their collective self-definition (Bourgois, 1998; Fordham, 1996; Gibson, 1989). Consequently, they may adopt an "oppositional outlook" toward the dominant group and mainstream institutions, regarding doing well in school as "acting white" or "selling out" to the system that functions to oppress them. They may also look down on their immigrant heritage as obsolete and old-fashioned and detach from and the support and control of their families and ethnic communities" (Zhou, 1997). Ironically, such symbolic expressions of empowerment may hinder, rather than facilitate, social mobility. However, Asian Americans have generally gained remarkable inroads into mainstream America. In their collective struggle to fight for equality in citizenship, civil rights, and representation, they have often adopted collective strategies to muster family and community resources for self-help and to move along the paths with least resistance, including ethnic entrepreneurship, overwork, and over-education.

Third, the immigrant family continues to play a significant role in structuring the lives of second-generation Asian Americans. Despite their diverse origins, children of Asian immigrants share certain common family experiences. Most prominently, the unduly familial obligation to fulfill the extraordinarily high parental expectations for educational and occupational achievement is a way to repay their parents and honor their families.

Many Asian immigrant parents migrate to provide better opportunities for their children even when they expect significant initial downward mobility. They are all too aware of their own limits in ensuring socioeconomic mobility for their children, and hence, turn to education as the surest path to move ahead. Thus, not only do they place an enormous amount of pressure on their children to excel in school, but they also provide the material means to assure success. For example, they move to neighborhoods with strong public schools, send their children to private after-school programs (including ethnic language programs, academic tutoring, and enrichment institutions in the ethnic community), spend time to seek out detailed academic information, and make decisions about schools and majors for their children (Zhou & Kim, 2006).

Although the parents feel that they are doing what is best for their children, the children—whose frame of reference is "American"—consider their parents unacculturated, old-fashioned, and traditional disciplinarians who are incapable of having fun and unwilling to show respect for their individuality. The children view the immigrant family and ethnic community as symbols of the old world— strictly authoritarian, severely demanding, and overwhelmingly stifling. At the same time, the children also experience their parents' daily struggles as new immigrants surviving in America, and consequently, develop a 'unique respect and sensitivity toward them.

In sum, opportunities and constraints go hand-in-hand. Second-generation Asian Americans have to straddle two social worlds unfolded by the dual processes of immigration and racialization (Zhou & Lee, 2004). On the one hand, they are intimately influenced and often intensely constrained by their immigrant heritage even though ethnic distinctiveness associated with homeland traditions and cultures blur with each succeeding generation (due to acculturation and rapid and high rates of intermarriage). Research has illustrated how the immigrant family and ethnic community have been the primary sources of support as well as the primary sites of conflict (Zhou & Bankstons, 1998). On the other hand, the lived experiences of second-generation Asian Americans are intrinsically linked with racialization. Race complicates intragroup dynamics and intergenerational relations. Because about two-thirds of the Asian American population is first generation, native-born Asians must now confront renewed images of Asians as "foreigners" while battling their unequal social status as racial minorities. Resembling the new immigrants, the more "assimilated" native-born find that they must actively and constantly distinguish themselves from the newer arrivals. For instance, comments about one's "good English" or inquiries about where one comes from are often taken as insensitive at best, and offensive or even insulting at worst, to native-born Asian Americans. By stark contrast, similar encounters may tend to be interpreted or felt more positively among foreign-born Asians. Different lived experiences between the generations are thus not only generational, but also cultural (Zhou & Lee, 2004).

7.6. Moving Ahead in Society: Culture Versus Structure

Like most Americans, the children of Asian immigrants regard education as the most important means to social mobility, and they have actualized the educational value in some remarkable ways. The higher than average levels of Asian American educational achievement are publicly known. The children of foreign-born physicians, scientists, and engineers and those of disadvantaged backgrounds, Chinese or Hmong, girls or boys, repeatedly appear on the lists of high school valedictorians and in competitive academic decathlon teams, and win prestigious awards and honors at the national, state, and local level (Portes & Rumbaut, 2001; Zhou & Xiong, 2005).

The children of Asian immigrants are also gaining admissions to prestigious universities in disproportionate numbers. For example, Asian Americans comprise roughly 12% of California's population but make up over one-third of the undergraduates at the University of California campuses at Berkeley, Los Angeles, and Irvine (UCB, 2004; UCI, 2004; UCLA, 2002). The nation's leading universities have also reported a dramatic increase in enrollment of Asian Americans, who make up 28% of the undergraduates at the Massachusetts Institute of Technology, 25% at Stanford, 19% at Harvard, and 17% at Yale (GoldSea, 2005). As of 2000, Asian Americans have attained the highest level of education of all racial groups in the United States: 44% of Asian American adults have attained bachelor's degrees or higher, and the ratio for those with advanced degrees (e.g., master's, Ph.D., M.D. or J.D.) is one in seven. Although some ethnic groups, such as Cambodians, Lao, and Hmong, still trail behind other East and South Asians in most indicators of achievement, they too show significant signs of upward mobility (Zhou & Xiong, 2005).

What contributes to the school success of Asian Americans? The cultural argument emphasizes the effects of an ethnic group's traits, qualities, characteristics, or behavioral patterns with which the group is either inherently endowed or which it develops in the process of immigrant adaptation (Fukuyama, 1993; Sowell, 1981; Steinberg, 1996). One view of the cultural argument regards an ethnic group's high achievement orientation, industriousness, perseverance, and ability to postpone immediate gratification for later rewards to be the cultural inventory facilitating social mobility. Another view of the cultural argument posits that cultural traits and related behavioral patterns are not intrinsic to an ethnic group but can exert an independent effect on social mobility once transmitted from the first generation and reconstructed in subsequent generations through interaction with the structural conditions of the host society. For example, urban ghettos gave rise to a particular way of living constrained by poverty, which in turn generated particular value systems that encourage fatalism, a lack of spiritual concerns and aspirations, and a present orientation fostering the desire for instant gratification. Poor families may rely on these values and behaviors as a means of coping with poverty, and gradually absorb them.

As a result, researchers holding the cultural argument tend to attribute the low achievement of Black, Hispanic, and Native American children to "deficiencies" in the home or the lack of cultural skills necessary for school success due to residential segregation and poverty (Coleman et al., 1966; Glazer & Moynihan, 1970; Lewis, 1966).

The structural argument, on the other hand, explain intergroup differences in educational and mobility outcomes by emphasizing the role of broader social structural factors, including a group's position in the class *and* racial stratification systems, labor market conditions, and residential patterns in the host society. These factors interact with individual socioeconomic characteristics and ethnic social structures to define the meaning of success, prescribe strategies for status attainment, and ultimately determine a group's chance of success.

For example, the children of Jewish immigrants fared better academically than their Italian counterparts who arrived in the United States at the same time. The Jewish success was not simply accounted for by the value Jews placed on education, but by their more advantageous class background — higher literacy, better industrial skills, and greater familiarity with urban living — and by the fact that they typically immigrated as families with the intention to settle, not to sojourn (Perlmann, 1988; Steinberg, 1981). Furthermore, because of middle-man minority status in the homelands, Jews had already developed a complex array of ethnic institutions and organizations, which allowed them to maintain extensive Jewish networks, synagogues, and other ties to cope with adversity and settlement problems (Goldscheider & Zuckerman, 1984). Upon arrival in the United States, the value Jews traditionally placed on education was activated, redefined, and given new direction when Jewish immigrants saw compelling social and economic rewards associated with educational achievement (Steinberg, 1981). In explaining Asian American school success, scholars holding the structural view argued that, because of the greater entry barriers into noneducational areas such as politics, sports, and entertainment, Asian Americans had to rely on education as the only effective means of upward social mobility. As a result, they devoted more energy to education and disproportionately succeeded in it (Sue & Okazaki, 1990).

I argue that cultural and structural factors constantly interact. The value of education must be supported not only by the family but also but the larger social environment. For immigrant children, this social environment is often formed by ethnic-specific social structures manifested in various economic, civic, sociocultural, and religious organizations in an ethnic community as well as in social networks arising from co-ethnic members' participation in these organizations. Therefore, an examination of specific ethnic social structures, namely ethnic language schools and afterschool establishments that target children and youth, can provide insight into how the community is sustained and how recourses are generated to support education. I illustrate this point through two ethnographic cases.

7.7.   Ethnic Social Environment Conducive to Education: Suburban Chinese Language Schools

In my UCLA Chinese Immigration class of 120 undergraduate students, I asked, "What is unique about growing up Chinese-American?" My Chinese American students (65% of the class) almost unequivocally responded, "Going to Chinese school." As in the past, going to Chinese school is a quintessential experience of the people of Chinese ancestry in the United States as well as in other parts of the world. Immigrants and their communities often consciously work to maintain their ethnic languages in the second generation as the basis for carrying on their cultural heritages (Fishman, 1980). In my view, what determines a child's development is not merely parental, racial, or socioeconomic status or other broader structure factors, such as neighborhoods and schools, but also the immediate social environment in which the child grows up. Chinese language schools, for example, constitute an important part of the immediate social environment that shape Chinese American children's educational experience. (Zhou & Li, 2003; Zhou & Kim, 2006).

Many Chinese immigrants today are from middle-class backgrounds and have achieved high levels of residential and occupational mobility, almost immediately upon arrival. More than half of Chinese immigrant families now live in white middle-class suburbs (Xie & Goyette, 2004). For Chinese immigrants, raising children in middle-class suburbs poses a set of challenges different from doing so in Chinatowns. The parents find it hard to simply impose the exceptionally high educational expectations upon their children, since the children's reference group is their middle-class American peers. A suburban Chinese mother in an interview stated, "My daughter was very resistant to my telling her to study more than she needed to. She seemed to have made up her mind of going to a community college with her other white friends. Whenever I mentioned the names of some prestigious colleges, she would talk back, 'what's wrong with going to community college.' I don't know what to say. I guess it would be alright, but how would I face other [Chinese] parents who boast about their children's Ivy League schools." In contrast, both parents and children in Chinatown look up to suburban whites as their reference point rather than native minorities in their neighborhoods.

In some ways, parental values and expectations regarding educational achievement needs the support and control of ethnic social structures even among middle-class Chinese immigrants. It is perhaps in this context that suburban Chinese language schools have developed since the 1970s and particularly rapidly since the early 1990s. First started by educated Taiwanese immigrants and then by international students and well-educated professional immigrants from mainland China, new Chinese schools emerged in suburbs rather than inner cities. For example, the majority of suburban Chinese schools affiliated with the Southern California United Chinese School Association were initially established by Taiwanese immigrants in the mid- or late 1970s. The Hua Xia Chinese School was established as a Saturday school in a northern New Jersey suburb in the early 1990s by immigrant Chinese from the mainland. It has now expanded into 14 branch campuses in suburbs along the northeastern seaboard from Connecticut to Pennsylvania, serving more than 5,000 students and shifting its admission to "everyone, regardless of his or her gender, race, color of skin, religion, nationality and blood ties." Similarly, the Hope Chinese School started as a small weekend Saturday school in a Washington D.C. suburb for professional Chinese immigrant families from mainland China in the early 1990s. The school has now grown into five campuses in suburban towns in Maryland and Virginia, enrolling more than 2,000 students (Zhou & Li, 2003).

Today's Chinese language schools are distinctive compared to those prior to World War II. First and foremost, the primary goal is to assist immigrant families in their efforts to push their children to excel in American public schools, to get into prestigious universities, and to eventually attain well-paying, high status professions that secure a decent living in the United States. Parents are enthusiastic about sending their children to Chinese language schools not because learning Chinese is the only goal. Rather, many parents are implicitly dissatisfied with American public schools. They believe that Chinese language schools and other ethnic supplementary institutions are instrumental in ensuring that their children meet parental expectations and academic success.

Second, unlike traditional Chinese schools that focused on Chinese language and culture, Chinese language schools today have a more comprehensive and well-rounded curriculum. In addition to the Chinese language, schools now offer a variety of academic programs and *buxiban* in such subjects as English (including English as a Second Language), social studies, math and sciences, as well as college preparation (i.e. SAT). They also offer extracurricular programs, such as youth leadership training, public speech, modern and folk dancing, chorus, music (piano, violin, drums, and Chinese string instruments), drama, Chinese painting, calligraphy, origami, martial arts, Chinese chess and Go, and sports (i.e., tennis, ping-pong ball, and basketball being the most popular).

Perhaps most importantly, today's Chinese language schools serve as an ethnic community, supporting immigrant family values that may often be regarded by the children "as stuff from the old world." When schools are in session, these institutions provide a cultural environment where both parents and children are surrounded by other Chinese people and cultural expectations. They may feel the external pressures to act Chinese and conform to the values and norms prescribed by the Chinese family. The spillover effects on children are also profound. First, Chinese language schools and other relevant ethnic institutions offer an alternative space where children can express and share their feelings of growing up in immigrant Chinese families. Moreover, these ethnic institutions provide unique opportunities for immigrant children to form a different set of peer group networks, giving them more leverage in negotiating parent-child relations at home. Furthermore, these ethnic institutions function to nurture ethnic identity and pride that may be rejected because of the pressure for assimilation. In Chinese schools, they are exposed to something quite different from what they learn in their formal schools. For example, they recite classical Chinese poems and Confucian sayings about family values, behavioral and moral guidelines, and the importance of schooling. They listen to Chinese fables and legends and learn to sing Chinese folk songs, which reveal various aspects of Chinese history and culture. Such cultural exposure reinforces family values and heightens a sense of "Chineseness," helping children to relate to the Chinese "stuff" without feeling embarrassed.

Together with other ethnic institutions specialized in academic and extracurricular programs for children, Chinese language schools have grown into an ethnic system of supplementary education which is complementary to formal education. Despite diversity in form and curriculum, Chinese language schools, non-profit and for-profit alike, have one thing in common. That is, they are Chinese language schools only in the name. They compete more and more intensely with one and other in offering services to immigrant families that are directly relevant to children's formal public education. This case study illustrates how the value of education is supported by an ethnic community's social structures and highlights the important effect of the immediate social environment between a child's home and formal school. As a Chinese school teacher remarked, "when you think of how much time these Chinese kids put in their studies after regular school, you won't be surprised why they succeed at such a high rate." It is this ethnic environment with enormous tangible and intangible benefits to the immigrant family that helps promote and actualize the value of education.

7.8.   Multilevel Social Integration: Bifurcation of Vietnamese Refugee Children

In my collaborative work with Carl Bankston III on the children of Vietnamese refugees, we argued that popular, and seemingly contradictory, views of Vietnamese children as "valedictorians" and "delinquents" were rooted in actual social tendencies (Bankston & Zhou, 1995a; Bankston & Zhou, 1995b; Zhou & Bankstons, 1998). Although this research was primarily based on a case study of a Vietnamese enclave in New Orleans, it sheds light on the understanding of this new ethnic group in the United States. The Vietnamese enclave that we studied in the mid-1990s was predominantly low-SES refugees from rural Vietnam, and most were new arrivals at the time of the study. They were settled as a group by Catholic Charities in a low-income black neighborhood. Despite their extreme disadvantages as refugees, the group reconstructed their community and reorganized their American lives under the support and direction of the Vietnamese Catholic church. Many children managed to make it through inadequate inner-city schools with great success owing not so much to the individual family but to the interconnectedness of families. But there was a visible number of children who became high school dropouts, gangsters, and delinquents and were excluded from the ethnic community.

This case study allowed us to develop a model of multi-level social integration to illustrate our argument that success was not a simple matter of culture, individual effort, or family SES, but involved social integration at various structural levels. Figure 7.1 shows a model of multi-level social integration. Note that the individual overlaps all of the systems that surround him or her, indicating that the individual simultaneously participates in his or her own family, ethnic community, the local social environment, and eventually the larger society. In this ideal representation, however, the family is at the very center of each level of social systems in which the individual participates, and each larger circle symmetrically contains each smaller circle. In this ideal case, the family is well integrated into the ethnic community, the ethnic community is well integrated into the local social environment, and the local social environment is well integrated into the larger society (Zhou & Bankstons, 1998). Successful integration into the larger society depends on the fit between familial and ethnic social systems, on the one hand, and on the fit between the ethnic social systems and the larger society, on the other. The local social environment, including both American

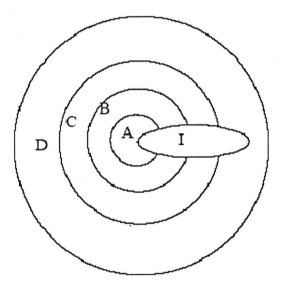

I   individual

A   family

B   ethnic community

C   local social environment

D   larger society

Figure 7.1. Model of Multilevel Social Integration: The Ideal Case.
Sources: Zhou & Bankstons, 1998, p. 204.

and Americanized peer groups, pulls young people toward orientations that may be at variance with those of the larger society. In order to avoid deviation from normative orientations, families function to pull young people into the ethnic community and the ethnic community steer them toward normative orientations consistent with those of the larger society.

In the case of the Vietnamese in New Orleans, problems in adaptation occurred either because an individual was insufficiently integrated into an effective family system, or because the family was insufficiently integrated into the ethnic community, or because the local social environment was at odds with the larger society. Living in a low-income neighborhood with high rates of crime and juvenile delinquency put children at a great risk of downward assimilation. In this situation, integration into the family and ethnic community systems was especially important because family and community could join forces in steering young people away from the marginal local social environment and helping them to bypass the problematic neighborhood to integrate to the mainstream society. In our earlier work, we found a direct correlation between individual and/or family disengagement in the ethnic community and delinquency. That is, the Vietnamese young people who moved toward the local social environment of the oppositional youth subculture and became delinquent were likely to be those who were from single-parent families or families that had little connection to the Vietnamese community (Zhou & Bankstons, 1998).

Recently, we have reexamined behavioral and attitudinal trends among Vietnamese youth, contrasting recently gathered data with data collected nearly ten years ago from the same Vietnamese enclave in New Orleans (Zhou & Bankston, 2006). This recent cohort of Vietnamese adolescents is mostly U.S. born and is growing up in an ethnic context quite different from the older cohort of the mid-1990s. We found that the trend of bifurcation continued but the ranks of "valedictorians" or "high achievers" were getting smaller, while those of "delinquents" were growing. Meanwhile, we found correlated trends of out-migration of more affluent families, less dependence of families on the ethnic community, and greater acculturation among children. Moreover, Vietnamese families living in the low-income neighborhood, despite longer length of US residence and greater familiarity with the US society, are less able than previously to channel their children through systems of ethnic social relations. The ethnic community is less unified than before because of the middle-class out-migration. This examination led us to conclude that delinquency is likely to become a more serious problem among Vietnamese adolescents living in low-income communities. While the media celebrated "Vietnamese valedictorians" in the earlier years, it appears they will become less common. The parents of Vietnamese youth today are likely to face similar kinds of problems that affect other low-income minority communities in the United States. As one resident of the Vietnamese enclave remarked in a recent interview, "it's so hard to keep up our culture and traditions when you've been in this country so long. Our children think that Vietnam is very far away and sometimes we just can't pass things onto them." Even with intact families and with an existing Vietnamese community, it is increasingly difficult for families or communities to function as sealed subsystems (Zhou & Bankston, 2006).

These results suggest that we should see acculturation and assimilation into American society as neither purely positive, nor purely negative. However, we do think that our findings suggest that the acculturation of new immigrant groups is interacting with family's SES and neighborhood contexts. While the children from high SES immigrant families in suburbs may likely achieve similar levels of educational success to those of their native peers, the children from low SES immigrant families in inner cities are likely to be attended by serious difficulties facing the children of their neighboring native minorities. In the latter case, an ethnic social environment with significant amount of community resources conducive to education may be particularly beneficial for upward social mobility.

7.9.   Conclusion and Recommendations

Like other immigrant families in the United States, Asian immigrant families set high expectations and instill in their children that educational achievement secures future livelihood and upholds family honor. Tremendous family and community pressures on achieving have yielded positive results. Compared with the general U.S. population, the children of Asian immigrants generally fare better in school regardless of their socioeconomic backgrounds. The educational achievement of Asian Americans appears to extend beyond secondary education into higher education. Indeed, the nation's best public high schools and universities have seen rapid increases in the Asian American enrollment in their freshmen classes.

However, the Chinese and Vietnamese cases show that the "right" cultural values of Confucianism is not enough to ensure educational success. In order to produce desirable educational outcomes, the intersection of culture and various structural factors, including ethnic social structures must occur. The family's educational goal is reinforced not by the individual family but by the entire ethnic community. In some ethnic communities, as in the case of Chinese, educationally-oriented ethnic language schools have constituted a key component of the Chinese immigrant community transcending geographic boundaries. These ethnic institutions serve as community centers for those who have seemingly assimilated, offering various after-school academic and extracurricular activities (i.e., tutoring, college preparation, music, art, ports) and developing supplementary education to assist families and children. In other communities, as in the case of Vietnamese, the ethnic community that once served as the locus of support and control has become weakened as a result of changing immigration dynamics, out-movement of co-ethnic middle class, and rapid acculturation.

There is also a downside of over-achievement. Because of family and community pressures for achieving and the burden of honoring the family, many children of Asian immigrants have to sacrifice their own personal interests to pursue what their parents think is best for them—a career in science, medicine, or technical professions. For example, a Chinese American college student gave up his promising singing career to enroll in medical school just to make his parents happy. The children of Asian immigrants also suffer from mental health problems that often go unnoticed until symptoms become chronic. For example, a Korean American high school senior made multiple suicidal attempts because she was not selected the valedictorian of her graduating class and was not admitted to the college of her parents' top choice. These undesirable outcomes should be given greater attention in future research.

Drawing on the Asian American educational experience, I offer the following recommendations:

First, "Asian" is a heterogeneous category that not only includes various national-origin or ethnic subgroups but also entails tremendous inter-ethnic and intra-ethnic differences in socio-economic status. Educators and policymakers should respect cultural diversity and be mindful not to homogenize all students of Asian origins.

Second, for the children of Asian immigrants, as for all other immigrant children, ethnicities based on national origins (i.e., a Chinese or Vietnamese identity) will recede under the pressure of assimilation. But assimilation may not lead to uniformly desirable outcomes. Educators and policymakers should be aware of "segmented" assimilation—into the middle-class mainstream, into the urban underclass, or into segregated ethnic enclaves. Ethnic enclaves may sometimes facilitate, rather than hinder, the assimilation of immigrant children into the middle-class mainstream. In ethnic communities with strong socio-economic recourses, various ethnic social structures (i.e., ethnic language schools, churches, private after-school programs) emerge to serve as a source of support for children's education. In socio-economically unprivileged communities, however, assimilation may mean downward social mobility (i.e., high school dropout, youth delinquency, gang affiliation, and oppositional cultures) because these communities lack resources necessary to help poor families to steer children away from local peer pressures and oppositional cultures. Educators and policymakers should look beyond the family into the social structures of the ethnic community and pay special attention to how these local social structures support or constrain the prospects of educational success.

Third, most immigrant families, Asians and non-Asians alike, place high value on education and consider it the most important path to upward social mobility. However, value cannot be actualized without the support of the family *and* the ethnic community. But the ability of the family and that of the ethnic community to influence children vary by national origins and generations. National-origin groups that constitute a significant middle-class with valuable resources (i.e., education, job skills, and financial assets) upon arrival in the United States have a leg up in the race to move ahead in their new homeland, while others lacking group resources trail behind. Educators and policymakers should be careful not to attribute school success or failure merely to culture, or to structure, but to the intersection of both cultural and structural factors.

Last but not least, the extraordinary levels of educational achievement seem to reaffirm the "model minority" image in the American public. But the model minority image implicitly casts Asian Americans as different from other Americans, white or nonwhite. In fact, much of the Asian success is due to selective immigration and community development. It remains an empirical question of whether the third or later generation Americans of Asian origins, who may not have the same family or ethnic community pressures or resources as today's second generation, will continue to stand out as the "model minority," or simply melt into mainstream America with little meaningful ethnic distinctiveness, or assimilate into a racial minority caught at the bottom of American racial hierarchy. So it is unfair to hold Asian Americans to higher standards and expect all of them to be good at math and science. Educators and policymakers should evaluate and judge Asian Americans by the same standards as they do other Americans.

In sum, while most immigrants, Asian, Latino or other alike, share the educational value of the American middle-class, not all have the same access to structural and cultural resources conducive to education. Even among children of Asian immigrants, access to both socio-economic and ethnic community resources vary. Educational policy should be attentive to variations on the intersection between culture and structure.

References

Bankston, C.L. & Zhou, M. (1995a). Effects of minority-language literacy on the academic achievement of Vietnamese youth in New Orleans. *Sociology of Education*, 68, 1–17.

Bankston, C.L. & Zhou, M. (1995b). Religious participation, ethnic identification, and adaptation of Vietnamese adolescents in an immigrant community. *The Sociological Quarterly*, 36, 501–512.

Bourgois, P. (1998). *In Search of Respect: Selling Crack in El Barrio*. New York: Cambridge University Press.

Coleman, J.S., Cambell, E.Q., Jobson, C.J., McParland, J., Mood, A.M., Weinfeld, F.D., & York, R.L. (1966). *Equality of Educational Opportunity*. Washington, DC: U.S. Government Printing Office.

Fishman, J. (1980). Language maintenance. In Thernstrom, S. (ed.), *Harvard Encyclopedia of American Ethnic Groups*. Cambridge: Harvard University Press, pp. 629–638.

Fordham, S. (1996). *Blacked Out: Dilemmas of Race, Identity, and Success at Capital High*. Chicago: The University of Chicago Press.

Fukuyama, F. (1993). Immigrants and family values. *Commentary*, 95, 26–32.

Gans, H.J. (1992). Second-generation decline: Scenarios for the economic and ethnic futures of the post-1965 American immigrants. *Ethnic and Racial Studies*, 15, 173–192.

Gibson, M.A. (1989). *Accommodation Without Assimilation: Sikh Immigrants in an American High School*. Ithaca, NY: Cornell University Press.

Glazer, N. & Moynihan, D.P. (1970). *Beyond the Melting pot: The Negroes, Puerto Ricans, Jews, Italians, and Irish of New York City*. Cambridge: MIT Press.

Goldscheider, C. & Zuckerman, A.S. (1984). *The Transformation of the Jews*. Chicago: University of Chicago Press.

GoldSea. (2005). *25 Great Asian American Universities*. Retrieved March 13, 2005, from goldsea.com/AAU/25/25.html.

Lai, E. & D. Arguelles (eds) (2003), *The New Faces of Asian Pacific America: Numbers, Diversity and Change in the 21st Century*. Jointly published by *AsianWeek*, UCLA's Asian American Studies Center, and the Coalition for Asian Pacific American Community Development.

Lewis, O. (1966, October). The culture of poverty. *Scientific American*, pp. 19–25.

Li, W. (1997). Spatial transformation of an urban ethnic community from Chinatown to Chinese ethnoburb in Los Angeles. *Ph.D Dissertation*. Department of Geography, University of Southern California.

Min, Pyong Gap (1995). *Asian Americans: Contemporary Trends and Issues*. Thousand Oaks, CA: Sage Publications.

Perlmann, J. (1988). *Ethnic Differences: Schooling and Social Structure Among the Irish, Italians, Jews, and Blacks in an American city, 1880–1935*. New York: Cambridge University Press.

Reeves, T.J. & Bennett, C. E. (2004). *We the people: Asians in the United States*. Census 2000 Special Report (censr17). Washington DC: US Census Bureau.

Perlmann, J. & Waldinger, R. (1997). Second generation decline? Immigrant children past and rresent – A reconsideration. *International Migration Review*, 31, 893–922.

Portes, A. & Rumbaut, R.G. (2001). *Legacies: The Story of the Immigrant Second Generation*. Berkeley: University of California Press.

Portes, A. & Zhou, M. (1993). The New second generation: Segmented assimilation and its variants. *The Annals of the American Academy of Political and Social Science*, 530, 74–96.

Sowell, T. (1981). *Ethnic America: A history*. New York: Basic Books.

Sue, S. & Okazaki, S. (1990). Asian American educational achievement: A phenomenon in search of an explanation. *American Psychologist*, 45, 913–920.

Steinberg, L. (1996). *Beyond the Classroom: Why School Reform has Failed and What Parents Need to do*. New York: Simon & Schuster.

Steinberg, S. (1981). *The Ethnic Myth: Race, Ethnicity, and Class in America*. Boston: Beacon Press.

University of California, Berkeley (UCB). 2004. *New Freshmen Enrolled by Ethnicity– Fall 1998 Thru Fall 2004*. Retrieved August 18, 2005, from *http://www.berkeley.edu/ news/media/releases/2004/12/02_enroll_table.shtml*.

University of California, Irvine (UCI). 2004. *Student Characteristics Summary–Fall 2004*. Retrieved August 18, 2005, from *http://www.oir.uci.edu/scs/*.

University of California, Los Angeles (UCLA). 2002. *Ethnic Enrollment–Fall 1973 Thru Fall 2002*. Retrieved August 18, 2005, from http://www.apb.ucla.edu/apbtoc.htm.

Xie, Y. & Goyette, K.A. (2004). A demographic portrait of Asian Americans. *The American People*, Census 2000. New York, Russell Sage Foundation and Washington DC: Population Reference Bureau.

Zhou, M. (1997). Growing up American: The challenge confronting immigrant children and children of immigrants. *Annual Review of Sociology*, 23, 63–95.

Zhou, M. (2004). Are Asian Americans becoming White? *Context* 3, 29–37.

Zhou, M. & Bankstons, C.L. (1998). *Growing Up American: How Vietnamese Children Adapt to Life in the United States*. New York: Russell Sage Foundation.

Zhou, M. & Bankstons, C.L. (2006). Delinquency and acculturation in the twenty-first century: A decade's change in a Vietnamese American community. In Martinez, R. & Valenzuela, A. (eds), *Immigration and Crime: Ethnicity, Race, and Violence*. New York: New York University Press, pp. 117–139.

Zhou, M. & Kim, S.S. (2006). Community forces, social capital, and educational achievement: The case of supplementary education in the Chinese and Korean immigrant communities. *Harvard Educational Review*, 76, 1–29.

Zhou, M. & Lee, J. (2004). The Making of culture, identity, and ethnicity among Asian American youth. In Lee, J. & Zhou, M. (eds), *Asian American Youth: Culture, Identity, and Ethnicity*. New York: Routledge, pp. 1–30.

Zhou, M. & Li, X. (2003). Ethnic language schools and the development of supplementary education in the immigrant Chinese community in the United States. In Suarez-Orozco, C. & Todorova, I.L.G. (eds), *New Directions for Youth Development: Understanding the Social Worlds of Immigrant Youth*. Jossey-Bass, pp. 57–73.

Zhou, M. & Xiong, Y. S. (2005). The multifaceted American experiences of the children of Asian immigrants: Lessons for segmented assimilation. *Ethnic and Racial Studies*, 28, 1119–1152.

Part 3
Socio-cultural Issues on Teaching, Learning, and Development

8
Educational Issues and Effective Practices for Hispanic Students

Hersh C. Waxman, Yolanda N. Padrón, and Andres García

The educational status of Hispanic[1] students in the United States is one of the most challenging educational issues. Although the number of Hispanic students in public schools has increased dramatically in recent decades, Hispanic students as a group have the lowest levels of education and the highest dropout rate. Furthermore, conditions of poverty, health, and other social problems have made it difficult for Hispanics to improve their educational status. This chapter summarizes some of the critical educational problems facing Hispanic students and provides some recommendations to alleviate the problems. The chapter is divided into four major sections. The first section focuses on the educational status of Hispanic students in the United States. The second section discusses factors associated with the underachievement of Hispanic students. This section includes problems associated with: (a) the need for qualified teachers, (b) inappropriate teaching practices, and (c) at-risk school environments. The third section examines factors associated with the success of Hispanic students. It provides a brief summary of instructional strategies, schools, and programs that have been found to significantly improve the academic achievement of Hispanic students. Finally, the chapter addresses some of the recommendations and conclusions from our current knowledge of effective practices and programs for Hispanic students.

---

[1] While this chapter specifically focuses on Hispanic students, some of the reports, studies, and articles reviewed use a variety of terms like immigrant students, English language learners (ELLs), language-minority students, and limited English proficient students (LEPs). Similarly, the term "Latino" is often used interchangeably with the term "Hispanic" in the literature. For purposes of this chapter, we have tried to consistently use the term, "Hispanic," but we have carefully tried not to misrepresent the literature cited.

8.1.   The Educational Status of Hispanic Students in the United States

Over the past 20 years, the enrollment of Hispanics in public elementary schools has dramatically increased (over 150%), compared to 20% for African American students and 10% for White students (U.S. Department of Education, 2000). Recent projections are that the Hispanic population and the numbers of preschool, school-age, and college-age populations will continue to dramatically increase (Chapa & De La Rosa, 2004).

The U.S. Hispanic population is quite diverse, representing various countries of origin, levels of primary language proficiency, prior educational experience, and socioeconomic status (García, 2001b). According to the 2000 U.S. Census, 59% of Hispanics were of Mexican origin, 10% were of Puerto Rican origin, and 4% were of Cuban origin. The remaining 28% were designated as "other" Hispanics. Nearly two-thirds (65%) of all Hispanics live in central cities of metropolitan areas, compared to non-Hispanic Whites (21%) (USDE, 2000). Hispanics constitute about 75% of all students enrolled in programs for limited English proficient students (LEPs), including bilingual education and English as second language (ESL) programs.

In terms of educational achievement, the National Assessment of Educational Progress (NAEP) scores for 17-year-old Hispanic students are well below that of their White peers in mathematics, reading, and science. The dropout rates for Hispanic students are also much higher than other ethnic groups. In 2000, 28% of all Hispanic 16- through 24-year-olds were dropouts (1.4 million)–more than double the dropout rate for African Americans (13%) and more than three times the rate for Whites (7%). Some researchers feel the attrition scores for Hispanics still are undercounted and fail to reveal an accurate picture of the problem (Montecel, Cortez, & Cortez , 2004). Montecel et al. (2004) used the U.S. Census Bureau data to determine that 43% of the Hispanic population did not receive a diploma and 26% dropped out before the ninth grade. Additionally, within the Hispanic student population, immigrants have a 44% dropout rate compared to first generation students (USDE, 2000). Only 64% of Hispanic kindergartners graduate from high school. Twenty-two percent enroll in college; of that 22%, only 10% complete 4 years of college (USDE, 2000).

In addition to the problems of underachievement and low educational attainment, many Hispanic students live in households and communities that experience high and sustained poverty. Thirty-four percent of Hispanic children live in single parent or no parent homes (USDE, 2000). Hispanic children are more than three times as likely to experience poverty than white students (Liagas & Snyder, 2003). Hispanic students also attend schools with more than twice as many poor classmates as those attended by White students (46% vs. 19%). Furthermore, Hispanic students primarily reside in urban cities and are immersed in neighborhoods of concentrated poverty where the most serious educational problems exist. Schools with high concentrations of poor students, for example, tend to be poorly maintained, structurally unsound, fiscally under funded, and staffed with large numbers of uncertified teachers (García, 2001b). Additionally, many Hispanic students are concentrated in campuses where they make up the majority of the student body. In fact, 38% of Hispanic students attend campuses where minority students make up 90% of the student body.

All the above socio-historical factors contribute to the complexity of issues that Hispanic students face in their quest for educational success. These factors also reveal the large achievement gap between White students and the growing and culturally diverse Hispanic student population. In the following section, we discuss critical educational factors related to the underachievement of Hispanic students.

8.2. Educational Factors Impacting the Underachievement of Hispanic Students

Although some educators have argued that the most serious concerns for Hispanic students are basic funding for programs that address their educational needs and political opposition to programs that focus on linguistically diverse students (Melendez, 1993), there are several "alterable factors" that have been found to contribute to the underachievement of Hispanic students. This section discusses three critical factors that have been related to the underachievement of Hispanic students, including: (a) the need for qualified teachers, (b) inappropriate instructional practices, and (c) at-risk school environments.

8.2.1. Need for Qualified Teachers

One of the most serious problems associated with the educational failure of Hispanic students involves the shortage of adequately qualified teachers and the lack of appropriate preparation of credentialed teachers (Gándara, Maxwell-Jolly, & Driscoll, 2005; Téllez & Waxman, 2006). Teachers of Hispanic ELLs, for example, have to address the "double demands" of acquiring a second language while learning traditional academic content (Gersten & Jiménez, 1998). Estimates have indicated that nearly half of the teachers assigned to teach Hispanic ELLs have not received any preparation specific to the education of ELLs. Presently, about 42% of all public school teachers in the US have at least one ELL student in their class, but less than 3% of these teachers are certified ESL or bilingual teachers (NCES, 2003). In other words, the number of teachers prepared to teach Hispanic ELLs falls far short of the tremendous need for such teachers.

There also have been a number of recent studies that have documented shortcomings in professional development opportunities targeted for teachers of Hispanic ELLs. In a profile showing the quality of our nation's teachers, for example, the National Center for Education Statistics found that most teachers of ELLs or other culturally diverse students did not feel that they were well prepared to meet the needs of their students (Lewis et al., 1999). In another national survey of classroom teachers, 57% of all teachers responded that they either "very much needed" or "somewhat needed" more information on helping students with limited English proficiency achieve to high standards (Alexander, Heaviside, & Farris, 1999). In a large-scale study of over 5,000 teachers in California, Gándara, Maxwell-Jolly, and Driscoll (2005) found that teachers had few professional development opportunities targeted to help them work effectively with ELLs. They also found that many teachers faced barriers communicating with their students and students' parents and there was a lack of appropriate materials and resources to meet their students' needs.

8.2.2.   *Inappropriate Teaching Practices*

Another critical problem related to the underachievement of Hispanic students has to do with current teaching practices. The most common instructional approach found in schools that serve Hispanic students is the direct instructional model, where teachers typically teach to the whole class at the same time and control all of the classroom discussion and decision-making (Waxman & Padrón, 2002). This teacher-directed instructional model emphasizes lecture, drill and practice, remediation, and student seatwork, consisting mainly of worksheet. These instructional practices constitute a "pedagogy of poverty" because they focus on low-level skills and passive instruction (Haberman, 1991; Waxman, Padrón, & Arnold, 2001).

Several studies have examined classroom instruction for Hispanic students and found that this "pedagogy of poverty" orientation exists in many classrooms with Hispanics, ELLs, and other minority students (Padrón & Waxman, 1993; Waxman, Huang, & Padrón, 1995). In a large-scale study examining the classroom instruction of 90 teachers from 16 inner-city middle schools serving predominantly Hispanic students, Waxman et al. (1995) found that students were typically involved in whole-class instruction (not interacting with either their teacher or other students). About two-thirds of the time, for example, students were not involved in verbal interaction with either their teacher or other students. There were very few small group activities and very few interactions with other students. Students rarely selected their own instructional activities, and were generally very passive in the classroom, often just watching or listening to the teacher, even though they were found to be on task about 94% of the time.

In another study examining mathematics and science instruction in inner-city middle-school classrooms serving Hispanic students, Padrón and Waxman (1993) found that science teachers participated in whole-class instruction about 93% of the time, while mathematics teachers participated in whole-class instruction about 55% of the time. Students in mathematics classes worked independently about 45% of the time, while there was no independent work observed in science classes. In the mathematics classes, there was no small group work observed, and students only worked in small groups in science classes about 7% of the time. Questions about complex issues were not raised by any of the mathematics or science teachers. Furthermore, teachers seldom (4% of the time) posed open-ended questions for students in science classes; they never posed these questions in the mathematics classes.

The results of these and other studies have illustrated that classroom instruction in schools serving predominantly Hispanic students often tends to be whole-class instruction with students working in teacher-assigned and generated activities, generally in a passive manner (i.e., watching or listening). In these classrooms, teachers also spend more time explaining things to students rather than questioning, cueing, or prompting students to respond. Teachers were not frequently observed encouraging extended student responses or encouraging students to help themselves or help each other. In summary, research has suggested that instructional inadequacies or "pedagogically induced" learning problems may account for many Hispanic students' poor academic achievement and low motivation (Fletcher & Cardona-Morales, 1990; García, 2001a).

8.2.3. At-Risk School Environments

García & Guerra (2004) argue that many efforts at reform fail because educators do not assume responsibility for students' failure. Many educators still have negative expectations or "deficit views" that place the blame for academic failure on the Hispanic student because they lack the necessary knowledge and/or language skills or they blame their parents who they believe does not care or support their child's education (García & Guerra, 2004; Valencia et al., 2001). While these negative expectations may be one of the fundamental explanations for the underachievement of Hispanic students, several researchers also have found that there are a number of organizational and institutional features of the school and classroom learning environment that are alienating and consequently drive students out of school rather than keep them in (García & Guerra, 2004; Valenzuela, 1999).

The term "at-risk school environment" describes these phenomena and suggests that the school rather than the individual student should be considered at risk. Waxman (1992) identified several characteristics of an "at risk environment" that includes: (a) alienation experienced by students and teachers, (b) low standards and low quality of education, (c) low expectations for students, (d) high noncompletion rates for students, (e) classroom practices that are unresponsive to students, (f) high truancy and disciplinary problems, and (g) inadequate preparation of students for the future. Valenzuela (1999), for example, found that many Hispanic students go through a subtractive schooling process that takes away their cultural identity and self-worth. For Hispanic students, these conditions as well as attending poorly maintained schools and having under-qualified teachers places them in an at-risk school environment. Hispanic students who attend these at-risk school environments merit our special attention because if we can alter their learning environment, we may be able to improve both their education and their overall chances for success in society.

This section acknowledges that the educational factors associated with underachievement are malleable, and it posits that the slightest positive changes in these areas may significantly improve teaching and learning conditions for Hispanic students. The following section summarizes some of the factors associated with the educational improvement for Hispanic students.

8.3.   Factors Associated with the Educational Success of Hispanic Students

Educators concerned with the schooling of Hispanic students have generally focused on the development of language skills. Recently, however, researchers have begun to investigate other critical issues, such as improving classroom instruction (Padrón & Waxman, 1999; Tharp et al., 2000), focusing on effective schools, and developing effective programs in schools serving predominantly Hispanic students (Slavin & Calderón, 2001; Slavin & Madden, 2001). This section examines effective (a) teaching practices, (b) school factors, and (c) community, language, and school-based intervention programs for Hispanic students.

8.3.1.   Effective Teaching Practices for Hispanic Students

Many educators have maintained that the best way to improve the education of Hispanic students is to provide them with better teachers and classroom instruction (Padrón & Waxman, 1999; Tharp et al., 2000). In order to determine which practices are most effective, educators need to focus on research-based instructional practices that have been found to be effective for Hispanic students. Teaching practices need to specifically address the concerns of Hispanic students who come from different cultures and speak different languages.

There have been several recent reviews that have synthesized research studies that have examined effective instructional practices for Hispanic students (Padrón & Waxman, 1999; Waxman & Padrón, 2002; Waxman, Padrón, & Arnold, 2001; Waxman & Téllez, 2002). These syntheses have identified a number of effective instructional strategies for teaching Hispanic students, including (a) culturally responsive teaching, (b) cooperative learning, (c) instructional conversation, and (d) cognitively guided instruction, and (e) technology-enriched instruction. The consensus across these reviews has been that education needs to be meaningful and responsive to students needs, as well as linguistically and culturally appropriate (Tharp et al., 2000). The following sections discuss each of the teaching practices.

Culturally responsive teaching. Culturally responsive teaching emphasizes the everyday concerns of students, such as critical family and community issues, and tries to incorporate these concerns into the curriculum. Culturally responsive instruction helps students prepare themselves for meaningful social roles in their community and larger society by emphasizing both social and academic responsibility. Furthermore, it addresses the promotion of racial, ethnic, and linguistic equality as well as the appreciation of diversity (Boyer, 1993). Culturally responsive instruction: (a) improves the acquisition and retention of new knowledge by working from students' existing knowledge base, (b) improves self-confidence and self-esteem by emphasizing existing knowledge, (c) increases the transfer of school-taught knowledge to real-life situations, and (d) exposes students to knowledge about other individuals or cultural groups (Rivera & Zehler, 1991). When teachers develop learning activities based on familiar concepts, they help facilitate literacy and content learning and help Hispanic students feel more comfortable and confident with their work (Peregoy & Boyle, 2000).

Cooperative learning. McLaughlin and McLeod (1996) described cooperative learning as an effective instructional approach that stimulates learning and helps students come to complex understandings by discussing and defending their ideas with others. One commonly accepted definition of cooperative learning is "the instructional use of small groups so that students work together to maximize their own and each other's learning" (Johnson & Johnson, 1991, p. 292). Instead of lecturing and transmitting material, teachers facilitate the learning process by encouraging cooperation among students (Bejarano, 1987). This teaching practice is student-centered and creates interdependence among students and the teacher (Rivera & Zehler, 1991).

As an instructional practice, cooperative grouping impacts Hispanic students in several different ways. Cooperative grouping: (a) provides opportunities for students to communicate with each other, (b) enhances instructional conversations, (c) decreases anxiety, (d) develops social, academic, and communication skills, (e) enhances self-confidence and self-esteem through individual contributions and achievement of group goals, (f) improves individual and group relations by learning to clarify, assist, and challenge each other's ideas, and (g) develops proficiency in English by providing students with rich language experiences that integrate speaking, listening, reading, and writing (Calderón, 1991; Christian, 1995; Rivera & Zehler, 1991). Furthermore, cooperative learning activities provide Hispanic students with "the skills that are necessary to function in real-life situations, such as the utilization of context for meaning, the seeking of support from others, and the comparing of nonverbal and verbal cues" (Alcala, 2000, p. 4).

Instructional conversation. Instructional conversation is a teaching practice that provides students with opportunities for extended dialogue in areas that have educational value as well as relevance for students (August & Hakuta, 1998). The instructional conversation is an extended discourse between the teacher and students. It should be initiated by students in order to develop their language and complex thinking skills, and to guide them in their learning process (Tharp, 1995).

August and Hakuta's (1998) comprehensive review of research found that effective teachers of Hispanic students provide students with opportunities for extended dialogue. Rather than avoiding discussion during instruction because students may not have the appropriate language proficiency skills, instructional conversations emphasize dialogue with teachers and classmates (Durán, Dugan, & Weffer, 1997). Thus, one of the major benefits of the use of instructional conversation for students who are learning English is to provide them with the opportunity for extended discourse, an important activity of second language learning (Christian, 1995).

Cognitively guided instruction. Cognitively guided instruction emphasizes the development of learning strategies that foster students' metacognitive development by the direct teaching and modeling of cognitive learning strategies. In addition, it teaches techniques and approaches that foster students' metacognition and cognitive monitoring of their own learning (Padrón & Knight, 1989; Waxman, Padrón, & Knight, 1991). From an instructional perspective, this approach emphasizes the need for teachers to focus on students' psychological processing as well as what is taught and how it is presented. This instructional approach can be very beneficial for Hispanic students who are not doing well in school because the effectively use of cognitive strategies may help to eliminate individual barriers to academic success.

One example of cognitively guided instruction is reciprocal teaching, a procedure where students are instructed in four specific comprehension-monitoring strategies: (a) summarizing, (b) self-questioning, (c) clarifying, and (d) predicting. Studies on reciprocal teaching have found that these cognitive strategies can successfully be taught to Hispanic students and that the use of these strategies increases reading achievement (Padrón, 1992, 1993). Another example of cognitively guided instruction is Chamot and O'Malley's (1987) instructional program for LEP students that focuses specifically on strategy instruction. They found that when cognitive learning strategies are modeled for the student and opportunities to practice the strategy presented, learning outcomes improved.

Technology-enriched instruction. Several studies and reviews of research have found that technology-based instruction is effective for Hispanic students (Cummins & Sayers 1990; Padrón & Waxman, 1996). Web-based picture libraries, for example, can promote Hispanic students' comprehension in content-area classrooms (e.g., science and mathematics) (Smolkin, 2000). Digitized books are now available and allow Hispanic students to request pronunciations of unknown words, request translations of sections, and ask questions (Jiménez & Barrera, 2000). Furthermore, some types of technology (e.g., multimedia) are effective for Hispanic students because they help students connect learning in the classroom to real-life situations, thereby creating a meaningful context for teaching and learning (Means & Olson, 1994). In addition, multimedia technology can be especially helpful for Hispanic students because it can facilitate auditory skill development by integrating visual presentations with sound and animation (Bermúdez & Palumbo, 1994).

In summary, all of these teaching practices incorporate more active student learning and change the teachers' role. Instead of delivering knowledge, the teacher's role is to facilitate learning (Padrón & Waxman, 1999). Glickman (1998) refers to this approach as "democratic pedagogy," describing it as instruction that "respects the students' own desire to know, to discuss, to problem solve, and to explore individually and with others, rather than learning that is dictated, determined, and answered by the teacher" (p. 52). These student- centered instructional practices represent a model of classroom instruction that has not been very common for Hispanic students and/or Hispanic ELLs.

8.3.2.   Effective School Factors for Hispanic Students

There have been a number of studies and reviews of the research that have examined effective school factors for Hispanic students. One recent synthesis (Waxman, Price, & Téllez, 2004), however, incorporated the findings from both, the studies and reviews, to examine school factors that influence the academic outcomes of Hispanic students. The results of this synthesis indicate that there are seven characteristics of effective schools for Hispanic students. These characteristics are: (a) valuing student's needs and culture, (b) effective instructional practices, (c) faculty professional development, (d) parental and community involvement, (e) continuous student assessment, (f) school leadership, and (g) school culture and expectations. The following sections summarize some of the key aspects of each characteristic or factor.

Valuing Student's Needs and Culture. Many of the studies on effective schools serving predominantly Hispanic students recognize that their students have unique needs that require more personal attention from teachers. Consequently, schools developed clusters of teachers that work with a particular group of students who are at risk of academic failure (Ancess, 2003; Minicucci et al., 1995). Making home visits, providing parent education, and distributing free school supplies are some of the ways that schools pay personal attention to students. Effective schools serving predominantly Hispanic students also value the students' culture, include it in the academic curriculum, and allow students to develop their own ethnic identity.

Effective Instructional Practices. Another important characteristic found in effective schools serving predominantly Hispanic students is that they provide a number of different instructional practices. A number of effective schools studies have found that the most productive instructional strategy is providing language support in the students' first language (L1) (Gonzalez, Huerta-Macias, & Tinajero, 2001; Miramontes, Nadeau, & Commins, 1997; Mora, 2000; Thomas & Collier, 1997, 2001). According to Thomas and Collier (2001), the academic achievement gap can almost be completely eliminated with instruction in both L1 and L2. English as a Second Language (ESL) instructional programs were also found to be somewhat effective in improving the academic performance of Hispanic ELLs (Miramontes et al., 1997; Thomas & Collier, 2001). Other instructional practices prevalent in effective schools were the use of collaboration, student-centered instruction, incorporating individual learning styles, providing more teacher support and classroom order, and having more instructional interactions with students.

Teachers' professional development. One very important component of effective schools is a collaborative relationship between teachers (Ancess, 2003;

Lopez, Scribner, & Mahitivanichcha, 2001; Short, 1994). The teachers in effective schools have been found to work together on curriculum, teaching practices, and other aspects of the school's functioning (Ancess, 2003; Lucas, Henze, & Donato, 1990; Mora, 2000). An important feature of this professional development is that it is ongoing, as well as focused on students' learning (Ancess, 2003; Mora, 2000). Not only does the professional development focus on students' learning needs, but it also emphasizes the teaching skills and practices that serve the students (August & Hakuta, 1998; Lucas, et al., 1990; Mora, 2000; Thomas & Collier, 1997; Waxman & Huang, 1994). Many teachers report that they need long-term professional development in order to: (a) use new methods of classroom instruction (e.g., cooperative grouping), (b) integrate educational technology in the subject they teach, and (c) address the needs of ELLs and other students from diverse cultural backgrounds (Lewis et al., 1999). Classroom teachers desire more: (a) information related to the teaching of Hispanic students, (b) time for training and planning, and (c) opportunities to collaborate and learn from other teachers (Téllez & Waxman, 2006).

Parent and community involvement. Parent and community involvement has been found to be an important component in numerous studies of effective schools for Hispanic students. The effective schools in these studies found ways to actively involve parents in their children's schooling. Furthermore, parent participation was found to be facilitated by empowering parents and other community members to get involved and to be actively engaged in student learning.

Student assessment. The student assessment component of research on effective schools for Hispanic students has two areas of use, (a) program and (b) student. At the program level, effective schools routinely use academic assessments of their students to measure improvements in students' learning as a means for program evaluation. This program level evaluation is then directly linked to teaching practice and professional development (August & Hakuta, 1998). At the student level, assessment is used to monitor individual student progress; however, all three of these studies have different points to make about individual student assessment. Miramontes et al. (1997), for example, found that assessments provide valuable information on students' language proficiency as well as development in L1 and/or L2 in conjunction with academic progress. Reyes, Scribner, & Scribner (1999) found that effective schools serving predominantly Hispanic students used assessment as a way to motivate students to succeed as well as a way to map out individualized learning procedures for students.

School Leadership. Effective school leadership for schools serving predominantly Hispanic students typically includes a self or shared governance structure (Ancess, 2003; Minicucci et al., 1995; Reyes et al., 1999). These studies found that the school community, parents, teachers, and other stakeholders have decision-making responsibility and this shared-decision making process is linked to the common goal of student success.

The role of the principal in the governance of these effective schools is really that of a supporter (August & Hakuta, 1998; Gonzalez et al., 2001; Maden, 2001; Reyes et al., 1999). Ancess (2003) explains that the principal acts as a guide to the school through changes and is a stabilizing force for the school community so that there is a certain amount of safety in taking risks for school improvement. Gonzalez et al., (2001) describes that the principal plays a pivotal role in student success by focusing on continuous improvement. According to August and Hakuta (1998), not only do these principals support the common vision and shared governance structures, but more specifically they support Hispanic students. Also, Maden (2001) found that a fundamental aspect of school leadership is the hiring, developing, supporting and maintaining of teachers.

School culture and expectations. This final characteristic of effective schools for Hispanic students, school culture and expectations, encompasses three aspects: (a) a caring school climate, (b) a focus on learning, and (c) high expectations. Many studies found that effective schools having caring relationships that are a pervasive part of the school culture (Ancess, 2003; Carter & Chatfield, 1986; Maden, 2001; Waxman & Huang, 1997). The next factor for success in the school culture is the focus on learning. Carter and Chatfield (1986), for example, found that effective schools honored the right to learn through a safe and orderly learning environment. Other studies found that the school faculty and staff held beliefs that education is empowering and thus they were dedicated to empowering Hispanic student through academic achievement (Lucas, et al., 1990). The final aspect of school culture and expectations is high expectations. Several studies have found that teachers, administrators, and parents need to set high expectations for academic learning and personal student development. (McKissack, 1999; Minicucci et al., 1995).

The findings from the present synthesis are important because they suggest that there are several alterable school factors that relate to improved academic achievement for Hispanic students. The seven characteristics of effective schools serving predominantly Hispanic ELLs also are quite similar to prior syntheses of effective schools research (Teddlie & Reynolds, 2000), with the exception of valuing students' needs and culture. This characteristic appears to be especially important because it highlights the need for schools serving predominantly Hispanics to be sensitive to students' primary language and culture.

8.3.3. Language and School-Based Intervention Programs for Hispanic Students

8.3.3.1. Language Programs

Special language programs (e.g., bilingual education) have traditionally been implemented to address Hispanic ELLs educational concerns, but recently many of these programs have been eliminated because of political ideologies rather than research-based decisions. Although there are a number of language programs that have been found to be effective in educating Hispanic ELLs, one of the most researched and controversial language program for Hispanic students is bilingual education. A recent review by Téllez, Flinspach, & Waxman (2005) summarizes the findings as well as focuses on the controversy. They examined three of the most recent research syntheses and reviews of the literature on bilingual education: Greene (1998), Rossell and Baker (1996), and Slavin and Cheung (2003, 2004).

Greene's (1998) review of the effects of bilingual education is a meta-analysis. It reviews many studies, calculating an "effect size" from each and then combining these values to determine an overall measure of success. Meta-analysis has become an important method for examining the effectiveness of programs and for exploring program effects across a wide range of students and contexts. Greene's study addresses a concern common to many meta-analyses, that a large number of the studies and evaluations are so flawed in their methods and designs that they cannot be included in the overall sample to be synthesized. After rejecting many studies for the meta-analysis, Greene calculated an overall effect size of .26. This value suggests that students who participate in bilingual education programs outscored their English-immersion counterparts by approximately 15 percentile points.

In contrast, Rossell and Baker (1996), using a very similar set of studies, concluded that bilingual education is no better than an English-only approach. The discrepant finding is partially due to the fact that Rossell and Baker use a vote-counting method, rather than meta-analytic techniques, to assess results across studies. They counted the studies in the review as favoring either bilingual instruction or English immersion and, based on the final vote count, argued that bilingual instruction was not better than English immersion. Hedges and Olkin (1980) discuss the problems with vote counting, including its uniform treatment of vastly different studies and its insensitivity to the degree of program effectiveness in each study. Disagreements about the appropriateness of the methods of research synthesis affect the interpretations of bilingual education research (Salazar, 1998).

In one of the most recent reviews of effective reading programs for English Language Learners (ELLs), Slavin and Cheung (2003) found that among 17 studies that met the scientifically-based research standards of the review, most of the studies found significant positive effects of bilingual reading performance and others found no difference. Nine of these studies were longitudinal and of those, five favored bilingual education, and four found no difference. There were no studies that found that an English-only favored ELLs.

Other recent meta-analyses of bilingual education also support the program's effectiveness. Rolstad, Mahoney, and Glass (2005), for example, examined evaluation studies in Arizona and found that they were overall positive effects for bilingual education on students' English outcomes and very large effects for outcomes in students' native language. Overall, while there have been some concerns about bilingual education, the research evidence clearly suggests that bilingual education is an effective language program. The next section describes some effective school-based programs for Hispanic students.

8.3.3.2. School-based Programs

In recent years, a number of school-based prevention and intervention programs have been found to be effective for Hispanic students. One critical component of most of these programs is the involvement of the community. Teachers and schools who effectively educate Hispanic students pool community resources in order to bridge the gap between them and the community.

Schools have incorporated intervention programs to address the educational needs of Hispanic students. Though some of the strategies vary due to the grade levels and purpose of the intervention programs, many still have similar characteristics. The programs find alternative ways to create successful results for the student, parents, and teachers. The programs all seek the introduction of community resources to assist students and families. Additionally, the programs have reorganized the type of instruction for students by providing an effective instruction and curriculum. Some of the programs include the following:

Coca Cola Valued Youth Program. This program was created in 1984 and has focused on working with students at risk of dropping out of middle and high school. The program works with over 250 schools in 25 cities. The purpose of the program is to provide elementary students with middle school or high school tutors. The tutors are paid a wage for their work with the elementary students. The program provides positive outcomes for both the tutor and the tutee. The program was considered an exemplary program by Department of Education for its effectiveness working with students (Montecel et al., 2004).

Achievement for Latinos through Academic Success (ALAS). The ALAS program was created to address the middle school students with low academic achievement, poor school attendance, and discipline problems. The program focused on providing these students intervention strategies directed at working with the student, the school, the family, and the community. The program had an intervention team consisting of teachers, counselors, social workers, and policemen/women ready to work with the students. Additionally, the program also incorporated the use of university faculty in order to reorganize curriculum and instruction for the students. The instructors worked with the teachers as a collaborative team addressing issues at home and school. An evaluation of the program revealed several positive findings. The evaluation focused on 50 ALAS students matched with 50 non-ALAS students. By the end of ninth grade, the ALAS students had more students enrolled, more students on track to graduate, better attendance and grades than the non-ALAS students (García, 2001a).

Mathematics, Engineering, Science Achievement (MESA). The MESA program is considered one of the older intervention programs created in 1970. The program focuses on producing trained scientific professionals in the workforce. These students pursue careers in computer science, math, and engineering. Additionally, the program serves low-academically performing students and provides various strategies for working with students such as providing career study, peer learning groups, parental involvement, and other services. MESA is located in elementary schools through colleges and universities throughout California. The programs effectiveness has been measured through a 90% student graduation rate, which went on to enroll in a college or university in 1996–1997 (Montecel et al., 2004).

Upward Bound. This program focuses on low socioeconomic teenage students who have the potential to become a first-generation college student. The program is administered by the Department of Education. The program works with the students by providing instructional assistance with their coursework after-school. Additionally, students are provided with personal counseling and college guidance. Assessments of the program indicate that students involved in the program are more likely to stay in school and had a greater chance of attending college than the comparison group (Montecel et al., 2004).

Success for All (SFA). SFA is one of the largest comprehensive reform programs for elementary schools serving students at risk of academic failure. The program's philosophy is that children must succeed academically and that it is possible to provide school personnel with the skills and strategies that they need to ensure academic success for students. A key goal of the program is that students must be able to read at grade level by the end of third grade. Therefore, SFA is an intervention that begins early in the student's academic life. It utilizes a great deal of tutoring. Tutoring takes place for 20-minute blocks and is done by certified teachers. Student progress is monitored on an ongoing basis. The program also includes a reading component for students whose native language is Spanish. Evaluations of SFA have indicated that the program has demonstrated consistent positive results for Hispanic students (Lockwood, 2001; Slavin & Madden, 2001)

Advancement Via Individual Determination (AVID). The AVID program (Mehan et al., 1996) is another successful program for older (Grade 6–12) Hispanic students. AVID places low-achieving students believed to have college potential in the same college preparatory courses as high-achieving students. AVID students receive special counseling, tutoring, and other academic support such as instruction in study skills, writing, and test-taking strategies. A comprehensive team of administrators, counselors, AVID teachers, and regular content-area teachers who work with AVID students also receive 1 week of training in the summer and monthly follow-up training during the school year on teaching practices (e.g., cooperative learning and inquiry-based practices) that are highlighted in the program. AVID has been successful in empowering students by reconnecting them to school. College enrollment rates and graduation rates for AVID students have dramatically increased as a result of the program.

Syntheses of research on effective school-based programs for Hispanic students have found that there are several common characteristics common to successful programs (Fashola et al., 2001; Lockwood, 2001). Effective programs typically: (a) have well-specified goals, (b) provide ample opportunity for teacher professional development, (c) begin early and are maintained throughout the schooling experience, (d) include ongoing assessment and feedback,

(e) incorporate the use of tutors and other support staff, and (f) focus on the quality of implementation. These programs focus on multiple variables when addressing the needs of Hispanic students within and outside campuses. Working to foster a positive relationship between the home and school also must take into consideration the students' culture and experiences within instructional practices (García, 2001a).

8.4.   Implications for Research on Effective Practices

One major limitation of the research on Hispanic students is that the majority of the studies are descriptive studies. There have been few experimental studies that have investigated the impact of effective educational practices on Hispanic students' educational outcomes. Future research needs to specifically design experimental studies that explicitly test interventions that promote effective outcomes for Hispanic students. Furthermore, there have been very few naturalistic, longitudinal studies conducted that have examined the success of effective practices on Hispanic students' long-term academic achievement and educational success. Mixed methods approaches also are needed to examine the effects of educational practices. Teacher self-report data, along with teacher, administrator, and student interview data could all be used to help supplement the survey data and systematic classroom observation data that are generally used in school and instructional effectiveness research. Such data could help us understand, from different perspectives, the complexity of issues surrounding the educational improvement of Hispanic students. More ethnographic studies also are needed in order to help us uncover "grounded theoretical" explanations of factors that impact schools for Hispanic students.

More systematic, long-term reviews of the research also are needed. These syntheses will contribute to our knowledge base and promote the use of procedural knowledge in policy and practice. It also will help us create a system of research-based educational reform to bring "what works" knowledge to scale. The educational problems faced by Hispanic students highlight the need for synthesizing existing research and suggest ways to improve their academic achievement.

8.5.   Conclusion and Recommendations

The research cited in the previous sections indicates that there are several educational practices and programs that significantly improve the academic success of Hispanic students. Many of these programs are supported by systematic, long-term studies and reviews of research. It is important to note that even if only a few factors associated with students' educational success are present, the programs seem to have a positive effect on student achievement and persistence in school. Changes in school practices, however, need to be accompanied by changes in policy that reflect the current diversity in classroom settings, and the best scientific evidence available. The following recommendations emerge from our review of the research:

- Some of the effective teaching practices for Hispanic students are: culturally responsive instruction, cooperative learning, instructional conversation, cognitively guided instruction, and technology-enhanced instruction.
- Some of the effective school factors for Hispanic students are: valuing student's needs and culture, effective instructional practices, teachers' professional development, parent and community involvement, student assessment, school leadership, and school culture and expectations.
- One of the most effective language programs for Hispanic students is bilingual education.
- Some of the effective school-based programs for Hispanic students are: Coca Cola Valued Youth Program, Achievement for Latinos through Academic Success (ALAS), Mathematics, Engineering, Science Achievement (MSEA), Upward Bound, Success for All (SFA), and Advancement Via Individual Determination (AVID).

This chapter described some of the research-based educational practices that have been found to be successful in improving the education of Hispanic students. Several key elements or components that have been successful in many different settings are discussed, but these are only suggestions, not "recipes" for improving schools. No program, however well implemented, will prove a panacea for all the educational problems of Hispanic students. For the most part, each school must concern itself with the resolution of its own specific problems (Schubert, 1980). In that sense, every school should be considered unique, and educators should choose among research-based practices and programs according to the needs of the Hispanic students that they serve. Furthermore, critical out-of-school factors that affect the outcomes of schooling for Hispanic students must also be addressed. If we only focus on school factors and ignore the importance of family and community influences on the education of Hispanic students, we will clearly fail in our endeavors.

The serious educational problems of Hispanic students highlight the need for schools to begin using scientific evidence to determine educational programs and practices. There is a critical need to develop a solid knowledge base on effective practices, leadership, and policy for Hispanic students that focuses on alterable practices that improve students' academic achievement. Strengthening links between evidence-based research and educational practices can benefit the growing population of Hispanic students in American schools and those who share responsibility for educating them. With greater understanding and support of the needs of Hispanic students and their teachers, schools can improve the quality of educational practices and ensure that no child, teacher, or school—is left behind.

References

Alcala, A. (2000). A framework for developing an effective instructional program for limited English proficient students with limited formal schools. *Practical Assessment, Research & Evaluation*, 7(9), 1–6.

Alexander, D., Heaviside, S., & Farris, E. (1999). *Status of Education Reform in Public Elementary and Secondary Schools: Teachers' Perspectives.* Washington, DC: U.S. Department of Education, National Center for Education Statistics.

Ancess, J. (2003). *Beating the Odds: High Schools as Communities of Commitment.* New York: Teachers College.

August, D. & Hakuta, K. (eds) (1998). *Educating Language-minority Children.* Washington, DC: National Academy Press.

Bejarano, Y. (1987). A cooperative small-group methodology in the language classroom. *TESOL Quarterly*, 21, 483–504.

Bermúdez, A.B. & Palumbo, D. (1994). Bridging the gap between literacy and technology: Hypermedia as a learning tool for limited English proficient students. *The Journal of Educational Issues of Language Minority Students*, 14, 165–184.

Boyer, J.B. (1993). Culturally sensitive instruction: An essential component of education for diversity. *Catalyst for Change*, 22(3), 5–8.

Calderón, M. (1991). Benefits of cooperative learning for Hispanic students. *Texas Research Journal*, 2, 39–57.

Carter, T.P. & Chatfield, M.L. (1986). Effective bilingual schools: Implications for policy and practice. *American Journal of Education*, 95, 200–232.

Chamot, A.U. & O'Malley, J.M. (1987). The cognitive academic language learning approach: A bridge to the mainstream. *TESOL Quarterly*, 21, 227–249.

Chapa, J. & De La Rosa, B. (2004). Latino population growth, socioeconomic and demographic characteristics, and implications for educational attainment. *Education and Urban Society*, 36, 130–149.

Christian, D. (1995). Two-way bilingual education. In Montone, C.L. (ed.), *Teaching Linguistically and Culturally Diverse Learners: Effective Programs and Practices.* Santa Cruz, CA: National Center for Research on Cultural Diversity and Second Language Learning, pp. 8–11.

Cummins, J. & Sayers, D. (1990). Education 2001: Learning networks and educational reform. *Computers in the Schools*, 7(1 & 2), 1–29.

Durán, B.J., Dugan, T., & Weffer, R.E. (1997). Increasing teacher effectiveness with language minority students. *The High School Journal*, 84, 238–246.

Fashola, O.S., Slavin, R.E., Calderón, M., & Durán, R. (2001). Effective programs for Latino students in elementary and middle schools. In Slavin, R.E. & Calderón, M. (eds), *Effective Programs for Latino Students*. Mahwah, NJ: Lawrence Erlbaum, pp. 1–66.

Fletcher, T.V. & Cardona-Morales, C. (1990). Implementing effective instructional interventions for minority students. In Barona, A. & García, E.E. (eds), *Children at Risk: Poverty, Minority Status, and other Issues in Educational Equity*. Washington, DC: National Association of School Psychologists, pp. 151–170.

Gándara, P., Maxwell-Jolly, J., & Driscoll, A. (2005). *Listening to Teachers of English Language Learners: A Survey of California Teachers' Challenges, Experiences, and Professional Development Needs*. Santa Cruz, CA: The Center for the Future of Teaching and Learning.

García, E. E. (2001a). *Hispanic Education in the United States: Raices Y Alas*. Lanham, MD: Rowman & Littlefield.

García, G.N. (2001b). The factors that place Latino children and youth at risk of educational failure. In Slavin, R.E. & Calderón, M. (eds), *Effective Programs for Latino Students*. Mahwah, NJ: Lawrence Erlbaum, pp. 307–329.

García, S.B. & Guerra, P.L. (2004). Deconstructing deficit thinking: Working with educators to create more equitable learning environments. *Education and Urban Society*, 36, 150–168.

Gersten, R. & Jiménez, R. (1998). Modulating instruction for language minority students. In Kameenui, E.J. & Carnine, D.W. (eds), *Effective Teaching Strategies that Accommodate Diverse Learners*. New York: Prentice Hall, pp. 161–178.

Glickman, C.D. (1998). Educational leadership for democratic purpose! What do we mean? *International Journal of Leadership in Education*, 1(1), 47–53.

Gonzalez, M.L., Huerta-Macias, A., &. Tinajero, J.V. (eds). (2001). *Educating Latino Students: A Guide to Successful Practice*. Lanham, MD: Scarecrow.

Greene, J. (1998). *A Meta-analysis of the Effectiveness of Bilingual Education*. Claremont, CA: Tomas Rivera Center.

Haberman, M. (1991). Pedagogy of poverty versus good teaching. *Phi Delta Kappan*, 73, 290–294.

Hedges, L.V. & Olkin, I. (1980). Vote-counting methods in research synthesis. *Psychological Bulletin*, 88, 359–369.

Jiménez, R.T. & Barrera, R. (2000). How will bilingual/ESL programs in literacy change in the next millennium? *Reading Research Quarterly*, 35, 522–523.

Johnson, D.W. & Johnson, R.T. (1991). Classroom instruction and cooperative grouping. In Waxman, H.C. & Walberg, H.J. (eds), *Effective Teaching: Current Research*. Berkeley, CA: McCutchan, pp. 277–293.

Lewis, L., Parsad, B., Carey, N., Bartfai, N., Farris, E., & Smerdon, B. (1999). *Teacher quality: A report on the preparation and qualifications of public school teachers* (Report No. 1999–080). Washington, DC: U.S. Department of Education, Office of Educational Research and Improvement, National Center for Education Statistics.

Liagas, C. & Snyder, T.D. (2003). *Status and trends in the education of Hispanics*. Washington, DC: US Department of Education, National Center for Education Statistics.

Lockwood, A.T. (2001). Effective elementary, middle, and high school programs for Latino youth. In Slavin, R.E. & Calderón, M. (eds), *Effective Programs for Latino Students*. Mahwah, NJ: Lawrence Erlbaum, pp. 101–124.

Lopez, G.R., Scribner, J.D., & Mahitivanichcha, K. (2001). Redefining parental involvement: Lessons from high-performing migrant impacted schools. *American Educational Research Journal*, 38, 253–288.

Lucas, T., Henze, R., & Donato, R. (1990). Promoting the success of Latino language-minority students: An exploratory study of six high schools. *Harvard Educational Review*, 60, 315–340.

Maden, M. (ed.). (2001). *Success Against the Odds – Five Years on: Revisiting effective schools in damaged areas*. London: Routledge/Falmer.

McKissack, E.A. (1999). *Chicano Educational Achievement: Comparing Escuela Tlatelolco, A Chicanocentric School and a Public High School*. New York: Garland.

McLaughlin, B. & McLeod, B. (1996). *Educating all our students: Improving education for children from culturally and linguistically diverse backgrounds (Vol. 1)*. Santa Cruz, CA: National Center for Research on Cultural Diversity and Second Language Learning.

Means, B. & Olson, K. (1994). The link between technology and authentic learning. *Educational Leadership*, 51(7), 15–18.

Mehan, H., Villanueva, I., Hubbard, L., & Lintz, A. (1996). *Constructing School Success: The Consequences of Untracking Low-Achieving Students*. Cambridge, UK: Cambridge University Press.

Melendez, M. (1993). Bilingual education in California: A status report. *Thrust for Educational Leadership*, 22(6), 35–38.

Minicucci, C., Berman, P., McLaughlin, B., McLeod, B., Nelson, & Woodworth, K. (1995). School reform and student diversity. *Phi Delta Kappan*, 77(1), 77–80.

Miramontes, O.B., Nadeau, A., & Commins, N.L. (1997). *Restructuring Schools for Linguistic Diversity: Linking Decision Making to Effective Programs*. New York: Teachers College.

Montecel, M.R., Cortez, J.D., & Cortez, A. (2004). Dropout-prevention programs: Right intent, wrong focus, and some suggestions on where to go from here. *Education and Urban Society*, 36, 169–188.

Mora, J.K. (2000). Policy shifts in language-minority education: A mismatch between politics and pedagogy. *The Educational Forum*, 64, 204–214.

National Center for Education Statistics. (2003) *Overview of Public Elementary and Secondary Schools and Districts: School Year 2001–2002*. Washington, DC: U.S. Department of Education.

Padrón, Y.N. (1992). Strategy training in reading for bilingual students. *Southwest Journal of Educational Research into Practice*, 4, 59–62.

Padrón, Y.N. (1993). The effect of strategy instruction on bilingual students' cognitive strategy use in reading. *Bilingual Research Journal*, 16(3 & 4), 35–51.

Padrón, Y.N. & Knight, S.L. (1989). Linguistic and cultural influences on classroom instruction. In Baptiste, H.P., Anderson, J., Walker de Felix, J., & Waxman, H.C. (eds), *Leadership, Equity, and School Effectiveness*. Newbury Park, CA: Sage, pp. 173–185.

Padrón, Y.N. & Waxman, H.C. (1993). Teaching and learning risks associated with limited cognitive mastery in science and mathematics for limited English proficient students. In Office of Bilingual Education and Minority Language Affairs (eds), *Proceedings of the Third National Research Symposium on Limited English Proficient Students: Focus on Middle and High School Issues* (Vol. 2, pp. 511–547). Washington, DC: National Clearinghouse for Bilingual Education.

Padrón, Y.N. & Waxman, H.C. (1996). Improving the teaching and learning of English language learners through instructional technology. *International Journal of Instructional Media*, 23, 341–354.

Padrón, Y.N. & Waxman, H.C. (1999). Effective instructional practices for English language learners. In Waxman, H.C. & Walberg, H.J. (eds), *New Directions for Teaching Practice and Research*. Berkeley, CA: McCutchan, pp. 171–203.

Peregoy, S.F. & Boyle, O.F. (2000). English learners reading English: What we know, what we need to know. *Theory into Practice*, 39, 237–247.

Reyes, P., Scribner, J., & Scribner, A.P. (1999). *Lessons From High-Performing Hispanic Schools: Creating Learning Communities*. New York: Teachers College.

Rivera, C. & Zehler, A.M. (1991). Assuring the academic success of language minority students: Collaboration in teaching and learning. *Journal of Education*, 173(2), 52–77.

Rolstad, K., Mahoney, K.S., & Glass, G.V. (2005). Weighing the evidence: A meta-analysis of bilingual education in Arizona. *Bilingual Research Journal*, 29(1), 43–67.

Rossell, C. & Baker, K. (1996). The educational effectiveness of bilingual education. *Research in the Teaching of English*, 30, 7–74.

Salazar, J.J. (1998). A longitudinal model for interpreting thirty years of bilingual education research. *Bilingual Research Journal*, 22, 1–11.

Schubert, W.H. (1980). Recalibrating educational research: Toward a focus on practice. *Educational Researcher*, 9(1), 17–24.

Short, D.J. (1994). Expanding middle school horizons: Integrating language, culture, and social studies. *TESOL Quarterly*, 28, 581–608.

Slavin, R.E. & Calderón, M. (eds). (2001). *Effective Programs for Latino Students*. Mahwah, NJ: Lawrence Erlbaum.

Slavin, R.E. & Cheung, A. (2003). *Effective Programs for English Language Learners: A Best-Evidence Synthesis*. Baltimore, MD: Johns Hopkins University, Center for Research on Education for Students Placed at Risk.

Slavin, R.E. & Cheung, A. (2004). How do English language learners learn to read? *Educational Leadership*, 61(6), 52–57.

Slavin, R.E. & Madden, N. (2001). Effects of bilingual and English as a second language adaptations of Success for All on the reading achievement of students acquiring English. In Slavin, R.E. & Calderón, M. (eds), *Effective Programs For Latino Students*. Mahwah, NJ: Lawrence Erlbaum. pp. 207–230.

Smolkin, L. (2000). How will diversity affect literacy in the next millennium? *Reading Research Quarterly*, 35, 549–550.

Teddlie, C. & Reynolds, D. (eds). (2000). *The International Handbook of School Effectiveness Research*. New York: Falmer.

Téllez, K., Flinspach, S.L., & Waxman, H.C. (2005). Resistance to scientific evidence: Program evaluation and its lack of influence on policies related to language education programs. In Hoosain, R. & Salili, F. (eds), *Language in Multicultural Education*. Greenwich, CT: Information Age, pp. 57–76.

Téllez, K. & Waxman, H.C. (eds). (2006). *Improving Educator Quality for English Language Learners: Research, Policies and Practices*. Mahwah, NJ: Lawrence Erlbaum.

Tharp, R.G. (1995). Instructional conversations in Zuni classrooms. In Montone, C.L. (ed.), *Teaching Linguistically and Culturally Diverse Learners: Effective Programs and Practices*. Santa Cruz, CA: National Center for Research on Cultural Diversity and Second Language Learning, pp. 12–13.

Tharp, R.G., Estrada, P., Dalton, S., & Yamauchi, L. (2000). *Teaching transformed: Achieving Excellence, Fairness, Inclusion, and Harmony*. Boulder, CO: Westview.

Thomas, W.P. & Collier, V. (1997). *School Effectiveness For Language-Minority Students*. Washington, DC: National Clearinghouse for Bilingual Education.

Thomas, W.P. & Collier, V. (2001). *A National Study of School Effectiveness For Language Minority Students' Long-Term Academic Achievement*. Santa Cruz, CA: National Center for Research on Education, Diversity & Excellence.

U.S. Department of Education (2000). *Key Indicators of Hispanic Student Achievement: National Goals and Benchmarks for the Next Decade* [on-line]. Available: http://www.ed.gov.pubs/hispanicindicators/

Valencia, R., Valenzuela, A., Sloan, K., & Foley, D.E. (2001). Let's treat the cause, not the symptoms: Equity and accountability in Texas revisited. *Phi Delta Kappan*, 83, 321–326.

Valenzuela, A. (1999). *Subtractive Schooling: U. S. Mexican Youth and the Politics of Caring*. Albany, NY: University of New York Press.

Waxman, H.C. (1992). Reversing the cycle of educational failure for students in at-risk school environments. In Waxman, H.C., Walker de Felix, J., Anderson, J., & Baptiste, H.P. (eds), *Students at Risk in at-risk Schools: Improving Environments for Learning*. Newbury Park, CA: Sage, pp. 1–9.

Waxman, H.C. & Huang, S.L. (1994). *Classroom Instruction Differences Between Effective and Ineffective Inner-City Schools for Language Minority Students*. Paper presented at the annual meeting of the American Educational Research Association, Montreal, Quebec.

Waxman, H.C. & Huang, S.L. (1997, April). *Classroom Learning Environment and Instructional Differences Between Effective, Average, and Ineffective Urban Elementary Schools for Latino Students*. Paper presented at the annual meeting of the American Educational Research Association, Chicago, IL.

Waxman, H.C., Huang, S.L., & Padrón, Y.N. (1995). Investigating the pedagogy of poverty in inner-city middle level schools. *Research in Middle Level Education*, 18(2), 1–22.

Waxman, H.C. & Padrón, Y.N. (2002). Research-based teaching practices that improve the education of English language learners. In Minaya-Rowe, L. (ed.), *Teacher Training and Effective Pedagogy in the Context of Student Diversity*. Greenwich, CT: Information Age, pp. 3–38.

Waxman, H.C., Padrón, Y.N., & Arnold, K.A. (2001). Effective instructional practices for students placed at risk of failure. In Borman, G.D., Stringfield, S.C., & Slavin, R.E. (eds), *Title I: Compensatory Education at the Crossroads*. Mahwah, NJ: Lawrence Erlbaum, pp. 137–170.

Waxman, H.C., Padrón, Y.N., & Knight, S.L. (1991). Risks associated with students' limited cognitive mastery. In Wang, M.C., Reynolds M.C., & Walberg, H.J. (eds), *Handbook of Special Education: Emerging Programs* (Vol. 4, pp. 235–254). Oxford, England: Pergamon.

Waxman, H.C., Price, D., & Téllez, K. (2004). *Research Synthesis On Effective Schools for English Language Learners*. Philadelphia: Laboratory for Student Success.

Waxman, H.C. & Téllez, K. (2002). *Research Synthesis On Effective Teaching Practices for English Language Learners* (Publication Series No. 3). Philadelphia: Laboratory for Student Success.

9
Improving the Schooling Experiences of African American Students
What school leaders and teachers can do

Gail L. Thompson

Many years ago, the congregation of an African Methodist Episcopal Church in southern California realized they had a big problem: At the end of the school term, none of the male high school seniors had enough credits to graduate (Thompson, 2002b). After this revelation, the congregation's and the pastor's sense of outrage was so great that the church developed a weekend tutorial program to assist struggling students. The general consensus was "If the schools can't meet our sons' academic needs, then we must do so ourselves."

Although this church's response was innovative and probably rare, its dilemma was not unusual: African American student underachievement is a national problem that has perplexed educators and researchers for decades. In recent years, the No Child Left Behind (NCLB) Act's emphasis on closing the achievement gap (U.S. Department of Education, 2001) and the fiftieth anniversary of the landmark Brown versus Board of Education legislation mandating school deseg-regation have added a new sense of urgency to closing this gap. However, according to Yale child psychiatrist, Dr. James P. Comer "…much of the public, as well as too many educators do not understand the conditions that support or serve as obstacles to learning" (2004, p. 14). This is all the more true when it comes to obstacles to learning for African American students, a constant theme in my own research and that of others.

Even though too many educators are unaware of ways in which they can improve African American student achievement, there is a substantial amount of research on this issue, and many African American students and parents (Thompson, 2002b; Thompson, 2003c) have strong opinions about what is needed to provide African Americans with optimal learning opportunities in school. In the remainder of this chapter, I describe some of this research based on my earlier work at underperforming-high-minority schools. I begin with a brief summary of research on the role of school leaders in improving African American student achievement and follow with an explanation of "Seven Things that African American Students Need from Their Teachers." Based on a review of research and my own work, the seven points emphasize what African American students need for optimal learning. I conclude the chapter by emphasizing the importance of professional development and providing recommendations for policy and practice.

9.1.   The Blind can't Lead the Blind: School Leadership that Makes a Positive Difference for African American Students

"Leadership sets the tone in organizations" is a message that I emphasize in my research. Other scholars have also stressed that in the absence of effective leadership, true school reform—which includes closing the achievement gap—is impossible (Comer, 2004; Fink & Resnick, 2001; Reitzug & Patterson, 1998; Tirozzi, 2001). As Leighton (1996) put it, "'Strong leadership' appears in virtually every list of attributes of successful schools" (p. 1). Whereas each individual K-12 teacher can improve student achievement within his or her *classroom*, in order for *school-wide* reform to occur, school leaders must be effective and proactive.

Although the media and some researchers constantly disseminate negative information about urban, high-poverty, and predominantly Black and Latino schools, a growing body of research, and even some news articles have revealed that numerous high-poverty-high-minority schools, including some predominantly Black schools, have improved student achievement. In fact, some have even become high-performing schools (Comer, 2004; Denbo, 2002). A recurring theme about these exemplary schools is that their styles may differ, but leaders engage in similar practices. In the next section, I summarize several of these practices.

9.2.   How Effective School Leaders Improve Student Achievement

A main theme in the literature about school leaders' role in improving achievement is that effective leaders are able to create a learning community that is built on respect for teachers, staff, students, and parents. Forming partnerships with the broader school community and soliciting input from individuals within and those outside of the school setting are an important component of school reform (Leighton, 1996). This not only includes welcoming input from other administrators, staff, teachers, and students, but parents as well. The relationships among adults and students in low-performing schools are often dysfunctional and impede learning, and historically the voices of students, Black and Latino parents, and teachers of color have been ignored (Comer, 2004; Delpit, 1995; Thompson, 2003a, b, c, 2004b). However, in order for optimal achievement to occur, effective leadership requires the ability to establish positive relationships that are built on a foundation of mutual respect for all of the school's constituents (Comer, 2004; Denbo, 2002).

In addition to being based on inclusiveness, the learning communities created by effective leaders are permeated by high expectations (Carter, 2000; Comer, 2004; Council of Chief State School Officers, 2002; Denbo, 2002; Simon Jr & Izumi, 2003; Thompson, 2002b; 2003c; 2004b; Yau, 2002). This climate of high expectations, which begins with explicitly stated measurable goals (Carter, 2000; Council of Chief State School Officers, 2002), leads to a school-wide "cultural transformation" where a rigorous curriculum results in higher achievement (Denbo, 2002), and where educators strongly believe that all students can succeed academically (Council of Chief State School Officers, 2002).

In his review and critique of research on high-achieving elementary schools with large percentages of low-income African Americans, Yau (2002) stated that in order for reform to occur, among other changes, school leaders must improve the school culture, provide support for teachers to be successful, increase parent involvement, and focus on the needs of students. This focus on student needs should lead to an increase in instructional and learning time, the use of test data to improve instruction, and efforts to boost students' self-esteem, and morale. Again, high expectations for the entire school community surfaced as a hallmark of high-achieving schools.

One of the best models of the essential components of a comprehensive school plan to improve African American student achievement was developed by Comer and members of the Yale Child Study team more than 30 years ago. Since then, the School Development Plan (SDP) that they piloted at two low-performing-high-poverty schools in New Haven, Connecticut, has been used by more than a thousand schools. The SDP is based on a holistic child-development approach to learning, a "no-fault" (not indulging in the "blame game" that is so common) perspective about school reform, an emphasis on positive relationships among adults and students, and a culture of high expectations that emphasizes focusing on students' strengths, instead of their weaknesses (Comer, 2004).

Another characteristic of effective leaders is that they use test results wisely (Carter, 2000; Comer, 2004; Council of Chief State School Officers, 2002; Denbo, 2002; Simon Jr & Izumi, 2003; Yau, 2002). However, although the wise use of test data can be beneficial in school reform, for too long many school leaders have used test data unwisely, particularly to bolster the widespread belief that African American students are cognitively inferior to Whites and Asians (Gould, 1981; Thompson, 2004b). As Comer (2004) stated, "But human behavior or performance, and its meaning, are too complex to be captured by numbers alone" (p. 19). Effective school leaders realize this and use data prudently.

In sum, in order to be effective, school leaders must begin with the right mind-set about students, parents, teachers, and the leader's own role in improving student achievement (Comer, 2004; Simon Jr & Izumi, 2003). The "no-fault" mind-set that Comer (2004) and others have described as essential to school reform, positive relationships, inclusiveness, providing support for teachers, the creation of a community of learners that is built on high expectations, and the wise use of test data to improve the curriculum and instruction are all among the key ingredients that school leaders must include in the recipe for reform that results in improving African American student achievement.

9.3.   Seven Things that African American Students Need from their Teachers

In order for school-wide reform to occur, outstanding leaders are crucial, but what occurs in each individual classroom is largely up to the teacher. Teacher preparation programs have historically failed to adequately prepare teachers to work successfully with students from diverse backgrounds (Carter, 2000; Delpit, 1995; Hale, 2001; Ladson-Billings, 1994, 2001; Thompson, 2004b; U.S. Department of Education, 2000), and many teachers, especially those in high-poverty and urban schools, leave the profession during the first five years of their teaching careers (CNN, 2003; Thompson, 2004b; U.S. Department of Education, 2000). Nevertheless, just as researchers have identified the characteristics of leaders of high-performing-high-poverty-high-minority schools, there is also a large body of research describing the characteristics of effective teachers of African Americans, and research focusing on how teachers can improve African American student achievement (Aronson, 2004; Boykin, 2002; Collins, 1992; Comer, 2004; Delpit, 1995; Denbo & Moore, 2002; Drew, 1996; Foster, 1998; Gay, 2000; Hale, 2001; Kunjufu, 1985; Ladson-Billings, 1994; Perry, Steele, & Hilliard, 2003; Thompson, 2002b; 2003c; 2004b; and many others). In the remainder of this section, I will synthesize some of this research by describing "Seven Things That African American Students Need from Their Teachers."

1.   African American Students Need Teachers Who Have The "Mrs. Tessem Mind-set."

One of the clearest messages in the literature about Black students is that the relationships they have with their teachers can have either a positive or a negative effect on their academic achievement (Collins, 1992; Comer, 2004; Delpit, 1995; Foster & Peele, 1999; Gay, 2000; Gunn Morris & Morris, 2000; Ladson-Billings, 1994; Thompson, 2002b; 2004b; Wimberly, 2002). African American students equate good teaching with certain strategies and practices. In addition to making the curriculum interesting and comprehensible, however, "More than anything...successful teachers of African American students must possess a certain mind-set. Instead of expecting deficits, teachers must look for the innate talents and gifts that all African American students arrive at school with..." (Thompson, 2002b, p. 165). Furthermore, the students want relation-ships with their teachers that are "...built on trust, mutual respect, and a sincere desire to provide African American students with the best caliber of instruction that teachers can offer" (p. 165).

One of the main characteristics that Ladson-Billings (1994) identified in the eight exemplary teachers of African American students that she studied was their ability to form positive relationships with their students that extended beyond the classroom. These teachers treated students humanely, developed a "connectedness" with them, and encouraged students to build positive relationships with each other through collaborative learning and a sense of responsibility for each other. In short, they were able to create a psychologically safe, comfortable, and supportive learning community.

In my own work, I contrasted Mrs. Tessem, my sixth grade teacher, with my previous elementary teachers in order to illustrate the differences between an effective teacher of African American students and ineffective ones. The main difference between Mrs. Tessem and the others was her skill in developing positive relationships with her students—poor Black children from one of the city's worse communities. Her ability to develop these relationships began with her mind-set about her job and her students. This mind-set consisted of eight core beliefs: (1) African American students are capable of academic success; (2) It was her job to equip students with strong academic skills; (3) Having high expectations was in her students' best interest; (4) The curriculum must be culturally relevant; (5) It is necessary to identify students' strengths and build on those strengths; (6) Life skills should be incorporated into the curriculum through current events and class discussions; (7) Effective teachers teach the "whole child"; and (8) It was imperative that she develop a "college-going mind-set" in her students (Thompson, 2004b).

Like Marva Collins (1992) and some of the educators that Comer (2004) and Ladson-Billings (1994) described, Mrs. Tessem is a prototype that teachers who truly desire to increase their efficacy with Black students can emulate. She is also an example of what can happen when a teacher is able to develop positive relationships with African American students. As I said in *Through Ebony Eyes...*:

Any decent teacher can become successful with well-behaved and high-achieving students. Only the phenomenal teachers who possess the Mrs. Tessem mind-set can succeed with underachievers, students from challenging backgrounds, and those who are perceived as discipline problems. Becoming a phenomenal teacher is not easy, but it is an option that is available to all teachers (2004c, p. 131).

2. *African American Students Need Teachers Who Equip Them With the Academic Skills That are Prerequisites for Academic Success.*

Many years ago, several television news programs featured stories about George Dawson, who learned to read at a third grade level about five years before his death. Shockingly, because of limited schooling as a result of racism and poverty during his childhood, Dawson didn't learn to read until he was 98 years old. In *Life is So Good*, Dawson and educator Richard Glaubman (2001) chronicled his remarkable journey to become literate. Although on the surface, Dawson's heartwarming story appears to be unusual, a deeper look at the realities of the U.S. K-12 school system suggests that his story is not so unusual. Despite the fact that most African American children aren't prevented from attending school due to economic circumstances or racism, many are passed through the school system year after year, with such weak academic skills that it's possible for them to actually graduate from high school and still be functionally illiterate. In fact, it is well known that far too many students, particularly Blacks and Latinos, are passed through the school system with weak reading, writing, and math skills (National Center for Education Statistics, 2003; Thompson, 2004b; Thompson & Louque, 2005). Functional illiteracy has been correlated with prison incarceration rates, school dropout rates, and poverty during adulthood (Thompson, 2004b). Weak math skills can become one of the greatest barriers to college admission and future economic success (Drew, 1996), and having poor writing skills can not only prevent students from earning good grades in their K-postsecondary education (Delpit, 1995; Thompson, 2004b; Thompson & Louque, 2005), but it can also have a negative impact on their future success in the workforce (National Commission on Writing, 2005). Therefore, one of the most obvious ways that teachers can improve African American students' academic achievement is to ensure that they have the skills that are prerequisites for academic success: good reading, writing, and math skills (Cooper, 2003; Delpit, 1995; Ladson-Billings, 2002; Thompson, 2004b).

In *Through Ebony Eyes...*(Thompson, 2004b), I explained that one of the easiest ways for teachers to teach basic skills is through the Theory of Small Wins. "The basic premise is that if individuals are permitted to learn new information in small steps, there is a greater likelihood they will comprehend it, because their stress over learning new material is greatly reduced" (pp. 52–53).

Ladson-Billings (1994) referred to this as "scaffolding," which enables students "to build upon their own experiences, knowledge, and skills to move into more difficult knowledge and skills" (p. 124).

It is also important for teachers who desire to increase their efficacy with African American students to realize that they can't afford to be sidetracked by the reading wars (Delpit, 1995; Thompson, 2004b). Instead, they must be willing to combine the best instructional practices available to ensure that students can decode words fluently and comprehend what they read (Delpit, 1995; Thompson, 2004b). These teachers should be knowledgeable about "The 8 Pieces of the Reading Puzzle" (phonological awareness, phonics, spelling, fluency, language, knowledge, cognitive strategies, and reading a lot) that McEwan (2002) identified.

Moreover, for too long math has been one of the most difficult subjects for many African American students to master (Drew, 1996; Thompson, 2002b; 2003c; 2004b), and in some cases, math phobia has become a problem that is passed on generationally (Thompson, 2003c). In order to help African Americans learn math content, teachers must make the curriculum interesting and comprehensible, and they must be patient and use diverse teaching strategies (Drew, 1996; Thompson, 2002b; 2003c). Teachers who over-rely on the textbook and who primarily use lecturing or a mechanical style of teaching (Comer, 2004) are likely to be ineffective at teaching most students the math content. Cooperative learning groups and the belief that African American students can excel at math are crucial factors in improving their math achievement (Drew, 1996, Thompson, 2002c; 2003c).

Additionally, because so many African American students have been short-changed academically by underqualified teachers, it is imperative that their teachers possess good skills themselves and remain current with research pertaining to their fields. Ongoing professional development is one way that school leaders can ensure that teachers remain current and receive the support they need (Thompson, 2004b).

3. African American Students Need Teachers Who Teach Them How to Use Their Education for Personal Empowerment.

In "Achieving in Post-Civil Rights America..." Perry (2003) wrote poignantly about the historical value of literacy among African Americans and how before and after the slavery era, Blacks equated literacy with freedom. According to Perry, "For African Americans from slavery to the modern Civil Rights movement...you pursued learning because this is how you asserted yourself as a free person, how you claimed your humanity" (p. 11). Furthermore, racial uplift, liberation, and preparation for leadership were related to one's motives for becoming literate (Perry, 2003). Unfortunately, today, many African American youths are unaware of this rich legacy and many see school as a waste of time when other factors are competing for their attention (Comer, 2004). At the same time, many teachers exacerbate the situation by using ineffective methods (Comer, 2004; Thompson, 2004b).

Consequently, another obvious way that teachers can improve African American student achievement is to instill in them the message that "A good education can lead to personal empowerment."

Making this message an ongoing component of lesson plans is possibly the easiest way to convey it. Lessons about the short- and long-term payoffs of a good education can be beneficial. These lessons should include details about the benefits of earning good grades, such as good grades are necessary for promotion to the next grade level, grades should indicate that the student has prerequisite skills and knowledge to advance to the next level of his/her education, and that high school graduation is a major benefit. Students also need to know that a high school diploma is not only necessary for most basic, low-paying jobs, but it's a requirement for admission to four-year-postsecondary institutions. In addition to storytelling and mini lessons, teachers can use guest speakers, literature, and research projects to teach students about the benefits of a good education (Thompson, 2004b).

4. African American Students Need Teachers Who Make the Curriculum Culturally Relevant.

Like many researchers, I'm convinced that one of the primary reasons why countless African American students underachieve in school is because the curriculum and traditional instructional practices are not only disconnected from their lives, history, and culture, but the curriculum also tends to portray a very one-sided portrait of African Americans (Delpit, 1995; Gay, 2000; Ladson-Billings, 1994; Thompson, 2003c; 2004b). According to the standard fodder that most students get in K-12 schools, "African Americans were slaves. Lincoln freed them, and then Martin Luther King and Rosa Parks sparked the Civil Rights movement." In general, that is basically what all students, not just African Americans, learn about Black history through the traditional K-12 curriculum (Thompson, 2004b). For this reason, it is little wonder that so many African American students become disillusioned with the school curriculum.

The theory of cultural discontinuity posits that the school culture is very different from traditional Black culture. In fact, the gulf between the school culture and traditional Black culture has historically been so wide that Hale (1986) maintained that for African American children, going to school for the first time is similar to visiting a foreign land. As a result, for more than a decade, researchers who challenge the exclusion and Euro-centrism that dominate the standard school curriculum have urged educators to make the curriculum culturally relevant (Corwin, 2001; Delpit, 1995; Gay, 2000; Ladson-Billings, 1994; Thompson, 2002b, 2003c, 2004b).

Delpit (1995), Ladson-Billings (1994), and Gay (2000) are just a few of the many scholars who have not only stressed the importance of a culturally relevant curriculum but have helped to define it as well. According to Ladson-Billings (1994), when culturally relevant teaching occurs, student achievement improves, students become socio-politically conscious, and they become culturally competent in their home culture. Using appropriate multi-cultural materials (Gay, 2000, Thompson, 2004b), connecting school and home experiences, emphasizing the legitimacy and value of each culture, and using diverse teaching strategies are some of the ways that teachers can make the curriculum culturally relevant (Gay, 2000).

5. African American Students Need Teachers Who Have Good Classroom Management Skills.

Researchers have repeatedly found that many teachers are more likely to perceive Black students as discipline problems at school than other students (CNN, 2003; Ferguson, 2001; Hale, 2001; Skiba & Peterson, 1999; Thompson, 2002b; 2003c; 2004b) Consequently, African Americans are disproportionately repre-sented among the students who are suspended and expelled from school (Skiba & Peterson, 1999; Thompson, 2002b; 2003c; 2004b). Researchers have also found that many teachers have weak classroom management skills (Delpit, 1995; Thompson, 2004b), and this may actually lead to student misbehavior. Classroom management is obviously linked to student achievement because if students are out of control, a teacher is unable to teach (Thompson, 2004b). Therefore, one way that teachers can increase the likelihood that African American students will be able to achieve their maximum potential in class is to ensure that teachers have good classroom management skills (Thompson, 2004b). In other words, as Ladson-Billings (1994) stressed, "The focus of the classroom must be instructional...the primary enterprise must be to teach" (p. 124).

Many African American students and parents equate seven practices with effective classroom management. Some of these practices have also been cited by other researchers, including Cooper (2003), Delpit (1995), Ferguson (2001),

Hale (2001), and Ladson-Billings (1994). African American students and parents believe that an effective classroom management system must be built (1) on fairness: Teachers must not punish African American students for behavior that they ignore in other students; (2) Teachers must have a positive attitude about African American students. "Teachers who expect African American students to be problematic will find that their beliefs may become a self-fulfilling prophecy" (Thompson, 2004b, p. 99); (3) Teachers must also be explicit and consistent. Wise teachers explain their class rules to both students and parents at the beginning of the school year to prevent misunderstandings; (4) Students also need effective instruction and a good curriculum. (5) Teachers should also focus on teaching and not be preoccupied with discipline. A classroom should not be run like a prison, and students shouldn't be expected to act like criminals. When teachers *look* for trouble, it can become a self-fulfilling prophecy (Ferguson, 2001); (6) Firmness rather than meanness is also needed. Teachers must be authoritative in a way that requires students to treat the teacher and other students respectfully but that is also respectful of students (Cooper, 2003; Delpit, 1995; Thompson, 2004b); and (7) Teachers must be patient with struggling students who may not learn subject matter as quickly as others. Impatience can create discipline problems when struggling students infer that the teacher is unwilling to give them the help they need (Thompson, 2002b; 2003c; 2004b). These simple strategies can enable any teacher to improve student achievement by having an orderly classroom in which learning is the main priority.

6. African American Students Need Teachers Who Develop a College-Going Mind-set in Students.

I once heard an African American Baptist pastor say that people often criticized him about his insistence that his three sons would eventually attend college. When asked, "But what if they don't want to go to college?" or "What if they aren't 'college material'?" the pastor would reply, "All of them are going and all of my children are college material."

This father's strong determination to see his sons attend college is similar to a dream shared by many Black parents and students. The majority of African American high school seniors whom I interviewed wanted to attend college when they graduated, and 92 percent of the African American parents who participated in another study that I conducted wanted their children to attend college. In another study, the U.S. Department of Education (2003) reported that 94 percent of the Black students planned to attend college and 96 percent of the Black parents expected their children to attend college. Wimberly (2002) also found that nearly 90 percent of the African American students planned to attend college. However, this dream of attending college is often thwarted for African American students by school factors within and outside of the classroom (Thompson, 2002b; 2003c; Wimberly, 2002). Therefore, an obvious way that educators can improve student achievement is to not only eradicate these barriers to college attendance but to also instill a college-going mind-set in African American students.

A primary barrier to attending college for African American students comes from school counselors. In many schools, African American students are less likely than others to receive the advisement they need from counselors regarding how to navigate the college admission process, or to be placed in college preparatory and advanced placement courses. For African American students whose parents never attended college, school counselors can be instrumental in helping them attain the goal of college admission (Thompson, 2002b; 2003c).

Another set of barriers are created in the classroom. One major obstacle stems from the sorting and tracking that is prevalent in the public school system (Ferguson, 2001; Hale, 2001; Oakes, 1999; Thompson, 2002b; 2004a). As early as kindergarten and first grade, educators begin to place labels on students and make assumptions about them that have long-term consequences (Hale, 2001; Thompson, 2002b). Consequently, Black students are disproportionately represented among special education students, underrepresented in Gifted and Talented Education Programs (Ford, 1995), and are more likely to be labeled as discipline problems than their peers.

Another barrier that arises in the classroom is that many teachers have low expectations of Black students (Delpit, 1995; Ladson-Billings, 2002; Thompson, 2004a; 2004b; Thompson & Louque, 2005). Low expectations can lead to students' receiving a substandard education that fails to prepare them for college. In the end, Black students who desire to attend college may not have the necessary reading, writing, or math skills that they need (Education Trust-West, 2004). This results in a high percentage of students of color being forced to attend community colleges rather than four-year postsecondary institutions, or students being placed in remedial classes at four-year institutions.

A third barrier that arises in the classroom is that many African American students are inadequately prepared to do well on standardized tests and college admission exams, such as the SAT and ACT (Corwin, 2001). In a study that I conducted at an underperforming high school, I learned that the majority of the participants—nearly 300 White, Latino, and African American students— believed that their teachers had failed to adequately prepare them for the required standardized tests (Thompson, 2007).

Clearly, one way that educators can eradicate these barriers is to develop a college-going mind-set in their students from elementary school onward. This would require teachers to adopt the mind-set that "All students have potential, all students deserve a college education, and it is not my job to decide who goes to college and who doesn't." Developing this college-going mind-set would also require teachers to have high expectations, be willing to give extra help to struggling students, discuss college with them on a regular basis, explain the benefits of college attendance to students, and provide adequate preparation for required standardized tests and college admission exams. Counselors would also have to do their part by providing accurate and consistent advisement to students about college, and by ensuring that students are placed in the proper courses. Finally, the culture of high expectations that is the hallmark of high-performing, high-poverty schools must permeate the entire school through a tone set by leaders and teachers. When all students—even those who may not plan to attend college—are exposed to a college preparatory curriculum, achievement increases and students are better prepared for success in college (Education Trust-West, 2004). As Carter stated, "…great schools make college the goal" (2000, p. 9).

7. African American Students Need Teachers Who Focus on the "Alterable Variables."

In underperforming schools throughout the nation, particularly predominantly Black, Latino, and low-income schools, there is at least one place on campus where the negative teachers congregate. It may be another teacher's classroom, the teachers' lounge, or some other place. Regardless of its location, the intent of the congregants is the same: They go to this place to complain and to listen to the complaints of their like-minded colleagues. In these "complaint rooms," teachers routinely criticize parents, students, and the community in which the school is located. One way that teachers can increase their own efficacy, and improve student achievement is to avoid these places. Instead, they can choose to focus on the "alterable variables" rather than on the "inalterable" ones.

In *Teach Them All to Read: Catching the Kids Who Fall Through the Cracks*, Elaine K. McEwan (2002), a former school principal and a reading expert, described the ingredients that are necessary to create a school culture that promotes reading achievement for all students. Among the "12 Traits of A Pervasive and Persuasive Reading Culture" that McEwan cited are strong instructional leadership by administrators and teachers; high expectations and accountability for students, teachers, and parents; comprehensive student assessment; the integration and coordination of special services for students with special needs; wise use of instructional time; ongoing staff development; and constant communication and coordination among teachers regarding curriculum and instruction. But McEwan also spoke extensively about the mind-set that educators must have in order to promote a high-achieving-reading culture in schools. This mind-set requires educators to "Focus on the alterable variables," a term McEwan attributed to Benjamin Bloom's work more than two decades ago. Concentrating on the alterable variables requires educators to pay attention to what is within their control rather than focusing on circumstances outside of their control. As a principal, when McEwan convinced her staff to adopt this attitude, student achievement improved and the entire school climate became more positive.

In his review of research on the causes of the achievement gap, Barton (2004) identified fourteen factors that were correlated to achievement. Eight of the factors (birth weight, lead poisoning, poor nutrition, being read to by a parent or caretaker, the amount of time children spent watching television, whether or not children lived in a two-parent home, student mobility, and parent participation in their children's education) were labeled as "Before and Beyond School" factors. Six factors (school safety, technology-assisted instruction, class size, teacher preparation, teacher experience and attendance, and the rigor of the curriculum) were labeled as "In School" factors. Because African American students are disproportionately represented among the children living in poverty in the U.S.

(U.S. Census Bureau, 2001), they are more likely than students from higher socioeconomic backgrounds to experience negative "Before and Beyond School" factors, a fact that may overwhelm many teachers. In spite of this, research has consistently shown that the quality of teaching and the curriculum that students receive, and what happens in the classroom are more important determinants of student achievement than other factors. Therefore, it would behoove educators, particularly teachers, to focus on what is within their power to change. The rigor of the curriculum, the amount of technology-assisted instruction that is available to students, teacher attendance, and how well prepared teachers are to deliver lesson plans are totally within each individual teacher's control. The other factors, class size, school safety, and the hiring of experienced and qualified teachers are factors that school leaders can control. Educators who sincerely want to improve African American student achievement will focus on these alterable variables and not waste time complaining about the factors they can't control, or indulging in the "blame game" (Comer, 2004; Thompson, 2004b; Thompson, Warren, & Carter, 2004). Moreover, educators who want to be proactive in trying to address some of the "Before and Beyond School" factors can at the very least provide parents with information and strategies to assist their children academically at home.

9.4. Conclusion

The literature on African American student achievement is clear in emphasizing that in order for true reform to occur in underperforming schools, systemic change is needed. Strong leaders who are able to improve the entire school culture are crucial, and changing the culture requires an inclusiveness that welcomes the voices and contributions of all members of the school community, especially African American parents and students, two groups who have historically been ignored and marginalized. It also entails the creation of "a culture of achievement" in which high expectations and preparation for college are the norms.

According to Carter (2000) "Improving the quality of instruction is the only way to improve overall student achievement" (p. 9). However, the quality of instruction can only improve and systemic change can only occur when school leaders and teachers receive ongoing, consistent, and thorough professional development (Guild, 2002; Thompson, 2004b). This will require educators to examine and address their own beliefs, attitudes, and behaviors that might impede student achievement. Furthermore, the professional development should also familiarize educators with current research and strategies, and provide support to increase their efficacy. Landsman (2004) recommended that educators meet regularly to discuss diverse cultures and related books. I urge educators to follow a "Three-Part, Long-Term Professional Development Plan" that each individual teacher can complete in the privacy of his/her home through reading, journal writing, and the creation and implementation of an action plan to improve African American student achievement (Thompson, 2004b). The bottom line is that school reform can't occur unless educators continue to grow professionally. Participating in ongoing professional development for school leaders and teachers is one way of ensuring that this growth occurs, as the following story illustrates.

9.5. A Final Story

In June 2005, I had a heartwarming telephone conversation with one of the most positive and enthusiastic school leaders I've ever spoken with. This woman, an African American principal at a predominantly Black Los Angeles elementary school, who referred to herself as "a missionary," made professional development a top priority at her school. "I'm on a mission," she said excitedly. "I've been at job level, but now I'm at mission level. I think we're a good school {but} we're on the verge of becoming a great school."

Most people would be surprised to learn that her school is located in a community that has one of the city's highest crime rates, highest unemployment rates, and highest concentration of children living in foster care. Nevertheless, these inalterable variables don't deter this principal from her dream of making her school a place "...where we truly are educating African American children, where we're doing it right." During the two years that she has served as principal of this particular school, her comprehensive school-improvement plan has included providing teachers with the resources and support they need, and ensuring that they have the correct mind-set about African American students. "The bottom line is my expectation is 'Children first.' I expect teachers to do their best...and I remind them 'Teaching is a service profession and you choose to be of service to children and communities.'" She went on to say, "What I tell teachers is 'To be at my school, you have to be more than a teacher. At times, on the same day, you'll have to be a social worker, a mom, a dad, and a big brother.'" When she meets resistance from teachers who are unwilling to accept this mission, the principal encourages them to find a job elsewhere.

In addition to mentoring teachers, she also makes her own and her teachers' professional development a top priority each year. Although she has served as a principal at various schools for six years and a vice principal for seven years, she is dedicated to continuing her own professional growth by keeping abreast of the most recent literature about African American student achievement. She also seeks to do this for her teachers. Each fall, she motivates them to attend professional development workshops and presentations for which they can earn extra pay, and each summer, she purchases a book for each teacher to read. "I'm going to keep giving {my teachers} what the experts are saying," she remarked.

9.6. Recommendations

I'll conclude this chapter with five recommendations. These recommendations can help school leaders, teachers, and policy makers improve the schooling experiences of African Americans and other students in underperforming schools.

First, the blind can't lead the blind. Like the aforementioned exemplary school leader, improving student achievement requires school leaders to set the appropriate tone and practice what they preach through their own ongoing professional development. The result should be the creation of a learning community that rests on a foundation of high expectations, inclusiveness of historically marginalized groups, and ongoing teacher support at the school site through professional development. When this becomes the norm rather than the exception in America's K-12 public schools, the achievement gap, undoubtedly, will be eradicated and true school reform will occur.

Second, in order for the systemic reform that is necessary to occur, school leaders and teachers also need the support of policy makers, social service organizations, and parents. In many inner cities throughout the nation, parents are overwhelmed by problems, such as unemployment, high crime rates, and other poverty-related issues. Until policy makers make a conscious effort to address the problems plaguing inner cities, many parents will be incapable of devoting more time to their children's education. Moreover, in communities in which jobs are scarce, it is often difficult for adolescents and their parents to truly believe that education can improve their economic circumstances. Therefore, policy makers must make the revitalization of inner cities a national priority. In addition to becoming more equitable in the distribution of small business loans and bringing jobs to inner cities, this would include improving the substandard conditions that are common in many inner-city schools. Adequate funding is necessary for ongoing professional development for school leaders and teachers, as well as funding to improve the infrastructures of dilapidated schools, funding for textbooks, science labs, classroom libraries, and a professional development library for teachers and parents. This library should contain educational journals and books that describe practical reading, writing, math, and classroom management strategies that parents and teachers can check out.

Third, another area that policy makers should continue to focus on relates to the quality of educators in schools. The widespread practice of staffing inner-city schools with anyone who is available must cease. Policy makers must not only give "lip service" to the notion of ensuring that every child has a qualified teacher; they must also enforce this policy and expand it to ensure that every school also has a qualified principal.

Fourth, policy makers must also re-examine the No Child Left Behind Act to determine if the high-stakes testing movement will truly produce the types of students that this nation needs. Like many other scholars, I believe that multiple types of assessments should be used to evaluate students. The ongoing national controversy over the NCLB Act should encourage policy makers to review the pros and cons of high-stakes testing and determine if it will actually result in true school reform, especially for underperforming schools.

Fifth, as Comer's work (2004) in inner-city schools has shown, when social service agencies become more connected with schools, there is a greater likelihood that basic human needs that can serve as impediments to academic achievement will be met. Because of the myriad problems in inner cities, each school should have trained therapists on site who can work with troubled children and their families. Parenting classes and workshops on specific ways that parents can assist their children academically should be available. A holistic child development approach like Comer's School Development Plan, could alleviate many problems that contribute to academic failure. Once again, this would require adequate funding for social service organizations in poor communities. More organizations are needed and additional personnel are needed.

The bottom line is that there is a lot more that can be done at the national, state, and local levels to improve underperforming schools. These schools are more likely to be attended by three of the most marginalized groups in the U.S. –poor children, Latinos, and African Americans. Actions speak louder than words. As long as our nation's leaders continue to merely *talk* about school reform and improving social conditions, America will remain a nation of "haves" and "have nots," and a nation that proclaims equality and justice for all while practicing a pernicious caste system in which some groups are treated like stepchildren and others are treated like royalty. Poor achievement will remain prevalent in predominantly Black, predominantly Latino, and predominantly low-income schools as long as the underlying issues that contribute to inequality of educational opportunity fail to become a national priority.

References

Aronson, J. (2004). The threat of stereotype: To close the achievement gap, we must address negative stereotypes that suppress student achievement. *Educational Leadership*, November, pp. 14–19.

Barton, P.E. (2004). Why does the gap persist: Researches 14 factors to student achievement and low-income and minority children are at a disadvantage in almost all of them. *Educational Leadership*, November, pp. 8–13.

Boykin, A.W. (2002). Talent development, cultural deep structure, and school reform: Implications for African immersion initiatives. In Denbo, S.J. & Moore Beaulieu, L. (eds) *Improving Schools for African American Students: A Reader for Educational Leaders*. Springfield, IL: Charles C. Thomas Publisher Ltd, pp. 81–94.

Carter, C.S. (2000). *No Excuses: Lessons From 21 High-Performing, High-Poverty Schools*. Washington DC: The Heritage Foundation.

CNN (January 13, 2003). *White Teachers Fleeing Black Schools*. www.CNN.com/EducationMonday.

Collins, M. (1992). *Ordinary Children, Extraordinary Teachers*. Charlottesville, VA: Hampton Roads Publishing Company, Inc.

Comer, J.P. (2004). *Leave No Child Behind: Preparing Today's Youth for Tomorrow's World*. New Haven, CT: Yale University Press.

Cooper, P.M. (2003). Effective white teachers of black children: Teaching within a community. *Journal of Teacher Education*, 54(5), 413–427.

Corwin, M. (2001). *And Still We Rise: The Trials and Triumphs of Twelve Gifted Inner City Students*. New York: HarperCollins.

Council of Chief State School Officers. (2002). *Expecting Success: A Study of Five High Performing, High Poverty Schools. www.ccsso.org*. Retrieved June 5, 2005.

Dawson, G. & Glaubman, R. (2001). *Life Is So Good*. New York: Penguin USA.

Delpit, L. (1995). *Other People's Children: Cultural Conflict in the Classroom.* New York: The New Press.

Denbo, S.J. (2002). Institutional practices that support African American student achievement. In Denbo, S.J. & Moore Beaulieu, L. (eds). *Improving Schools for African American Students: A Reader for Educational Leaders.* Springfield, IL: Charles C. Thomas Publisher Ltd, pp. 55–71.

Denbo, S.J. & Moore Beaulieu, L. (eds). (2002). *Improving Schools for African American Students: A Reader for Educational Leaders.* Springfield, IL: Charles C. Thomas Publisher, LTD.

Drew, D.E. (1996). *Aptitude Revisited: Rethinking Math and Science Education for America's Next Century.* Baltimore: The Johns Hopkins University Press.

Education Trust-West. (2004). The A-G curriculum: College-prep? Work-prep? *Life-Prep.* Oakland, CA: Education Trust-West.

Ferguson, A.A. (2001). Bad boys: Public schools in the making of Black masculinity. *Ann Arbor,* MI: The University of Michigan Press.

Fink, E. & Resnick, L.B. (2001). Developing principals as instructional leaders. *Phi Delta Kappan,* April, 598–606.

Ford, D. (1995). Desegregating gifted education: A need unmet. *Journal of Negro Education,* 64(1), 53–62.

Foster, M. (1998). *Black Teachers On Teaching.* New York: New Press.

Foster, M. & Peele, T.B. (1999). Teaching Black males: Lessons from the experts. In Polite, V.C. & Davis, J.E. (eds) *African American Males in School and Society: Practices and Policies for Effective Education.* New York: Teachers College Press, pp. 8–19.

Gay, G. (2000). *Culturally Responsive Teaching: Theory, Research, and Practice.* New York: Teachers College Press.

Gould, S.J. (1981). *The Mismeasure of Man.* New York: Norton.

Guild, P.B. (2002). An educational leader's guide to culture and learning style. In Denbo, S.J. & Moore Beaulieu, L. (eds). *Improving Schools for African American Students: A Reader for Educational Leaders.* Springfield, IL: Charles C. Thomas Publisher Ltd, pp. 103–113.

Gunn Morris, V. & Morris, C.L. (2000). *Creating Caring and Nurturing Educational Environments for African American Children.* Westport, CT: Bergin and Garvey.

Hale, J.E. (1986). *Black Children: Their Roots, Culture, and Learning Styles.* (Rev. ed.). Baltimore: The Johns Hopkins University Press.

Hale, J.E. (2001). *Learning While Black: Creating Educational Excellence for African American Children.* Baltimore: The Johns Hopkins University Press.

Kunjufu, J. (1985). *Countering the Conspiracy to Destroy Black Boys.* Chicago: African American Images.

Ladson-Billings, G. (1994). *The Dreamkeepers: Successful Teachers of African American Children.* San Francisco: Jossey-Bass.

Ladson-Billings, G. (2001). *Crossing Over to Canaan: The Journey of New Teachers in Diverse Classrooms.* San Francisco: Jossey-Bass.

Ladson-Billings, G. (2002). I ain't writin' nuttin': Permissions to fail and demands to succeed in urban classrooms. In Delpit, L. & Kilgour Dowdy, J. (eds). *The Skin That We Speak: Thoughts On Language and Culture in the Classroom.* New York: The New Press, pp. 109–120.

Landsman, J. (2004). Confronting the racism of low expectations: Racism in educators' attitudes—and in how students are placed in advanced classes—still robs minority students of chances for success. *Educational Leadership,* November, 28–32.

Leighton, M.S. (1996). *The Role of Leadership in Sustaining School Reform: Voices From the Field.* Washington, DC: U.S. Department of Education.

McEwan, E.K. (2002). *Teach Them All to Read: Catching the Kids Who Fall Through the Cracks.* Thousand Oaks, CA: Corwin Press, Inc.

National Center for Education Statistics (2003). http://nces.ed.gov/nationsreportcard. Retrieved June 28, 2005.

National Commission on Writing for America's Families, Schools, and Colleges (2005). *A Powerful Message From State Government. www.writingcommission.org.* Retrieved July 5, 2005.

Oakes, J. (1999). Limiting students' school success and life chances: The impact of tracking. In Ornstein, A.C. & Behar-Horenstein, L.S. (eds) *Contemporary Issues in Curriculum* (2nd edn). Needham Heights, MA: Allyn & Bacon, pp. 224–237.

Perry, T. (2003). Achieving in post-civil rights America: The outline of a theory. In Perry, T., Steele, C., & Hilliard, A.G. III (eds) *Young, Gifted, and Black: Promoting High Achievement among African American Students.* Boston: Beacon Press, pp. 87–108.

Perry, T., Steele, C., & Hilliard, A.G. III (2003). *Young, Gifted, and Black: Promoting High Achievement Among African American Students.* Boston: Beacon Press.

Reitzug, U.C. & Patterson, J. (1998). I'm not going to lose you! Empowerment through caring in an urban principal's practice with students. *Urban Education,* 33(2), 150–181.

Simon, W.E. Jr & Izumi, L. (April 23, 2003). *High-Poverty but High-Performing Schools Offer Proof That Minority Students From Poor Families Can Thrive.* Orange County Register online *www.pacificresearch.org.* Retrieved June 7, 2005.

Skiba, R. & Peterson, R. (1999). The dark side of zero tolerance: Can punishment lead to safe schools? *Phi Delta Kappan* online. *www.pdkintl.org/kappan/kski9901.htm.*

Thompson, G. (2002a). *African American Students in Schools: Research and Effective Instructional Practices: Introduction to a Themed Issue of Educational Horizons.* Spring, pp. 105–108.

Thompson, G.L. (2002b). *African American Teens Discuss Their Schooling Experiences.* Westport, CT: Bergin & Garvey.

Thompson, G. (2002c). Teachers' cultural ignorance imperils student success. *USA Today,* May, 29, 13A.

Thompson, G.L. (2003a). No parent left behind: Strengthening ties between educators and African American parents. *Urban Review,* 35(1), 7–23.

Thompson, G. (2003b). Predicting African American parents' and guardians' satisfaction with teachers and public schools. *Journal of Educational Research.* May/June 96(5), 277–285.

Thompson, G.L. (2003c). *What African American Parents Want Educators to Know.* Westport, CT: Praeger.

Thompson, G.L. (2004a). Home to school to work transitions for African Americans: Eliminating barriers to success. In Halpern, D. (ed.) *Changing the Metaphor: From Work-Family Balance to Work-Family Interaction.* Malwah, NJ: Lawrence Erlbaum Publishers, pp. 117–133.

Thompson, G.L. (2004b). *Through Ebony Eyes: What Teachers Need to Know But Are Afraid to Ask About African American Students.* San Francisco: Jossey Bass.

Thompson, G., Warren, S., & Carter, L. (2004). It's not my fault: Predicting high school teachers who blame parents and students for students' low achievement. *The High School Journal* 87(3), 5–14.

Thompson, G.L. & Louque, A.C. (2005). *Exposing the Culture of Arrogance in the Academy: A Blueprint for Increasing Black Faculty Satisfaction in Higher Education*. Sterling, VA: Stylus Publishing.

Thompson, G.L. (2007). *Up Where We Belong: Helping African American and Latino Students Rise in School and in Life*. San Francisco: Jossey Bass.

Tirozzi, G.N. (2001). The artistry of leadership: The evolving role of the secondary school principal. *Phi Delta Kappan*, February, 434–439.

U.S. Census Bureau. (2001). *Statistical Abstract of the United States*. www.census.gov/hhes/www/img/incpov01/fig08.jpg

U.S. Department of Education. (2000). *Eliminating Barriers to Improving Teaching*. Washington, DC: U.S. Department of Education.

U. S. Department of Education (2001). *No Child Left Behind*. Washington, DC: Office of the Secretary.

U. S. Department of Education (2003). *Getting Ready to Pay For College: What Students and Their Parents Know About the Cost of College Tuition and What They Are Doing To Find Out*. Washington, DC: Institute of Education Sciences.

Wimberly, G. (2002). *School relationships foster success for African American students: ACT Policy Report*. Iowa City, Iowa.

Yau, R. (2002). High-achieving elementary schools with large percentages of low-income African American students: A review and critique of the current research. In Denbo, S.J. & Moore Beaulieu, L. (eds). *Improving Schools For African American Students: A Reader For Educational Leaders*. Springfield, IL: Charles C. Thomas Publisher Ltd, pp. 193–217.

10
The Truth and Myth of the Model Minority: The Case of Hmong Americans

Stacey J. Lee

Asian Americans are one of the fastest growing groups in the United States, and the Asian American category represents tremendous diversity (Reeves & Bennett, 2003). Individuals classified as Asian American come from different ethnic, linguistic, social class, religious, and generational backgrounds. Despite the growth of Asian America and the diversity of the Asian American population, many educators and educational policymakers know little about Asian American students and often rely on stereotypic representations of Asian American students as "model minorities." According to the model minority stereotype, Asian Americans are academically and economically successful because they work hard and follow Asian cultural norms that emphasize the importance of education. Asian American students are depicted as valedictorians, violin prodigies, and computer geniuses.

While aggregate data on Asian American students appear to confirm the model minority image, when data is disaggregated by ethnicity a more complicated picture appears. Although there are Asian American students who are highly successful, the model minority stereotype hides variation in academic and economic achievement across ethnic groups and among individuals. With respect to economic status, some Asian Americans have achieved professional success while others struggle to survive economically. In terms of education, some Asian American groups have higher levels of educational attainment than the national average while other Asian American groups have significantly lower levels of educational attainment than the national average.

The model minority stereotype has a significant impact on how educational policy makers view Asian American students. It influences what they do and do not do to support Asian American students. Assumptions regarding the academic success of Asian Americans that are often confirmed by aggregate data, lead policy makers to ignore the specific needs and concerns of Asian American students (Pang, Kiang, & Pak, 2003). Teachers and other education professionals in schools also commonly evaluate Asian American students according to the standards of the model minority. Students able to live up to the standards are held up as examples for others to follow, and those unable to meet them are deemed failures or substandard for their race (Lee, 1996).

This chapter will highlight the variation in educational achievement and attainment across various Asian American ethnic groups. The central focus will be on the educational experiences of the Hmong, a Southeast Asian ethnic group that has experienced considerable difficulty in U.S. schools. Particular attention will be paid to the cultural and structural barriers that Hmong American students face in their pursuit of education. Furthermore, the paper will reveal the way the model minority stereotype negatively affects Asian American students who struggle in school. Finally, the chapter will conclude with a discussion regarding implications and recommendations for policy and practice.

10.1. Beyond Aggregate Data

As noted earlier, the assumptions regarding the model minority achievement of Asian Americans are based on aggregate data. When data on Asian Americans are disaggregated by ethnic groups, however, the differences among Asian Americans are quite apparent. An examination of disaggregated data reveals that the experiences of some Asian American groups directly challenge the model minority stereotype. Census 2000 data, for example, reveal that 53.3% of Cambodians, 59.6% of Hmong, 49.6% of Lao, and 38.1% of Vietnamese over 25 years of age have less than a high school education. By contrast, 13.3% of Asian Indians, 12.7% of Filipinos, 8.9% of Japanese, and 13.7% of Koreans over 25 years of age have less than a high school education (Reeves & Bennett, 2004).

Educational attainment and achievement appear to be closely related to social class. Although the model minority stereotype characterizes Asian Americans as economically successful, the reality is far more complex. For example, Asian Americans and Pacific Islanders are more likely than whites to have incomes of $75,000 or more, but they are also more likely than whites to have incomes below $25,000 (Reeves & Bennett, 2003). Asian American ethnic groups with high rates of poverty experience low rates of educational attainment, and those with high levels of educational attainment have high median incomes.

Asian Indians have the highest levels of economic and educational attainment among Asian American ethnic groups. Nearly 64% of Asian Indians over 25 have earned a bachelor's degree. In 1999 Asian Indian families had a median income of $70,849, compared to a median income of $50,046 for all families in the US (Reeves & Bennett, 2004). The economic and educational successes of Asian Indians are due in part to the fact that the majority of post-1965 Indian immigrants were highly educated professionals (Zhou, 2004). Many Indian immigrants also arrived in the United States fluent in English, a fact that made their transition to life in the United States easier. In short, many Asian Indians arrived in the United States with substantial human capital that they could translate into mainstream success.

According to 2000 Census data, Korean Americans are another relatively successful Asian American group. Only 13.7% of Korean Americans over 25 have less than a high school education, and 43.8% of Korean Americans over 25 have a bachelor's degree or more (Reeves & Bennett, 2004). Like many Asian Indians, many of the Korean immigrants who came to the U.S. between 1965 and 1972 were well-educated professionals. Although there are many Korean students who are academically successful, there is some growing evidence that low-income Korean youth are struggling in our schools (Lew, 2003).

While educational attainment among East Asian (e.g., Chinese, Korean, Japanese) and South Asian groups (e.g., Indian, Pakistani) is high, educational attainment among Pacific Islanders (e.g., Hawaiian) and Southeast Asian groups (e.g., Cambodian, Hmong, Lao, Vietnamese) is relatively low. According to the 2000 Census, only 13.8% of Native Hawaiians and other Pacific Islanders have bachelor's degrees (Ro, 2002). Not insignificantly, 17.7% of Native Hawaiians and other Pacific Islanders lived under the poverty line, compared to 12.4% of the U.S. population overall. Compared to other major ethnic groups in Hawaii, Native Hawaiian students have the lowest graduation rates and are overrepresented in special education. Native Hawaiian students' scores on standardized tests are below national norms (Tibbets, 1999).

Southeast Asians experience high rates of poverty (e.g., 29.3% of Cambodians, 37.8% of Hmong, 18.5% of Lao), and relatively low rates of educational attainment (Reeves & Bennett, 2004). Although there is considerable variation in the levels of educational attainment and achievement among Southeast Asian Americans, the percentage of Southeast Asian Americans that have earned a bachelor's degree is lower than the percentage for Black, Hispanic and American Indian/Alaskan Native adults. For example, the percentage of Blacks over 25 that have earned a bachelor's degree or more is 14% (McKinnon & Bennett, 2005). Vietnamese American students are the most successful of the Southeast Asian groups. According to 2000 Census data, 9.4% of Vietnamese American adults over 25 have a bachelor's degree or more. Hmong Americans have the lowest levels of educational attainment among the Southeast Asians. According to 2000 Census data, 59.6% of Hmong American adults over 25 have less than a high school education and only 7.5% of Hmong American adults over 25 have earned bachelor's degrees.

The educational problems faced by Southeast Asians and Pacific Islanders are masked by aggregate data that lumps all Asian Americans into one category. In their examination of the Massachusetts Comprehensive Assessment System (MCAS) data, for example, Pang, Kiang, & Pak (2003) reveal that aggregate data on Asian Americans hides the problems that some populations are having on the high stakes exam. Specifically, they discovered that school districts with high concentrations of Southeast Asian students had higher numbers of Asian American students who received failing scores on the MCAS than school districts with largely Chinese and South Asian populations (Pang, Kiang, & Pak, 2003).

10.2.   The Hmong Case

In the remainder of this chapter I will focus on the educational experiences of Hmong Americans. After a brief review of the early experiences of Hmong refugees, the paper will focus on the current state of Hmong American education. In discussing the current experiences of Hmong American students, I will draw primarily on my interview-based research on Hmong college women (Lee, 1997), and on my ethnographic research on Hmong American students at a high school in Wisconsin (Lee, 2001, 2005). My study on Hmong college women focused on the experiences of women who were among the first in their ethnic group to pursue four-year college degrees (Lee, 1997). This research highlighted the factors that contributed to their educational success and revealed the cultural and structural barriers they faced in their pursuit of education. My research on Hmong American high school students focused on how Hmong American students' experiences in school shaped their understandings of what it means to be Hmong in the United States (2001, 2002, 2005). Particular attention was paid to the way race and racism informed their identities. One of the central findings in this research involved the growing educational concerns faced by second-generation Hmong American youth.

10.2.1.   Background

The first Hmong came to the United States as refugees from Laos over 25 years ago. During the Vietnam War Hmong soldiers served as U.S. allies in the fight against communism in Laos. After the U.S. withdrew from Southeast Asia the Hmong in Laos were targets of persecution, and waves of Hmong refugees fled to Thailand, where they spent months and even years before being resettled. According to the 2000 Census, there are 186,310 people who identify as Hmong living in the United States. The largest Hmong American communities are in California (65,095), Minnesota (41,800) and Wisconsin (33,791).

Much of the early reports on Hmong refugees in the United States emphasized the cultural differences between the Hmong and mainstream Americans. Hmong culture was described rural, preliterate, patriarchal, traditional and even primitive. Both journalists and academics suggested that the Hmong were among the most culturally different group to come to the United States (Beck, 1994; Fass, 1991; Sherman, 1988). The Hmong were understood to be ill equipped to deal with life in a modern society such as the United States, and the high rates of poverty and low levels of educational attainment among early Hmong refugees were viewed to be the result of their culture.

Early research on the educational experiences of Hmong refugees pointed to the many problems faced by Hmong American students in K-12 education, including high dropout rates (Goldstein, 1985; Rumbaut & Ima, 1988). Cultural differences were identified as the primary barriers to Hmong educational achievement. In one early study on Hmong refugee students, Trueba, Jacobs, & Kirton (1990) found that the collaborative culture within Hmong communities clashed with the individualistic and competitive culture of U.S. schools. The fact that most early Hmong refugees were illiterate and had little familiarity with formal education also created problems for Hmong refugees. Furthermore, poverty and limited English language skills also posed serious barriers for Hmong students.

Hmong girls experienced particularly serious problems in school during the early years of resettlement. An emphasis on early marriage and motherhood led many girls to drop out of middle and high school. Although Hmong families encouraged their sons to pursue education, girls continued to gain status during this period through marriage and motherhood (Goldstein, 1985). In commenting on the academic difficulties faced by Hmong girls, Rumbaut and Ima (1988) pointed to the "patrilineal and patriarchal norms that tend to devalue females among the Hmong" (p. xiv).

The Hmong population continues to suffer from high rates of poverty and low rates of educational attainment. Like many immigrant and refugee populations, the Hmong community is young, with a median age of 16.1. Despite the troubles faced by the Hmong community in the United States, there is evidence that some Hmong are achieving upward mobility. According to the 2000 Census, Hmong Americans have made gains in educational attainment, household income and homeownership since the 1990 Census (Pfeifer & Lee, 2004). While 62% of Hmong families were below the poverty level in 1990, 34.8% of Hmong families were below the poverty level in 2000. In 2000, 38.74% lived in owner occupied housing, up from 13% in 1990. A growing number of Hmong men and women have gone on to pursue higher education (Fass, 1991; Lee, 1997; Ngo, 2000).

10.2.2. Signs of Progress

More recent research on Hmong American students suggests that a growing number of Hmong American students are doing well and even going on to pursue higher education. Today there are many Hmong American professionals including doctors, lawyers, teachers, pharmacists, professors, social workers and public officials. Economic conditions in the United States and the Hmong community's understandings of these conditions have led the Hmong to invest in education as a way to achieve social mobility like many other immigrant groups. That is, the community holds an instrumental understanding of education whereby education is understood to be a way to escape poverty and gain greater social status.

The Hmong community's commitment to education can be seen in the activities of Hmong organizations across the country. For example, there are numerous national and local Hmong organizations dedicated to promoting educational success among Hmong youth. There are two Hmong Charter Schools in the U.S., one in Milwaukee and one in Minneapolis. Both charter schools reflect the Hmong community's interest in providing their children with an education that sets high educational expectations and reflects their culture (Adler, 2004).

Girls and women have made particularly remarkable strides in their pursuit of education. Some Hmong American women are choosing to postpone marriage until after college and others who have followed more traditional marriage patterns are returning to school (Fass, 1991; Lee, 1997; Ngo, 2000). Although there are still more Hmong men who have completed higher educations than Hmong women, recent research shows that many in the Hmong community now believe that Hmong women are more successful in higher education than Hmong men (Vang, 2004). Vang writes, "The Hmong community's perception that Hmong women are becoming more successful than Hmong men in studying at college and obtaining higher education degrees is something that appears to be widely accepted" (p. 24).

In my research on Hmong college women I found that while the women faced cultural, economic and racial barriers in their pursuit of higher education they were convinced that education was necessary for life in the United States. Many of the women had grown up in poor families and they viewed education as the way to escape poverty. Like other immigrants and refugees, the Hmong women in my study had a folk theory of success that led them to believe that through hard work and an education they could achieve middle class status and other aspects of the American Dream (Ogbu, 1987). One Hmong college woman explained that she and her sister had always dreamed of going to school because they saw education as the route to economic success. She stated:

I mean, we knew that we want, like money. We wanted money, we wanted success in life and we knew that the only way we can get money or success is by education.

This same woman went on to explain,

Well, I guess, my family, we weren't too rich. We didn't have a lot of money. So, I mean, I want money. I want to be success — successful. And I wanted to support, like have enough money to have children and take care of them, too, you know. So I mean, well you in this society you really need money if you want to go anywhere. We knew that we can get money through you know, good education..." (Lee, 1997, p. 813).

In addition to economic motivations for pursuing education, the women in my study were motivated by a desire for increased independence in their relationships with men. They assumed that education would empower women to take control over their own lives. One Hmong woman, an undergraduate at a major university, asserted that education made women more confident:

Having a confidence too, that comes from being educated...I think that is what has allowed women to speak out more...And if, you know, a woman thinks that well, I've made it here in college and I'm doing well and I'm learning all these things and I have a lot more information and knowledge about that and I can speak out about those things whereas our mothers, they were never educated and they never had the opportunity to ever speak out because I think part of the reason was because they didn't have any confidence in what they were saying. And it was always the man who knew more...

Not insignificantly, this woman believed that her generation of women has more opportunities than her mother's generation, and they assume the increased opportunities that they have are related to life in the United States.

The strict gender roles placed on Hmong girls and women may be another factor in their academic success. As in other immigrant and refugee communities, Hmong girls and young women are more strictly controlled by their parents than boys and young men. While Hmong boys and young men are often allowed to spend time socializing with their peers after school, girls and young women are expected to go home and perform household chores and care for younger siblings. One college student suggested Hmong girls were used to working harder than Hmong boys because "Parents are more strict on the girls, and they allow the guys to go play more." Other women suggested that boys simply have more opportunities to "get into trouble." In her ethnographic study on Dominican, West Indian and Haitian youth, Lopez (2003) found a similar pattern of greater parental restrictions on girls than boys. Lopez concludes, "men's exemption from the adult responsibilities imposed on their female counterparts left them deprived of the emotional supports readily available to women" (p. 114). Based on my research on Hmong high school students, I would argue that the parental restrictions placed on Hmong girls both limit them and motivate them. Girls reported that their household chores often prevented them from spending enough time on their homework. Some girls, however, were motivated to work even harder in order to do well in school and escape gender inequality.

In general, Hmong girls and women possess a positive dual frame of reference whereby they compare their opportunities in the US with their opportunities in their native countries and conclude that life is better in the US (Ogbu, 1987). The Hmong girls and women in my two studies possessed positive dual frames of reference with regard to gender opportunities for women. That is, they believed that life in the US offers them greater gender equality than they would have in Thailand or Laos. In discussing the opportunities for Hmong women in the US, one woman remarked: "I think because Hmong women have never had the opportunity to speak out and do things ever before, that now that they have the opportunity to do so, they're taking full advantage of it." In particular, Hmong girls and women were optimistic about the role of education in providing them with greater gender equality when they got married. They assumed that education would bring them greater gender equality than their mother's experienced.

My research on Hmong American high school students suggests that schools also play a significant role in the success of Hmong girls (Lee, 2005). I observed that teachers were often willing to provide extra help to Hmong girls that they did not provide to Hmong boys. The teachers' perceptions of the subordinate position of women in Hmong culture appeared to influence their desire to help Hmong girls. Teachers were generally most concerned about Hmong girls who were relative newcomers to the United States because they saw them as being most vulnerable to traditional gender roles. In discussing the differences between Hmong girls and boys, one teacher remarked, "I think the girls have to grow up faster in terms of taking on home responsibilities. I think the workload is inequitable outside of school. And then this whole issue of, you know, who gets to decide when you marry, who you marry..." (Lee, 2005, p. 93). This teacher and others were motivated to provide Hmong girls, particularly newcomers, with extra assistance because they believed that education would allow the girls to lead more independent lives. The girls' faith in education and their optimistic view of life in the United States were confirmed by their positive relationships with teachers. In contrast to their generally sympathetic attitude towards Hmong girls, teachers were noticeably wary of Hmong boys and few teachers made efforts to connect with them.

In short, successful Hmong students have a positive dual frame of reference that makes them relatively optimistic about life in the U.S., and they have internalized a belief in the value of education. A growing number of Hmong girls and women, in particular, appear to be on track for educational success.

10.2.3. *Continuing Barriers to Success*

Although some Hmong students are doing well in school and even going on to pursue higher education, many continue to experience academic difficulties. Within Hmong communities across the country there is a growing concern regarding second-generation youth who are increasingly alienated from school (Thao, 1999). In my ethnographic research on Hmong American students at a high school in Wisconsin, teachers repeatedly told me that Hmong students were increasingly "at risk" for academic failure (Lee, 2001; 2005). Teachers and administrators pointed to what they perceived to be the alarming growth in the truancy among Hmong students as evidence of the problem. One of the Hmong bilingual resource specialists explained that there were significant differences between Hmong newcomers who were still learning English and adjusting to American culture and American born Hmong who were acculturated. She identified the newcomers who were in ESL as good kids and the American born kids as "bad" kids:

We don't have problems with those ESL kids. Because, they are, I don't know, they seem, maybe they're not Americanized or you know, so they are still,...let's say, good kids. So they are working hard and trying to graduate from UHS. The other problems, I think the problem that most of the Hmong students face are students who are in the mainstream – they are facing truancy. (Lee 2005, p. 52).

According to this bilingual resource specialist, many second-generation students had become "bad kids" and were having problems with truancy. She explained that "bad kids" could be identified by their "Americanized" clothes, specifically the baggy pants and oversized shirts associated with Hip Hop style. Similar to many scholars of immigration, the bilingual resource specialist linked Americanization, particularly the adoption of Hip Hop style, with negative attitudes about education.

Teachers' observations regarding the growing academic alienation among second-generation Hmong youth were largely accurate. Many second-generation youth adopted a Hip Hop style and exhibited oppositional attitudes towards school. Hmong boys, in particular, appeared to be questioning whether education was the most efficient way for them to achieve economic success. Through interviews with Hmong youth and observations of the youth inside and outside of classrooms, I discovered that Hmong American students faced significant barriers at the school and in the larger society that contributed to their alienation. That is, my ethnographic data challenges the teachers' belief that Americanization is the sole cause of the problems faced by second-generation Hmong students.

At the macro-level, poverty and racism negatively affected the way second-generation students viewed themselves and their future opportunities. As in the greater Hmong American community, many of the second-generation students in my study were from low-income families. Most lived in subsidized housing and received free and/or reduced price lunch. Although Hmong students who were relative newcomers to the U.S. were relatively optimistic about their ability to escape poverty, second-generation youth appeared to have internalized a belief that to be Hmong is to be poor. One student remarked, "All Hmong people are poor and live in shabby houses" (Lee, 2005, p. 71). Sadly, this student was not hopeful about escaping poverty. Second-generation students also complained that non-Hmong people looked down on Hmong culture, stereotyped Hmong people as lazy welfare recipients, and stereotyped Hmong youth as gang members. According to these students, White people were the most likely to stereotype Hmong people and consequently they viewed Whites, including teachers, with suspicion.

Inside of the school, second-generation students encountered teachers who, for the most part, knew little about Hmong students' backgrounds. With the exception of members of the ESL department, teachers knew little about how to work with second language students. Although most mainstream teachers knew little about their Hmong students, they were quick to point out that Hmong students were less successful than other Asian American students, particularly East Asian students. The differences in achievement between East and Southeast Asian students were understood to be the result of cultural or attitudinal differences. One guidance counselor, for example, commented that East Asian students were "more serious" about school than Southeast Asian students. He went on to say, "A lot of them are not intellectually motivated. These are the Southeast Asians I'm talking about now. They are polite, they're nice, they never tell me what, where to go and that sort of thing. I'm a counselor. But they don't have a background of working hard academically, and they don't feel like it now" (Lee, 2005, p. 45). As this quote demonstrates, East Asians were cast as model minorities and Southeast Asian students were understood to be somehow culturally deficient.

A significant number of second-generation Hmong students asserted that their teachers were racist and didn't care about them. While the Hmong students who were relative newcomers to this country were enrolled in the school's ESL program where they received academic, social and emotional support, the second-generation students were in mainstream classes where their educational needs were largely ignored. The chair of the ESL department, for example, reported that mainstream teachers regularly abdicated responsibility for their Hmong students by referring them back to ESL at the first sign of academic difficulty. According to the chair of the ESL department, most mainstream teachers assumed that it was the sole responsibility of the ESL department to serve all Hmong students, including those who were no longer in ESL. Her assertions were confirmed by my observations and through my conversations with mainstream teachers who regularly referred me to the ESL department whenever I asked them about Hmong students. Not insignificantly, the practice of referring Hmong students to the ESL department confirmed the Hmong students' suspicions that most teachers are racist and uncaring. Significantly, boys were more likely than girls to complain about their teachers and I would suggest that this was because teachers were more critical of Hmong boys, often stereotyping them as dangerous gang members.

The school's largely Eurocentric curriculum also alienated second-generation Hmong students. In interviews, students regularly asserted that they wanted to learn about Hmong culture and history. That is, students were asking for a culturally relevant pedagogy that reflected their experiences (Ladson-Billings, 1995). One second-generation Hmong student reported that she had tried to talk to teachers about starting a Hmong language class, but was told that there would not be enough interest. When I asked her what she thought about the school's response she noted that she knew that she and her friends would take the class. She commented that she would much rather take a Hmong language class than the French class that she is currently enrolled in because "Hmong is my culture." This girl and most second-generation Hmong youth had been dominant Hmong speakers when they entered kindergarten, but were now dominate English speakers. Because they were no longer fluent Hmong speakers many had difficulties communicating with their parents. It is important to point out, however, that while they spoke fluent English many second-generation youth still struggled with academic English. These second-generation Hmong students are the victims of a subtractive process of education that strips them of crucial cultural resources thereby making them more susceptible to academic failure (Valenzuela, 1999).

While teachers at the high school seemed to assume that Hip Hop culture and Americanization were to blame for the growing academic troubles faced by second-generation Hmong youth, my research suggests Hmong youth embrace Hip Hop culture as a response to the problems they faced at school and in the larger society. Second-generation Hmong students understood they faced racial and class barriers at school and in the larger society, but they did not know how to constructively confront these barriers. For some Hmong youth, Hip Hop culture became a form of resistance to race and class exclusion they experienced as low-income youth of color. Significantly, second-generation youth recognized that Hip Hop style was interpreted in racialized terms, and was associated with African Americans. While they did not socialize with African American students and certainly did not identify themselves as Black, they did relate to what they perceived to be the oppositional nature of Hip Hop culture. In summary, my argument is that the embrace of an oppositional style is not the problem, but the symptom of the problem. A growing number of second-generation Hmong youth in my study were attempting to articulate a critique of the schooling they were offered.

10.3.   Parental Involvement & Social Capital

In my study, Hmong American students were disadvantaged by a school culture that expected and responded to a certain type of parental involvement. As in many schools across the United States, teachers defined involved parents as those who are involved in the day-to-day activities of their children's educations, including their academic learning. Research on immigrant communities, however, reveals that Hmong parents have culturally different ideas about appropriate involvement in their children's education. In her research on parent-teacher relationships at a Hmong charter school, for example, Adler (2004) found that when Hmong parents came to conferences they were primarily concerned with their children's behavior, not their academic performance. When I asked Hmong students about their parents' involvement in their education, I learned that most parents simply told their children to go to school and stay out of trouble.

Hmong parents lack educational backgrounds and English language skills to participate in the school or to help their children with homework. As in many low-income immigrant and refugee families, parents relied on their children to serve as interpreters and translators. Several Hmong students explained that they used to sign their own report cards because their parents couldn't read them. Furthermore, Hmong parents lacked the social capital that would have allowed them to negotiate the system. That is, they did not belong to social networks that can provide them with the necessary information regarding how school works and how to advocate for their children. It is important to point out that in communities with larger and more established Hmong American communities there are Hmong leaders who have been successful in advocating for Hmong students. As noted earlier, the Hmong charter schools were established in response to Hmong communities.

Like their parents, Hmong American students in my study lacked important information regarding how to negotiate the school. Furthermore, they did not belong to the social networks where they could gain information (Stanton-Salazar, 1997). I found, for example, that Hmong students lacked the necessary information regarding how to negotiate the choice-based de-tracking policy that the school had instituted. Under a choice-based de-tracking system, differences in class levels remain untouched, but students are allowed to choose which classes they take. Although the principal suggested that this system would lead to greater equity, I found that Hmong students lacked the knowledge to make educated choices regarding course selection.

Hmong students assumed that all English classes were the same, not recognizing the differences between courses in Shakespeare and courses in popular literature. Several students reported that they were taking vocational education classes because they assumed that colleges would like it if they had business courses. Because second-generation Hmong students socialized almost exclusively with other second-generation Hmong students they often ended up sharing inaccurate information about course selection. In their examination of choice based de-tracking, Yonezawa and Wells (2005) assert, "Choice-based detracking asks students to move up the educational hierarchy yet ignores the fact that the spaces low-and middle-track students occupy in tracked educational structures and cultures contain within them powerful barriers and norms that make moving up quite difficult" (47–48). My data confirms Yonezawa and Wells' critique. The Hmong American students in my study were disadvantaged by the school culture and organization. Furthermore, they and their parents lack the knowledge and the social capital to negotiate the educational system.

In short, many second-generation Hmong students are in danger of academic underachievement. Long term experiences with racism and class inequality appear to be taking a toll on second-generation Hmong students, particularly boys and young men. The second-generation Hmong students in my study face a Eurocentric curriculum and teachers who know little about Hmong students. With the growing Hmong population, cultural and structural barriers need to be addressed for future Hmong newcomers and American-born Hmong students.

10.4.   Conclusions and Recommendations

The educational experiences of Hmong American high school and college students challenge simplistic understandings of Asian Americans as model minorities. While a growing number of Hmong American students are doing well in school and achieving middle class status, many second-generation Hmong American students are struggling against cultural and structural barriers. In order to uncover the diverse experiences of Asian American students, including Hmong American students, educational policy makers must collect and pay attention to disaggregated data. In the absence of disaggregated data and/or single group studies, the concerns of smaller Asian American ethnic groups will be ignored. My research suggests that we need to uncover the voices of various Asian American groups. The following suggestions grow out of my research with Hmong American students:

1. Provide teachers and educational policymakers with more education regarding the diversity of Asian American populations.
2. Collect disaggregated data on Asian American populations.
3. Educate teachers and policymakers regarding the dangers inherent in the model minority stereotype.
4. Recognize the way that gender, class and other issues may affect diversity within ethnic groups.

5. Educate all teachers regarding the unique educational needs of second-language students.
6. Work with teachers to create culturally relevant pedagogy and curriculum.
7. Build school – community collaborations where information can flow in two directions.
8. Educate Hmong parents, and other low-income immigrant and refugee parents, about their rights as parents and about expectations regarding parental involvement.
9. Provide Hmong American students, and other students from low-income immigrant and refugee backgrounds, access to information regarding how to negotiate the U.S. educational system.
10. Provide students with constructive ways of resisting race and class inequality.

References

Adler, S.M. (2004). Home-school relations and the construction of racial and ethnic identity of Hmong elementary students. *The School Community Journal*, 14(2), 57–75.

Beck, R. (1994, April). The ordeal of immigration in Wausau. *Atlantic Monthly*, pp. 84–97.

Fass, S. (1991). *The Hmong in Wisconsin: On the Road to Self-Sufficiency*. Milwaukee: Wisconsin Policy Research Institute.

Goldstein, B. (1985) Schooling for Cultural Transitions: Hmong girls and boys in American high schools. Unpublished Doctoral Dissertation. Madison: University of Wisconsin.

Ladson-Billings, G. (1995). Toward a culturally relevant pedagogy. *American Educational Research Journal*, 32, 465–491.

Lee, S. (1996). *Unraveling the Model Minority Stereotype: Listening to Asian American Youth*. New York: Teachers College Press.

Lee, S. (1997). The road to college: Hmong American women's pursuit of higher education. *Harvard Educational Review*, 67, 803–831.

Lee, S. (2001). More that "model minorities" or "delinquents": A look at Hmong American high school students. *Harvard Educational Review*, 71(3), 505–528.

Lee, S. (2005). *Up Against Whiteness: Race, School and Immigrant Youth*. New York: Teachers College Press.

Lew, J. (2003). Korean American High School Dropouts: A case study of their experiences and negotiations of schooling, family and communities. In Books, S. (ed.). *Invisible Children in the Society and its Schools* (2nd edn), Mahwah, NJ: Lawrence Erlbaum Associates.

Lopez, N. (2003). *Hopeful Girls, Troubled Boy: Race and Gender Disparity in Urban Education*. New York: Routledge.

McKinnon, J. & Bennett, C. (2005). *We the People: Blacks in the United States: August 2005*, Current Population Reports. U.S. Census Bureau.

Ngo, B. (2000). Obstacles, miracles and the pursuit of higher education: The experiences of Hmong American college students. Unpublished Master's thesis. University of Wisconsin-Madison.

Ogbu, J. (1987). Variability in minority school performance: A problem in search of an explanation. *Anthropology & Education Quarterly*, 18(4), 312–334.

Pang,V.O., Kiang, P., & Pak, Y. (2003).Asian Pacific American Students: Challenging A Biased Educational System. In Banks, J. (ed.). *Handbook of Research on Multicultural Education* (2nd edn). San Francisco: Jossey Bass, pp. 542–563.

Pfeifer, M. & Lee, S. (2004). Hmong population, demographic, socioeconomic, and educational trends in the 2000 census. In Hmong National Development Inc. & Hmong Cultural Resource Center (eds). *Hmong 2000 Census Publication: Data & Analysis.* Washington, DC: Hmong National Development Inc., pp. 3–11.

Reeves, T. & Bennett, C. (2003). *The Asian American and Pacific Islander Population in the United States. March 2002*, Current Population Reports. U.S. Census Bureau.

Reeves, T. & Bennett, C. (2004). *We the People: Asians in the United States. December 2004*, Census 2000 Special Reports. U.S. Census Bureau.

Ro, M. (2002). *Overview of Asian Americans and Pacific Islanders in the United States and California.* Washington, DC: Center for Policy Alternatives. Available online at http://www.communityvoices.org/PolicyBriefs.aspx.

Rumbaut, R. & Ima, K. (1988). *The Adaptation of Southeast Asian Refugee Youth: A Comparative Study.* Washington, DC: Office of Refugee Resettlement.

Sherman, S. (1988) The Hmong: Laotian refugees in the "land of giants." *National Geographic*, 174, 586–610.

Stanton-Salazar, R. (1997). A Social Capital Framework for Understanding the Socialization of Racial Minority Children and Youths. *Harvard Educational Review*, 67(1), 1–40 Spring.

Tibbets, K. (1999). *Native Hawaiian Educational Assessment, 1999* (Report No. 99-00:9). Honolulu, NI: Office of Program Evaluation and Planning, Kamehameha Schools, Bishop Estate.

Thao, P. (1999). *Mong Education at the Crossroads.* New York: University Press of America, Inc.

Trueba, H.T., Jacobs, L., & Kirton, E. (1990). *Cultural Conflict and Adaptation: The Case of Hmong Children in American Society.* New York: The Falmer Press.

Valenzuela, A. (1999). *Subtractive Schooling: U.S.-Mexican Youth and the Politics of Caring.* Albany, NY: State University of New York Press.

Vang, H. (2004). Hmong American women's educational attainment: Implications for Hmong American women and men. In Hmong National Development Inc. & Hmong Cultural Resource Center (eds). *Hmong 2000 Census Publication: Data & Analysis.* Washington, DC: Hmong National Development Inc., pp. 23–25.

Yonezawa, S. &. Well, A. (2005). Reform as Redefining the spaces of schools: An examination of detracking by choice. In Weis, L. & Fine, M. (eds). *Beyond Silenced Voices: Class, Race, and Gender in United States Schools* (Rev ed), Albany, NY: State University of New York Press.

Zhou, M (2004). Coming of age at the turn of the twenty-first century: A Demographic Profile of Asian American Youth. In Lee, J. & Zhou, M. (eds). *Asian American Youth: Culture, Identity and Ethnicity.* New York: Routledge, pp. 33–50.

11
Conclusion and Recommendations

Susan J. Paik

The national invitational conference included researchers, practitioners, and policy makers from different disciplines who contributed to this chapter. The conference was a way to bring together the experts on the three groups to provide solutions to the problems and discuss the strengths of different communities. Based on the papers and plenary sessions, work groups were formed to develop consensual recommendations. Since much of the research discourse is often focused on the differences among Latino, Black, and Asian groups, one of the goals of the conference was also to discuss the similarities across the groups in developing recommendations. While differences certainly exist in making such comparisons, the hope was that a discussion of commonalities might provide further understanding.

As the work groups collaborated on these issues, we expected discussion on "this group versus that group." However, a "collective" voice notably emerged as the conferees focused the discussion on the needs of all minority children, particularly disadvantaged minority children. Examples were presented in discussing specific groups, but most of the recommendations centered on the well-being and capability of all students. Consequently, general recommendations were reported from all groups at the end of the conference. While there were differences on some issues among the three groups as specified in the prior chapters, the conferees largely felt that all children can learn given supportive conditions in their immediate environment. The commonalities across all groups were bridged in the form of resources and support needed by all minority children to succeed in school. The purpose of this chapter is to present those areas of consensus in how minority children can best be served.

Although numerous recommendations came in a variety of forms, such as being philosophical, practical, research and policy-oriented on all levels, much of the discussion centered on understanding and providing for the needs of minority students and their families. Due to the interdisciplinary perspectives of the book and conference, the recommendations altogether represented a comprehensive, integrated, holistic view. In short, most of the themes and recommendations focus on their immediate environments – the family and school, and inevitably examine the community contexts and resources for minority children.

While many of the conference recommendations were largely agreed upon, there were also some differing points, which were also included in the list. Specific recommendations and nuances regarding Latino, Black, and Asian students can be found in each of the respective chapters and should be taken in context of the chapter.

This chapter first briefly summarizes the integrative themes of both the prior chapter recommendations, as well as the consensual recommendations from the conference. The chapter then provides a list of consensual recommendations including examples from the conferees. And finally, it is important to note that the recommendations in this chapter should not merely be confined to the list or subtopic, but should be viewed as a starting point for developing and executing plans to increase our understanding and support of minority students.

11.1.   Integrative Themes

Rather than presenting three sets of recommendations in symmetry with each section, the recommendations from the authors and conferees were carefully reviewed and synthesized into the following seven major themes. The list includes the building blocks, resources, and social capital needed to support minority learning:

1) Systemic Change
2) Diversity Awareness
3) Research & Policy Action
4) School Factors
5) Family Involvement
6) Community Support
7) Social Networks

Systemic Change. As noted in Chapter 1, we must adopt the belief of Rosa Parks that all children can learn and achieve. In building a foundation, the conferees agreed that this belief is the basic building block for change to occur and must be adopted by all stakeholders.

Research consistently tells us that real change must be systemic on all levels— across and within institutions, whether it is in the home, school, community, state, and/or national levels. Practice and policy must go hand in hand as national efforts are important in sustaining local efforts. Given the needs of disadvantaged minority children, economic and political support would also greatly benefit those in low SES communities as found in the research by Ron Taylor (Ch. 3). Delgado-Gaitan (Ch. 2) also informs us that effective change must involve "commitment, communication, collaboration and continuity." We echo this on all levels. In addition, we must go beyond the "One size fits all" model in working with the specific needs of minority communities.

Diversity Awareness. Given the ethnic composition of our schools, diversity of individuals and communities should be considered more than ever. The chapters in the book remind us about the richness and diversity among and within cultural groups represented in the classroom. The chapters discuss the variations and subgroups of Latino, Black, and Asian communities. Consequently, one of the resounding themes and recommendations focuses on the importance of better understanding Latino, Black, and Asian students. As a result, stakeholders need to be educated at all levels.

Teachers, school officials, and policymakers need to be continually educated about the larger social context of families, such as students' backgrounds, ethnic diversity, SES differences, gender issues within the cultural context, educational needs of second language learners, and other contextual factors. The research by Lee (Ch. 10) reminds us to consider the bigger picture of economic, racial, and cultural barriers of minority groups. Recommendations from this section include diversity awareness in the form of courses in teacher training or professional development in the schools.

Schools should also provide safe, learning environments to support racially bias-free environments for all students. Rong and Brown (Ch. 6) emphasize the importance of respecting the wide range of identities and cultural competencies of students (immigrant and non-immigrant alike). Many of the chapters encourage school officials to recognize that racial and ethnic identity can make a difference for individual development and educational attainment. Furthermore, schools should also foster and exchange healthy cultural interactions and address issues of racism. Recommendations include creating supportive environments such as incorporating culturally relevant pedagogy and curriculum, projects, and events that value students' diverse backgrounds.

Research and Policy Action. Researchers, policymakers, and practitioners consistently tell us that good research is needed to understand the alterable factors that promote achievement and well-being on the three groups. Disciplined inquiry on all three groups should incorporate data-driven implications for real change and policy action. Given NCLB's accountability to report separate achievement scores, recommendations also include disaggregating data to understand within group differences.

School Factors. Poor minority children often attend poor schools. These communities tend to lack resources and face many challenges. Recent research has shown, however, that some high poverty schools can be high achieving schools. The Center for Public Education (2005) reviewed 17 studies based on their rigor and relevancy including the well-known study by Education Trust (Jerald, 2001) that analyzed over 4500 high-poverty-high-achieving schools in 47 states and the District of Columbia. Similar to the recommendations from the authors and conferees, the review found ten common features of these high achieving schools:

- A culture of high expectations and caring for the students
- A safe and disciplined environment
- A principal who is a strong instructional leader

- Hard-working, committed, and able teachers
- A curriculum focused on academic achievement that emphasizes basic skills in math and literacy (based on local/state standards)
- Increased instructional time
- On-going, diagnostic assessment (built-in accountability systems)
- Parents as partners in learning
- Professional development to improve student achievement
- Collaboration among teachers and staff

Research has shown that even poor schools can achieve given supportive environments also confirmed by the work of Thompson (Ch. 9) and Waxman, Padrón, and Andrés (Ch. 8). Describing effective factors that promote learning environments, they both agree that change must also be systemic.

Family Involvement. While school factors are obviously important, we agree with Thompson that the voices of minority parents and students must also be heard. Waxman, Padrón, and Andrés also add, "If we only focus on school factors and we ignore the importance of family and community influences, we will clearly fail in our endeavors." We begin this section with parents as they are the first teachers to their children.

"Parents as partners in learning" is one of the common features included in the list above that make high achieving schools. In 2000, the National Goals emphasized that "every school will promote partnerships that will increase parental involvement and participation..." More recently, NCLB defined parent participation as "regular, two-way, and meaningful communication." Parent participation and involvement is still largely an untapped resource in the schools, where communication must be fostered and increased from both parties.

Although research has consistently reported that parenting practices make a difference for student success as confirmed by the prior chapters, many parents may be too busy or unaware of such practices. Often, these parents do not know how to navigate the school system or are unaware of helpful social services. Helping parents to understand how to navigate the system will be critical to all other forms of parent involvement and partnership. Parent participation in the schools may reinforce some of these practices in the home. Some studies even show that there is an increase in parental self-esteem, as well as in emotional adjustment and achievement for students.

Collaborative efforts must involve understanding the culture of the home and ethnic community. Pang (Ch. 4) informs us of the diversity even within cultures and emphasizes the importance of involving parents in school activities, committees, and the classroom. She adds further that providing interpreters, English and other classes to get parents more involved, and disseminating a school newsletter in different languages will increase communication between families and schools. Further recommendations include workshops, events, and programs for parents to collaborate, as well as be informed about their child's education.

Community Support. Community support is critical for families and schools. Further insight into the ethnic community may also provide understanding of minority students. Similar to Taylor's perspective that one must look at the larger social context of the family, Zhou (Ch. 7) presents specific case studies to remind us to "look beyond the family into the social structures of the ethnic community". Taking into consideration other issues, she informs the reader that family and community resources can make a difference for student success. Like parent involvement, community resources are also an untapped resource for many families and schools. Locating and developing important services in communities are particularly important to low SES families.

Recommendations include locating services and programs for students and families. Delgado-Gaitan (Ch. 2) describes family-school-community partnerships and its role in building the community. Waxman, Padrón, and Andrés (Ch. 8), and Ream and Stanton-Salazar (Ch. 5) also describe effective programs in working with some minority groups. Examples of effective programs are suggested in their chapters.

Social Networks. As John Donne, the famous philosopher once stated, "Man is not an island, entirely unto himself". Likewise, a student, parent, teacher, principal, researcher, policymaker are part of an embedded system. Each person has a role to fulfill in this system and must work in concert with other parts of the system.

Ream and Stanton-Salazar inform us that effective programs must be built on a social paradigm. It is through social relationships that disadvantaged students can benefit greatly. Their work on the *mobility/social capital dynamic* inform us of the importance of stable relationships that help "root" students into a social system. Most important and most relevant to all the factors presented in this chapter, this recommendation has powerful implications for students as they develop healthy social networks in the larger community. These relationships include peers, parents, teachers, counselors, schools, programs, and communities. Effective training and knowledge of communities are also needed to know how to utilize resources. Effective families, schools, communities, and programs require "commitment, communication, continuity, and collaboration" on all levels.

11.2. National Invitational Conference: Consensual Recommendations and Next Steps

The following themes emerged from the notes that were shared orally at the end of the conference. For the purpose of clarity and accessibility, we consolidated repetitive recommendations within a category, reorganized the material, developed subcategories, and provided examples in bullet-points. Some points were included more than once on different topics. The preliminary list provides recommendations and next steps for research, policy, and practice.

11.2.1. Research

1. Conduct rigorous empirical research on improving and understanding minority learning.

For example:

- Continue research and discussion on the various challenges in separate communities
- Research educational programs and their true effectiveness
- Research the effects of teaching/teacher education and how it can best be measured

2. Create more effective links between researchers and practitioners. Practitioners can exchange information and actively engage in dialogue with researchers.
3. Develop connections with universities to conduct on-site research in schools and districts.

11.2.2. Policy

1. Seek opportunities to effectively communicate with and involve all stakeholders.
   For example:

- States should provide opportunities for parents and other stakeholders to participate in focus groups regarding proposed education legislation
- Include educators on policymaking teams
- Communicate with district leadership to discuss policy, hiring practices, teacher preparation

2. Evaluate the impact of all policies and programs to address needs.
   For example:

- Align curriculum and tests with state standards
- Address the basic health needs of students in underserved communities and school districts
- Provide equity in funding
- Address teacher retention/student mobility issues

3. School officials should use data for educational evaluation and development of new policies and practices.

11.2.3. Practice

Supportive environments are critical to all stakeholders, especially students. The recommendations are organized by (1) social networks, (2) students, (3) parents and families, (4) teachers and administrators, (5) professional development, and (6) curriculum/tests/data.

Social Networks and Partnerships
1. Build coalitions to bring families, schools, and communities together.
   For example:

   - Develop family-school partnerships and other collaborative links
   - Develop parent/community liaisons, especially in low SES schools
   - Create clear goals, tasks, and positions for those involved

2. Create effective community-based programs in the schools (school-to-community/school-to-school).
3. Determine ways to connect students to the school community to build student attachment to school.

Students in the Classroom
4. Provide academic, social, and emotional support to students on an individual basis.
   For example:

   - Align curriculum and tests with state standards
   - Address the basic health needs of students
   - Teach social skills/role playing as a means to student success
   - Identify what students know and can do and integrate findings into school programs

5. Provide a safe and healthy learning environment for students.
   For example:

   - Have students complete "school environment" survey (including classrooms)
   - Interview students for a better understanding

Parents and Families
6. Build leadership capacity systematically to engage parents and facilitate communication between parents and schools.
7. Eliminate barriers (e.g., language, etc.) to parental engagement.
   For example:

   - Disseminate pertinent information to parents, particularly low-income immigrants, in native languages, to foster continuous communication between parents and schools.
   - Develop programs to involve parents in the schools, including programs that teach parents to navigate the school environment effectively.

Teachers and School Administrators
8. Educators should feel and be encouraged to feel a sense of ownership of the work of monitoring policy and procedures that affect student achievement.
9. Address teacher retention/student mobility issues.
10. Give teachers and administrators the authority to make decisions regarding students.

Professional Development/Diversity Awareness
11. Provide cultural training for teachers to understand the cultural backgrounds of their students and how culture influences the teaching–learning process (should be addressed in teacher education and continuing teacher education programs, including alternative teacher/administrator education programs). For example:

   - Use culturally competent/responsive coaches (coaches' individual recommendations can be included in student improvement plans)
   - Extend "other cultural" requirements to all teachers and students
   - Teachers should undergo pre-service training, job-embedded development (possibly by other teachers) to identify their own biases and learn how to overcome them so they may best serve all of their students.

12. Provide thorough and systematic professional development for teachers, addressing issues relevant to diverse student populations and poor quality teacher preparation programs.
13. Determine how staff development meetings can be used more effectively. For example:

   - Transfer research to practice and disseminate information to parents, community organizations, places of worship, work places, etc.
   - Use videotapes of good practice
   - Develop professional learning teams

Curriculum/Tests/Data
14. Align curriculum and tests with state standards.
15. Educators and administrators must take testing seriously.
16. Move beyond single measure test and allow for multiple assessments of achievement.
17. School officials should use data for educational evaluation and development of new policies and practices.

11.3.   Conclusion

In closing, the last of the consensual recommendations are as follows:

1. Change belief systems: all stakeholders—teachers, administrators, support staff, parents, and community leaders must *believe* that all children can learn.

2. Remember that we live in an age of globalized economy—the education our students receive must keep pace with students around the world.
3. Engage in conversations about the purpose of schooling—how that translates into policy and practice; are all stakeholders on the same page?

This volume discusses the challenges and strengths of Latino, Black, and Asian students, and provides strategies for educational policy, practice, and research. As minority populations continue to grow in the United States, it is important to understand culturally diverse students and their families in order to support their schooling experiences. Since families and schools are the two most important institutions to children, enhancing their involvement is critical to individual development and school success. Research has shown that early and continuous efforts make for large differences in student learning and achievement. Collaborative efforts are needed in order to support the three most visible minority groups in the U.S. Educational problems will undoubtedly persist and concerns will continue to grow given the dismal statistics on achievement, retention, and enrollment. Educating all students well is not only an important endeavor for all stakeholders, but a national call that demands our best efforts.

References

Center for Public Education. (2005). *Research Review: High-Performing, High-Poverty Schools*. Retrieved July 20, 2006 from *www.centerforpubliceducation.org/site/*.
Jerald, C.D. (2001). *Dispelling the Myth Revisited: Preliminary Findings From A Nationwide Analysis of "High-Flying" Schools*. Washington, DC: Education Trust.

About the Editors

Susan J. Paik is an Associate Professor in the School of Educational Studies at Claremont Graduate University. She has participated in education projects in Africa, Asia, Central America, Europe, and the U.S, where she founded and directed an urban program for minority children and youth. Dr. Paik has not only presented her work at AERA annually, but at the Oxford University in England, the University of Cape Town in South Africa, and the University of Bologna in Italy, as well as other invited professional meetings in Australia, Germany, South America, Spain, and the U.S. She has been designated as a Young Scholar by the Koret K-12 Task Force at Stanford University. She has been the recipient of numerous awards, fellowships, grants, such as an AERA-NSF-IES grant, NIMH fellowship grant for prevention, Center for Urban Educational Research and Development (CUERD) fellowship, Chancellor's Service Award, Teaching Incentive Award, and Early Outreach Award for her dedication and service to inner city youth by the University of Illinois. Among many published articles, she is the author of a research monograph called *Educational Productivity in South Korea and the United States*, and co-editor of a special journal issue on family and school partnerships published by the International Journal of Educational Research. She is the co-author of a booklet called *Effective Educational Practices* published by UNESCO and translated and disseminated to over 150 countries. Dr. Paik is the editor of *Advancing Educational Productivity: Policy Implications from National Databases* (IAP, 2004).

Herbert J. Walberg was on the faculty of Harvard University and is now Emeritus University Scholar and Research Professor of Education and Psychology at the University of Illinois at Chicago and Distinguished Visiting Fellow at Stanford University. He chairs the Beck Foundation, MetaLytics, and the Heartland Institute, and serves as a member of several other boards. An editor or author of more than 50 books, he has contributed more than 300 papers to peer-reviewed psychology and education journals, and he has written extensively for educators and policy makers. Dr. Walberg currently edits a series of booklets on effective education practices for the International Academy of Education that the United Nations Educational, Scientific, and Educational Organization distributed in hard copy in more than 150 countries and on the Internet for downloading and re-publication. He is a fellow of the American Psychological Association, the American Association for the Advancement of Science, and the Royal Statistical Society. In 2004, the U.S. Senate confirmed his presidential appointment to the National Board for Education Sciences, which provides guidance and oversight for federal research for education.

About the Authors

Frank Brown is the Cary C. Boshamer Distinguished Professor of Education and Dean Emeritus, University of North Carolina at Chapel Hill. He holds the Ph.D. in Policy, Planning, and Administration from the University of California at Berkeley. His research interests include urban education, educational law and finance. He is author or editor of more than 12 books and more than 200 peer-reviewed journal publications. He has held office in the American Education Research Association, Education Law Association and the Educational Finance Association and served as editor or a member of the editorial boards of 14 academic journals.

Concha Delgado Gaitan's ethnographic research examines issues of family and community literacy. The culmination of her collaboration with underrepresented communities has resulted in her scholarly publications, including her books: (1) *The Power of Community; (2) Protean Literacy; (3) Crossing Cultural Borders; (4) Literacy for Empowerment; (5) School and Society*; (6) *Involving Latino Families in the School* and, (7) *Creating Culturally Responsive Classroom.* In 2000, she received the George and Louise Spindler award for her contributions to Anthropology and Education. She is a former professor of Sociocultural Studies in Education at the University of California, Santa Barbara and U.C. Davis.

Andres García is a doctoral student in Educational Leadership and Cultural Studies Department at the University of Houston. He also is a bilingual teacher in the Houston Independent School District. He received the University of Houston Mexican American Alumni Award. His research interests include Hispanic and minority studies, research methods, and accountability testing.

Stacey J. Lee is a Professor of Educational Policy Studies at the University of Wisconsin – Madison. She received her Ph.D. in 1991 from the University of Pennsylvania. Lee's research focuses on the ways race, class and gender inform the experiences of immigrant youth. She is the author of *Unraveling the Model Minority Stereotype: Listening to Asian American Youth* and *Up Against Whiteness: Race, School and Immigrant Youth.*

Yolanda N. Padrón is a Professor of Bilingual Education in the College of Education and Human Development at Texas A & M University. She recently was the Co-Director of the U.S. Department of Education, National Center for Research on Education, Diversity, and Excellence. Her research focuses on bilingual education, students at risk of failure, and instruction for English language learners. She has published articles on those topics in journals such as *Bilingual Research Journal, TESOL Quarterly*, and *Journal of Education for Students Placed At Risk*.

Valerie Ooka Pang is a Professor in the School of Teacher Education at San Diego State University. She has published several books such as *Multicultural Education: A Caring-centered, Reflective Approach*. In addition Pang has published in various journals including *Harvard Educational Review, The Kappan, The Journal of Teacher Education, Action in Teacher Education, and Social Education*. Pang has consulted with organizations such as Sesame Street, Family Communications (Producers of Mr. Roger's Neighborhood), and ScottForesman. Pang was a senior Fellow at the Annenberg Institute at Brown University and honored by organizations such AERA and the University of Washington's College of Education.

Robert K. Ream is an Assistant Professor in the Graduate School of Education at UC Riverside. Dr. Ream joined the faculty at UCR in 2004 after postdoctoral fellowships at Princeton University and the RAND Corporation. His research addresses educational stratification and Latino social demography, drawing from the theoretical work on social capital. His first book, *Uprooting Children: Mobility, Social Capital, and Mexican American Underachievement*, was published in 2005 by LFB Scholarly Publishing, New York, in the book series, "The New Americans: Recent Immigration and American Society."

Xue Lan Rong is an Associate Professor at University of North Carolina at Chapel Hill. Her research interests include issues on immigration and schooling, and international education. Authoring more than 17 articles, 15 chapters, and one book, she has presented over 60 conference papers in national and international conferences. Her publications include *The Continuing Decline in Asian American Teachers* (AERA, 1997), *The Effects of Immigrant Generation and Ethnicity of Educational Attainment Among Young African and Caribbean Blacks in the United States* (Harvard Educational Review, 2001), and *Educating Immigrant Students* (Sage-Corwin, 1998).

Ricardo D. Stanton-Salazar is an Associate Professor in the Rossier School of Education at the University of Southern California; he holds a joint appointment in the Department of Sociology. His research focuses on theories and models of social capital and educational equality, network-building strategies of minority and immigrant youth, and designing educational environments. In 2004, Stanton-Salazar was a resident research fellow at the Woodrow Wilson International Center for Scholars in Washington, D.C. His book, *Manufacturing Hope &*

Despair: The School and Kin Support Networks of U.S.-Mexican Youth, is published by Teachers College Press.

Ronald D. Taylor is an Associate Professor in the Psychology Department at Temple University. Dr. Taylor is a developmental psychologist and received his Ph.D. from the University of Michigan. His research interests include family relations and social and emotional adjustment of ethnic minority adolescents. Recent work has focused on the processes mediating the association of families' economic resources with adolescents' psychosocial well-being. He has numerous publications in peer-reviewed journals and has edited volumes including *Social and Emotional Adjustment and Family Relations in Ethnic Minority Families* and *Addressing the Achievement Gap: Findings and Applications*.

Gail L. Thompson is an Associate Professor in the School of Educational Studies at the Claremont Graduate University. In addition to *African American Teens Discuss Their Schooling Experiences* (Bergin & Garvey: Greenwood Publishers, 2002), she has also written three other books–*What African American Parents Want Educators to Know* (Praeger: Greenwood Publishers, 2003); *Through Ebony Eyes: What Teachers Need to Know but are Afraid to Ask About African American Students* (Jossey Bass, 2004), and *Exposing the Culture of Arrogance in the Academy: A Blueprint for Increasing Black Faculty Satisfaction*, which she co-authored with Dr. Angela Louque (Stylus, 2005).

Hersh C. Waxman is a Professor of Teaching, Learning, and Culture in the College of Education and Human Development at Texas A & M University. He was a Principal Researcher in the National Center for Research on Education, Diversity, and Excellence, and for the Mid-Atlantic Regional Educational Laboratory for Student Success. His research focuses on equity, excellence, and social justice issues that appear in the *Journal of Educational Research, Urban Education*, and others. His books include *Observational Research in U. S. Classrooms: New Approaches for Understanding Cultural and Linguistic Diversity* (Cambridge, 2004), *Educational Resiliency: Student, Teacher, and School Perspectives* (Information Age, 2004), and *Preparing Quality Educators for English Language Learners* (Lawrence Erlbaum, 2006).

Min Zhou is a Professor of Sociology and the founding chair of the Department of Asian American Studies at the University of California, Los Angeles. Her main areas of research are immigration; ethnic and racial relations; and the new second generation. She is the author *of Chinatown: The Socioeconomic Potential of an Urban Enclave* (Temple University Press, 1992), co-author of *Growing up American: How Vietnamese Children Adapt to Life in the United States* (Russell Sage Foundation Press, 1998), co-editor of *Contemporary Asian America* (New York University Press, 2000), and co-editor of *Asian American Youth: Culture, Identity, and Ethnicity* (Routledge, 2004).

University Advisory Committee
for The University of Illinois at Chicago
Series on Issues in Children's
and Families' Lives

Carl C. Bell
Department of Psychiatry

Barry R. Chiswick
Department of Economics

Victoria Chou
Dean, College of Education

Christopher M. Comer
Dean, College of Liberal Arts and
Sciences

Rachel Gordon
Department of Sociology

Creasie Finney Hairston
Dean, Jane Addams College of
Social Work

Donald Hellison
College of Education

Mary Utne O'Brien
Department of Psychology

David Perry
Director, Great Cities Institute

Gary E. Raney
Department of Psychology

Olga Reyes
Department of Psychology

Gerald S. Strom
Department of Political Science

R. Michael Tanner
Provost and Vice Chancellor for
Academic Affairs

Patrick H. Tolan
Director, Institute for Juvenile
Research

Steven Tozer
College of Education

B. Joseph White
President, University of Illinois

National Advisory Committee for The University of Illinois at Chicago Series on Issues in Children's and Families' Lives

Edmund W. Gordon
Professor Emeritus
Yale University

Thomas P. Gullotta
Chief Executive Officer
Child and Family Agency of
Southeastern Connecticut

Robert J. Haggerty
Professor of Pediatrics
University of Rochester

Anne C. Petersen
Senior Vice President for Programs
W.K. Kellogg Foundation

Ruby N. Takanishi
President
Foundation for Child Development

William J. Wilson
Malcolm Wiener Professor of Social
Policy, Harvard University

Edward Zigler
Sterling Professor of Psychology
Yale University

Index